9th Workshop on Multiword Expressions

(MWE 2013)

Atlanta, Georgia, USA
13 – 14 June 2013

ISBN: 978-1-62748-993-5

Printed from e-media with permission by:

Curran Associates, Inc.
57 Morehouse Lane
Red Hook, NY 12571

CURRAN ASSOCIATES INC. proceedings.com

Some format issues inherent in the e-media version may also appear in this print version.

Printed by Curran Associates, Inc. (2013)

For permission requests, please contact the Association for Computational Linguistics at the address below.

Association for Computational Linguistics
209 N. Eighth Street
Stroudsburg, Pennsylvania 18360

Phone: 1-570-476-8006
Fax: 1-570-476-0860

acl@aclweb.org

Additional copies of this publication are available from:

Curran Associates, Inc.
57 Morehouse Lane
Red Hook, NY 12571 USA
Phone: 845-758-0400
Fax: 845-758-2634
Email: curran@proceedings.com
Web: www.proceedings.com

NAACL HLT 2013

9th Workshop on Multiword Expressions
MWE 2013

Proceedings of the Workhop

13-14 June 2013
Atlanta, Georgia, USA

Introduction

The *9th Workshop on Multiword Expressions (MWE 2013)*[1] took place on June 13 and 14, 2013 in Atlanta, Georgia, USA in conjunction with the 2013 Conference of the North American Chapter of the (NAACL HLT 2013), and was endorsed by the Special Interest Group on the Lexicon of the Association for Computational Linguistics (SIGLEX)[2]. The workshop has been held almost every year since 2003 in conjunction with ACL, EACL, NAACL, COLING and LREC. It provides an important venue for interaction, sharing of resources and tools and collaboration efforts for advancing the computational treatment of Multiword Expressions (MWEs), attracting the attention of an ever-growing community working on a variety of languages and MWE types.

MWEs include idioms (*storm in a teacup, sweep under the rug*), fixed phrases (*in vitro, by and large, rock'n roll*), noun compounds (*olive oil, laser printer*), compound verbs (*take a nap, bring about*), among others. These, while easily mastered by native speakers, are a key issue and a current weakness for natural language parsing and generation, as well as real-life applications depending on some degree of semantic interpretation, such as machine translation, just to name a prominent one among many. However, thanks to the joint efforts of researchers from several fields working on MWEs, significant progress has been made in recent years, especially concerning the construction of large-scale language resources. For instance, there is a large number of recent papers that focus on acquisition of MWEs from corpora, and others that describe a variety of techniques to find paraphrases for MWEs. Current methods use a plethora of tools such as association measures, machine learning, syntactic patterns, web queries, etc.

In the call for papers we solicited submissions about major challenges in the overall process of MWE treatment, both from the theoretical and the computational viewpoint, focusing on original research related to the following topics:

- Manually and automatically constructed resources
- Representation of MWEs in dictionaries and ontologies
- MWEs and user interaction
- Multilingual acquisition
- Crosslinguistic studies on MWEs
- Integration of MWEs into NLP applications
- Lexical, syntactic or semantic aspects of MWEs

Submission modalities included Long Papers and Short Papers. From a total of 27 submissions, 15 were long papers and 12 were short papers, and we accepted 7 long papers for oral presentation and 3 as posters: an acceptance rate of 66.6%. We further accepted 5 short papers for oral presentation and 3

[1] http://multiword.sourceforge.net/mwe2013
[2] http://www.siglex.org

as posters (66.6% acceptance). The workshop also featured 3 invited talks, by Jill Burstein (Educational Testing Service, USA), Malvina Nissim (University of Bologna, Italy) and Martha Palmer (University of Colorado at Boulder, USA).

Acknowledgements

We would like to thank the members of the Program Committee for the timely reviews and the authors for their valuable contributions. We also want to thank projects CAPES/COFECUB 707/11 Cameleon, CNPq 482520/2012-4, 478222/2011-4, 312184/2012-3 and 551964/2011-1.

Valia Kordoni, Carlos Ramisch, Aline Villavicencio
Co-Organizers

Organizers:

Valia Kordoni, Humboldt-Universität zu Berlin, Germany
Carlos Ramisch, Joseph Fourier University, France
Aline Villavicencio, Federal University of Rio Grande do Sul, Brazil

Program Committee:

Iñaki Alegria, University of the Basque Country, Spain
Dimitra Anastasiou, University of Bremen, Germany
Doug Arnold, University of Essex, UK
Giuseppe Attardi, Università di Pisa, Italy
Eleftherios Avramidis, DFKI GmbH, Germany
Timothy Baldwin, The University of Melbourne, Australia
Chris Biemann, Technische Universität Darmstadt, Germany
Francis Bond, Nanyang Technological University, Singapore
Antonio Branco, University of Lisbon, Portugal
Aoife Cahill, Educational Testing Service, USA
Helena Caseli, Federal University of São Carlos, Brazil
Ken Church, IBM Research, USA
Matthieu Constant, Université Paris-Est Marne-la-Vallée, France
Paul Cook, The University of Melbourne, Australia
Béatrice Daille, Nantes University, France
Koenraad de Smedt, University of Bergen, Norway
Markus Egg, Humboldt-Universität zu Berlin, Germany
Stefan Evert, Friedrich-Alexander Universität Erlangen-Nürnberg, Germany
Afsaneh Fazly, University of Toronto, Canada
Joaquim Ferreira da Silva, New University of Lisbon, Portugal
Chikara Hashimoto, National Institute of Information and Communications Technology, Japan
Kyo Kageura, University of Tokyo, Japan
Su Nam Kim, Monash University, Australia
Ioannis Korkontzelos, University of Manchester, UK
Brigitte Krenn, Austrian Research Institute for Artificial Intelligence, Austria
Evita Linardaki, Hellenic Open University, Greece
Takuya Matsuzaki, National Institute of Informatics, Japan
Yusuke Miyao, National Institute of Informatics, Japan
Preslav Nakov, Qatar Computing Research Institute - Qatar Foundation, Qatar
Joakim Nivre, Uppsala University, Sweden
Diarmuid Ó Séaghdha, University of Cambridge, UK
Jan Odijk, Utrecht University, The Netherlands
Yannick Parmentier, Université d'Orléans, France
Pavel Pecina, Charles University Prague, Czech Republic
Scott Piao, Lancaster University, UK

Adam Przepiórkowski, Polish Academy of Sciences, Poland
Magali Sanches Duran, University of São Paulo, Brazil
Agata Savary, Université Francois Rabelais Tours, France
Ekaterina Shutova, University of California at Berkeley, USA
Mark Steedman, University of Edinburgh, UK
Sara Stymne, Upsalla University, Sweden
Stan Szpakowicz, University of Ottawa, Canada
Beata Trawinski, University of Vienna, Austria
Yulia Tsvetkov, Carnegie Mellon University, USA
Yuancheng Tu, Microsoft, USA
Kyioko Uchiyama, National Institute of Informatics, Japan
Ruben Urizar, University of the Basque Country, Spain
Tony Veale, University College Dublin, Ireland
David Vilar, DFKI GmbH, Germany
Veronika Vincze, Hungarian Academy of Sciences, Hungary
Tom Wasow, Stanford University, USA
Eric Wehrli, University of Geneva, Switzerland

Additional Reviewers:

Silvana Hartmann, Technische Universität Darmstadt, Germany
Bahar Salehi, The University of Melbourne, Australia

Invited Speakers:

Jill Burstein, Educational Testing Service, USA
Malvina Nissim, University of Bologna, Italy
Martha Palmer, University of Colorado at Boulder, USA

Table of Contents

Conference Program

Thursday, June 13 – Morning

09:00-09:15	Opening Remarks
	Oral Session 1: Resources and Applications
09:15–09:40	*Managing Multiword Expressions in a Lexicon-Based Sentiment Analysis System for Spanish* Antonio Moreno-Ortiz, Chantal Perez-Hernandez and Maria Del-Olmo
09:40–10:05	*Introducing PersPred, a Syntactic and Semantic Database for Persian Complex Predicates* Pollet Samvelian and Pegah Faghiri
10:05–10:30	*Improving Word Translation Disambiguation by Capturing Multiword Expressions with Dictionaries* Lars Bungum, Björn Gambäck, André Lynum and Erwin Marsi
10:30-11:00	**COFFEE BREAK**
11:00–12:00	**Invited Talk 1** *Complex Predicates are Multi-Word Expressions* Martha Palmer
	Oral Session 2: Compositionality
12:00–12:25	*The (Un)expected Effects of Applying Standard Cleansing Models to Human Ratings on Compositionality* Stephen Roller, Sabine Schulte im Walde and Silke Scheible
12:30-14:00	**LUNCH BREAK**

	Oral Session 2: Compositionality (contd.)
14:05–14:30	*Determining Compositionality of Word Expressions Using Word Space Models* Lubomír Krčmář, Karel Ježek and Pavel Pecina
14:30–15:30	**Invited Talk 2** *Modelling the Internal Variability of MWEs* Malvina Nissim
15:30-16:00	**COFFEE BREAK**
	Oral Session 3: Short Papers
16:00–16:15	*Automatically Assessing Whether a Text Is Cliched, with Applications to Literary Analysis* Paul Cook and Graeme Hirst
16:15–16:30	*An Analysis of Annotation of Verb-Noun Idiomatic Combinations in a Parallel Dependency Corpus* Zdenka Uresova, Jan Hajic, Eva Fucikova and Jana Sindlerova
16:30-17:40	**Poster Session**
16:30-16:40	Poster Boosters *Automatic Identification of Bengali Noun-Noun Compounds Using Random Forest* Vivekananda Gayen and Kamal Sarkar *Automatic Detection of Stable Grammatical Features in N-Grams* Mikhail Kopotev, Lidia Pivovarova, Natalia Kochetkova and Roman Yangarber *Exploring MWEs for Knowledge Acquisition from Corporate Technical Documents* Bell Manrique-Losada, Carlos M. Zapata-Jaramillo and Diego A. Burgos *MWE in Portuguese: Proposal for a Typology for Annotation in Running Text* Sandra Antunes and Amália Mendes *Identifying Pronominal Verbs: Towards Automatic Disambiguation of the Clitic 'se' in Portuguese* Magali Sanches Duran, Carolina Evaristo Scarton, Sandra Maria Aluísio and Carlos Ramisch *A Repository of Variation Patterns for Multiword Expressions* Malvina Nissim and Andrea Zaninello

Friday, June 14 – Morning

	Oral Session 4: Identification and Classification
09:10–09:35	*Syntactic Identification of Occurrences of Multiword Expressions in Text using a Lexicon with Dependency Structures*
	Eduard Bejček, Pavel Straňák and Pavel Pecina
09:35–10:00	*Combining Different Features of Idiomaticity for the Automatic Classification of Noun+Verb Expressions in Basque*
	Antton Gurrutxaga and Iñaki Alegria
	Oral Session 5: Short Papers
10:00–10:15	*Semantic Roles for Nominal Predicates: Building a Lexical Resource*
	Ashwini Vaidya, Martha Palmer and Bhuvana Narasimhan
10:15–10:30	*Constructional Intensifying Adjectives in Italian*
	Sara Berlanda
10:30-11:00	**COFFEE BREAK**
11:00–12:00	**Invited Talk 3**
	The Far Reach of Multiword Expressions in Educational Technology
	Jill Burstein
	Oral Session 5: Short Papers (contd.)
12:00–12:15	*Construction of English MWE Dictionary and its Application to POS Tagging*
	Yutaro Shigeto, Ai Azuma, Sorami Hisamoto, Shuhei Kondo, Tomoya Kouse, Keisuke Sakaguchi, Akifumi Yoshimoto, Frances Yung and Yuji Matsumoto
12:15-12:30	Closing Remarks

Managing Multiword Expressions in a Lexicon-Based Sentiment Analysis System for Spanish

Antonio Moreno-Ortiz and **Chantal Pérez-Hernández** and **M. Ángeles Del-Olmo**
Facultad de Letras
Universidad de Málaga
29071 Málaga. Spain
{amo, mph, mariadelolmo@uma.es}

Abstract

This paper describes our approach to managing multiword expressions in Sentitext, a linguistically-motivated, lexicon-based Sentiment Analysis (SA) system for Spanish whose performance is largely determined by its coverage of MWEs. We defend the view that multiword constructions play a fundamental role in lexical Sentiment Analysis, in at least three ways. First, a significant proportion conveys semantic orientation; second, being units of meaning, their relative weight to the calculated overall sentiment rating of texts needs to be accounted for as such, rather than the number of component lexical units; and, third, many MWEs contain individual words that carry a given polarity, which may or may not be that of the phrase as a whole. As a result, successful lexicon-based SA calls for appropriate management of MWEs.[1]

1 Introduction

In recent years, *sentiment analysis* or *opinion mining* has become an increasingly relevant sub-field within natural language processing that deals with the computational treatment of opinion and subjectivity in texts. The fact that emotions and opinions condition how humans communicate and motivate their actions explains why the study of evaluative language has attracted a great deal of attention from a wide range of disciplines (Pang and Lee, 2008).

With the advent of the Web 2.0 and the widespread use of social networks, it is easier than ever before to gain access to vast amounts of sentiment-laden texts. User reviews are particularly interesting for companies as a tool for product improvement. Different opinions and trends in political or social issues can be identified, to the extent that many companies have decided to add sentiment analysis tools to their social media measurement and monitoring tools with a view to improving their business.

With regard to MWEs, their relevance to Natural Language Processing in general, and to Sentiment Analysis in particular, can hardly be overstated since they constitute a significant proportion of the lexicon of any natural language. It is estimated that the number of MWEs in the lexicon of a native speaker has the same order of magnitude as the number of single words (Jackendoff, 1997) and even these ratios are probably underestimated when considering domain-specific language, in which the specialized vocabulary and terminology are composed mostly by MWEs. As Erman and Warren (2000: 29) point out, the fact that half of spoken and written language comes in preconstructed multiword combinations makes it impossible to consider them as marginal phenomena. Further, a large number of such expressions

[1] This work is funded by the Spanish Ministry of Science and Innovation (Lingmotif Project FFI2011-25893).

express emotions and opinions on the part of the speaker, so it follows that any lexicon-based approach to sentiment analysis somehow needs to account for multiword constructions.

2 Sentiment Analysis in perspective

Sentiment Analysis approaches mainly fall into one of two categories, which are usually referred to as the lexicon-based approach and the machine-learning approach. The latter is undoubtedly more popular for many reasons, an important one being a faster bootstrapping process, but also reasonably good performance (Pang and Lee, 2005; Aue and Gamon, 2005). In fact, machine learning techniques, in any of their flavors, have proven extremely useful, not only in the field of sentiment analysis, but in text mining and information retrieval applications in general, as well as a wide range of data-intensive computational tasks. However, their obvious disadvantage in terms of functionality is their limited applicability to subject domains other than the one they were designed for. Although interesting research has been done aimed at extending domain applicability (Aue and Gamon, 2005), such efforts have shown limited success. An important variable for these approaches is the amount of labeled text available for training the classifier, although they perform well in terms of recall even with relatively small training sets (Andreevskaia and Bergler, 2007).

In contrast, lexicon-based approaches rely on dictionaries where lexical items have been assigned either *polarity* or *valence*, which has been extracted either automatically from other dictionaries, or, more uncommonly, manually. Although the terms *polarity* and *valence* are sometimes used interchangeably in the literature, especially by those authors developing binary text classifiers, we restrict the usage of the former to non-graded, binary assignment, i.e., positive / negative, whereas the latter is used to refer to a rating on an *n*-point semantic orientation scale. The works by Hatzivassiloglou and Wiebe (2000), and Turney (2002) are perhaps classical examples of such an approach. The most salient work in this category is Taboada et al. (2011), whose dictionaries were created manually and use an adaptation of Polanyi and Zaenen's (2006) concept of Contextual Valence Shifters to produce a system for measuring the semantic orientation of texts, which they call SO-CAL(culator). This is exactly the approach we used in our Sentitext system for Spanish (Moreno-Ortiz et al., 2010).

Hybrid, i.e., semi-supervised, approaches have also been employed, as in Goldberg and Zhu (2006), where both labeled and unlabeled data are used. Extraction of lexical cues for semantic orientation (i.e., polarity) is usually performed semi-automatically, for example by Mutual Information scores obtained from adjectives or adverbs, which are the most obvious word classes to convey subjective meaning. To a lesser extent, nouns (e.g. Riloff et al., 2003) and verbs (e.g. Riloff and Wiebe, 2003) have also been used to identify semantic orientation. It is worth noting at this point that no mention has been made thus far of MWE's. The reason is simply that they have by and large been ignored, probably due to the increased complexity that dealing with them involves.

Sentiment Analysis approaches can also be classified according to output granularity. Most systems fall in the *Thumbs up or Thumbs Down* approach, i.e., producing a simple positive or negative rating. Turney's (2002) work, from which the designation derives, is no doubt the most representative. A further attempt can be made to produce not just a binary classification of documents, but a numerical rating on a scale. The rating inference problem was first posed by Pang and Lee (2005), and the approach is usually referred to as *Seeing Stars* in reference to that work, where they compared different variants of the original SVM binary classification scheme aimed at supporting *n*-ary classification. Gupta et al. (2010) further elaborated on the multi-scale issue by tackling multi-aspect, i.e., pinpointing the evaluation of multiple aspects of the object being reviewed, a feature we regard as essential for high-quality, fine-grained sentiment analysis, but one that requires very precise topic identification capabilities.

2.1 Sentiment Analysis for Spanish

Nor surprisingly, work within the field of Sentiment Analysis for Spanish is, by far, scarcer than for English. Besides, most studies focus on specific domains, typically movie reviews.

Cruz et al. (2008) developed a document classification system for Spanish similar to Turney's (2002), i.e. unsupervised, though they also tested a supervised classifier that yielded better results. In both cases, they used a corpus of movie reviews taken from the Spanish Muchocine website. Boldrini et al. (2009) carried out a preliminary study in which they used machine learning techniques to mine opinions in blogs. They created a corpus for Spanish using their Emotiblog system, and discussed the difficulties they encountered while annotating it. Balahur et al. (2009) also presented a method of emotion classification for Spanish, this time using a database of culturally dependent emotion triggers. Finally, Brooke et al. (2009) adapted a lexicon-based sentiment analysis system for English (Taboada et al., 2011) to Spanish by automatically translating the core lexicons and adapting other resources in various ways. They also provide an interesting evaluation that compares the performance of both the original (English) and translated (Spanish) systems using both machine learning methods (specifically, SVM) and their own lexicon-based semantic orientation calculation algorithm, SO-CAL, mentioned above. They found that their own weighting algorithm, which is based on the same premises as our system, achieved better accuracy for both languages, but the accuracy for Spanish was well below that for English.

Our system, Sentitext (Moreno-Ortiz et al., 2010; 2011), is very similar to Brooke et al.'s (2009) in design: it is also lexicon-based and it makes use of a similar calculation method for semantic orientation. It differs in that the lexical knowledge has been acquired semi-automatically and then manually revised from the ground up over a long period of time, with a strong commitment to both coverage and quality. It makes no use of user-provided, explicit ratings that supervised systems typically rely on for the training process, and it produces an index of semantic orientation based on weighing positive against negative text segments, which is then transformed into a ten-point scale and a five-star rating system.

Yet another way in which our system differs from most other systems, including Taboada et al.'s (2011), is in the relevance given to multiword expressions vis-à-vis individual words.

3 Sentitext: a SA system for Spanish

Sentitext is a web-based, client-server application written in C++ (main code) and Python (server). The only third-party component in the system is Freeling (Atserias et al., 2006; Padró, 2011), a powerful, multi-language NLP suite of tools, which we use for basic morphosyntactic analysis. Currently, only one client application is available, developed in Adobe Flex,[2] which takes an input text and returns the results of the analysis in several numerical and graphical ways, including visual representations of the text segments that were identified as sentiment-laden. For storage, we rely on a relational database (MySQL), where lexical information is stored.

Given that it is a linguistically-motivated sentiment analysis system, special attention is paid to the representation and management of the lexical resources that Sentitext uses for its analysis. The underlying design principle is to isolate lexical knowledge from processing as much as possible, so that the processors can use the data directly from the database. The idea behind this design is that all lexical sources can be edited at any time by any member of the team, which is facilitated by a PHP interface specifically developed to this end. We believe this approach is optimal for lexicon-based systems, since it allows improvements to be easily incorporated simply by updating the database by means of a user-friendly interface.

3.1 Data sources

Sentitext relies on three major sources: the individual word dictionary (*words*), the multiword expressions dictionary (*mwords*), and the context rules set (*crules*), which is our implementation of Contextual Valence Shifters (Polanyi and Zaenen, 2006).

The individual word dictionary currently contains over 9,400 items, all of which are labeled for valence. The acquisition process for this dictionary was inspired by the bootstrapping method recurrently found in the literature (e.g., Riloff and Wiebe, 2003, Aue and Gamon, 2005). We adapted this methodology in the following way: first, we established a set of 22 antonymic pairs of words to be used as seed words, which we fed to the Spanish version of the OpenOffice thesaurus in order to track its contents for sentiment-carrying words. However, rather than doing this automatically, we built an interactive tool that presented a user with consecutive rounds of candidate words to be added to the dictionary, thus providing the means to

[2] This application can be accessed and tested online at http://tecnolengua.uma.es/sentitext

block wrong polarity assignments, caused mainly by polysemy, that would propagate to subsequent sets of synonymous words. The resulting dictionary was thoroughly revised manually and actual valences were added by lexicographers using the GDB tool. In Section 4, we elaborate on this process of manual valence assignment in relation to the MWEs dictionary, which does not differ from the one used in the word dictionary. Lexical items in both dictionaries in our database were assigned one of the following valences: -2, -1, 0, 1, 2. However, since the word dictionary contains only sentiment-carrying items, no 0-valence word is present.

The SA system most similar to ours (Taboada et al., 2011) uses a scale from -5 to +5, which makes sense for a number of graded sets of near synonyms such as those given as examples by the authors (p. 273). In our opinion, however, as more values are allowed, it becomes increasingly difficult to decide on a specific one while maintaining a reasonable degree of objectivity and agreement among different (human) acquirers, especially when there is no obvious graded set of related words, which is very often the case. In fact, our initial intention was to use a -5 to 5 scale, but this idea was abandoned, as the difficulty for assigning such fine-grained valences became apparent in actual practice on a large scale dictionary.

This does not imply that valence values for actual words and MWEs in context are limited to these. In a lexicon-based SA system that computes a sentiment rating based on weighing positive against negative text segments there should be a way to distinguish not only between, for example, the adjectives "good" and "bad", but also deal with the semantics of qualifiers, as in "very good", and "extremely good". This is where context rules come into play.

3.2 Context rules

It is important to understand the way our context rules work in order to appreciate how closely they interact with the other lexical data sources, especially the multiword dictionary. Simply accounting for negative and positive words and phrases found in a text would not be enough. There are two ways in which their valence can be modified by the immediately surrounding context: the valence can change in degree (intensification or downtoning), or it may be inverted altogether. Negation is the simplest case of valence inversion.

The idea of Contextual Valence Shifters (CVS) was first introduced by Polanyi and Zaenen (2006), and implemented for English by Andreevskaia and Bergler (2007) in their CLaC System, and by Taboada et al. (2011) in their Semantic Orientation CALculator (SO-CAL). To our knowledge, apart from Brooke et al.'s (2009) adaptation of the SO-CAL system, Sentitext is the only sentiment analysis system to implement CVS for Spanish *natively*.

Our CVS system is implemented in what we call Context Rules, which are expressed as the following data structure:

1. Unit Form: Freeling-compliant morphosyntactic definition of the item being modified (e.g.: "AQ" for qualifying adjectives).
2. Unit Sign: polarity of the item being modified (e.g. "+").
3. CVS Definition: modifier definition (e.g.: *very*,"very").
4. CVS Position: position of the modifier (e.g. "L" for left).
5. CVS Span: maximum number of words where the modifier can be found in the modified item.
6. Result: valence result of the modification. This result can be expressed as either an operator or a set valence. An operators is one of the following
   - INV (valence/polarity INVersion)
   - INT*n* (valence INTensification of *n*)
   - DOW*n* (valence DOWntoning of *n*).

The *n* argument in the last two operators is the degree by which the operator is to be applied. The result can also be a set valence, in which case it looks like any valence expressed in the dictionaries.

This system allows us to describe fairly elaborate context rules; for instance, having multiword modifiers such as those in (1) and (2) below. A context rule for type (1) constructions would cause the polarity of the negative adjective to be inverted, whereas a rule for type (2) constructions would intensify the valence of the negative adjective.

(1) *no tener nada de* (be not at all) + negative adjective:
"Ese no tiene nada de tonto/estúpido/..."
("He's not at all dumb/stupid/...")

(2) *(ser) un completo* (be a complete) + negative adjective:
"Es un completo idiota" ("He's a complete idiot")

The implementation of this kind of context rules gives us greater flexibility than simply having a repository of MWEs. Without context rules, it would be very difficult to represent (and successfully process for SA) these types of MWEs, where part of them is defined by the existence of a given semantic prosody that triggers a certain polarity (e.g., adjectives denoting a negative quality).

3.3 Computing Sentiment

Sentitext returns a number of metrics in the form of an XML file which is then used to generate the reports and graphical representations of the data. The crucial information is a *Global Sentiment Value* (GSV), which is a numerical score (on a 0-10 scale) for the sentiment of the input text. Other data include the total number of words, total number of lexical words (i.e., content, non-grammatical words), number of neutral words, etc.

To arrive at the global value, a number of scores are computed. The most important is what we call *Affect Intensity*, which modulates the GSV to reflect the percentage of sentiment-conveying words that the text contains. Before we explain how this score is obtained, it is worth stressing the fact that we do not count words (whether positive, negative, or neutral): we count identified text segments that correspond to lexical units (i.e., meaning units from a lexical perspective). A segment is one of the following:

1. A single word or MWE as found in the text (or rather, its lemmatized form), either neutral or otherwise. MWEs are not marked in any special way in Sentitext's output, except for the fact that the individual words it is composed of appear in the lemmatized form in which they are stored in the database.
2. A single word or MWE identified as a sentiment-conveying lexical item, whose valence has been modified by a context rule, either by inversion or by intensification.

As we mentioned before, items in our dictionaries are marked for valence with values in the range -2 to 2. Intensification context rules can add up to three marks, for maximum score of 5 (negative or positive) for any given segment.

The simplest way of computing a global value for sentiment would be to add negative values on the one hand and positive values on the other, and then establish it by simple subtraction. However, as others have noted (e.g., Taboada et al., 2011), things are rather more complicated than that. Our Affect Intensity measure is an attempt to capture the effect that different proportions of sentiment-carrying segments have in a text. We define the Affect Intensity simply as the percentage of sentiment-carrying segments. Affect Intensity is not used directly in computing the global value for the text, however: we first adjust the upper and lower limits (initially -5 and 5). The adjusted limit or *Upper Bound* equals the initial limit unless the Affect Intensity is greater than 25 (i.e., over 25% of the text's lexical items are sentiment-carrying). Obviously, this figure is arbitrary, and has been arrived at simply by trial and error. The Upper Bound is obtained by dividing the Affect Intensity by 5 (since there are 5 possible negative and positive valence values).

A further variable needs some explaining. Our approach to computing the GSV is similar to Polanyi and Zaenen's (2006) original method, in which equal weight is given to positive and negative segments, but it differs in that we place more weight on extreme values. This is motivated by the fact that it is relatively uncommon to come across such values (e.g. "extremely wonderful"), so when they do appear, it is a clear marker of positive sentiment. Other implementations of Contextual Valence Shifters (Taboada et al., 2011) have put more weight only on negative segments when modified by valence shifters (up to 50% more weight), operating under the so-called "positive bias" assumption (Kennedy and Inkpen, 2006), i.e., negative words and expressions appear more rarely than positive ones, and therefore have a stronger cognitive impact, which should be reflected in the final sentiment score.

In our implementation, equal weight is placed on positive and negative values. However, we do not simply assign more weight to both extremes of the scale (-5 and 5), we place more weight increasingly to each value by multiplying them by different factors, from -12.5 to 12.5 in 2.5 increments[3].

[3] Our rating scale is based on a 0-10 scale, i.e., a 11-point scale, which is the most familiar for Spanish users, commonly used for grading. Sentitext outputs its rating using such a scale, and then this is converted to 5-star rating system.

What we aim to achieve with these increments is to give more weight to extreme values. For example, a text segment that has been assigned a valence of +4, which warrants a 10 factor, would end up having twice as much weight as two +2 segments (5 factor): 10x4x1=40; 5x2x2=20. The reason for this is that such extreme values are rarely found and, when they are, they invariably signal strong opinion.

The resulting method for obtaining the Global Sentiment Value for a text is expressed by Equation 1 below,

$$GSV = \frac{(\sum_{i=1}^{5} 2.5i \cdot i \cdot N_i + \sum_{i=1}^{5} 2.5i \cdot i \cdot P_i) \cdot UB}{5 \cdot (LS - NS)} \quad (1)$$

where N_i is the number of each of the negative valences found, and P_i is the equivalent for positive values. The sum of both sets is then multiplied by the Upper Bound (*UB*). *LS* is the number of lexical segments and *NS* is the number of neutral ones. Although not expressed in the equation, the number of possible scale points (5) needs to be added to the resulting score, which, as mentioned before, is on a 0-10 scale.

This formula was arrived at by trial and error and heuristics, starting from the simple addition and weighing of positive and negative valences. We found that accounting for the proportion of neutral-to-polarity segments was clearly necessary, because otherwise a fully neutral text with a few polarity segments would be analyzed as highly positive or negative, which is usually not the case. Similarly, opinion texts commonly show a number of mild opinion expressions, but if extreme values are found, they largely determines the overall opinion of the text.

Although we think that the positive bias path is worth exploring, we have not to date made comparisons with our current method. In the following section we describe previous performance tests of our system and mention some other ways in which it could be improved.

3.4 Performance

Sentitext was designed, from the beginning, with domain independence in mind. However, our first formal evaluation of the system (Moreno-Ortiz et al., 2010) was performed using a set of user reviews from the Spanish Tripadvisor website. The results of our experiment showed that good performance on a domain-specific corpus implied even better performance on general language texts.

Table 1 below shows a tendency toward low recall of negative segments, which we think may be caused by the "positive bias" effect mentioned in the previous section. In any event, these figures are more than reasonable for a sentiment analysis system.

Dataset	Precision	Recall
Global segments	0,848	0,616
Positive segments	0,838	0,669
Negative segments	0,864	0,525

Table 1: Precision and recall results in global, positive and negative segment valences.

A second evaluation (Moreno-Ortiz et al., 2011) was carried out using a greater variety of types of user reviews: movies, books and music, consumer goods, and electronics. We also introduced new features, such as a slightly modified system for calculating the GSV (modified Affect Intensity threshold) and conversion of the 0-10 score to a 5-point star-rating system. Introducing the star-rating system posed interesting questions, such as defining what is a miss and what is a hit, when comparing Sentitext's results to human ratings. Performance results were consistent with the previous evaluation, and confirmed a tendency to obtain better results for reviews of non-content objects (i.e. not books and movies), such as electronics.

A recent evaluation (Moreno-Ortiz and Pérez-Hernández, 2013) has been carried out using a large set of Twitter messages. This work was developed for the TASS workshop (Villena-Roman et al., 2013), where a double challenge was proposed by the organizers that consisted of classifying over 60,000 tweets according to their polarity in 3 levels + none and 5 levels + none, respectively. This time performance was significantly poorer, which we attribute to both the nature of the texts, and the imposed distinction between neutral and no polarity, which we find irrelevant[4]. It has served,

[4] In this scheme, no polarity means that no lexical segments carrying polarity were found, whereas neutral means that positive and negative text segments cancel each other out. Our Affect Intensity measure could easily be used for this, but such a distinction is not really useful for most applications, and usually not taken into account in the literature.

however, as proof that our GSV calculation needs to be modified in order to account for extremely short texts.

4 MWEs in Sentitext

Our criteria for the lexical representation of MWEs were largely determined by our choice of tools for basic morphosyntactic analysis, i.e., tokenization, part-of-speech tagging, and lemmatization. Freeling has the advantage of offering a very flexible MWE recognition engine.

An important advantage of using Freeling is that, being open source, the lexical resources it uses for its analysis are installed in the system in the form of text files, which allows for relatively easy editing. This is particularly useful for the acquisition of MWEs, since, although Freeling includes only a reduced set of common phrases, it is fairly straightforward to update the text file that contains them.

As for the criteria we have employed for the inclusion of an item in our database, we follow Baldwin and Kim's (2010) loose definition of *MWEhood* and typology of idiomaticity. They distinguish between lexical, semantic, pragmatic, and statistic idiomaticity, where MWEs may display one or more of those types. Some of them are idiomatic at more than one level, whereas others at one (statistical idiomaticity, in the case of collocations, for example).

4.1 Annotation schema

As of February 2013, the Sentitext MWE lexicon contains over 19,000 entries, most of which are, as expected, noun phrases. The full distribution according to syntactic category is shown in Table 2 below.

MWE Category	Number	Proportion
Noun Phrases	10,421	55%
Verb Phrases	4,768	25%
Adverbial Phrases	2,255	12%
Interjections[5]	781	4%
Adjectival Phrases	436	2%
Prepositional phrases	237	1%
Conjunctions	122	1%

Table 2: Distribution of MWE categories in the Sentitext lexicon.

Freeling uses the EAGLES tagset recommendations for morphosyntactic annotation of corpora (EAGLES, 1996), which have consistently proved their viability in the past. The EAGLES recommendations do not impose a particular representation scheme for MWEs, and Freeling takes a simple compositional approach in which MWEs are sequences of categorized individual words.

Each morphological tag is composed of different data fields, depending on which morphosyntactic category it belongs to; some categories, like interjections, have just one field, while others have up to seven fields (e.g., verb phrases), some of which may be instantiated at runtime. For example, the morphologically invariable MWE *gafas de sol* ("sunglasses") is represented as

(3) gafas_de_sol,gafas_de_sol,NCMS000

where the tag "NCMS000" specifies that it is: N = noun, C = common, M = masculine, S = singular. Whereas in (4) below (*oso polar*, "polar bear"), the MWE is defined as a noun phrase composed of two lemmas that can be instantiated to any valid words form at runtime.

(4) <oso>_<polar>,oso_polar,$1:NC

4.2 Acquisition and valence assignment

Our *mwords* dictionary was obtained mainly from dictionaries and corpora, and the initial collection was subsequently enhanced during the extensive application testing process. We regard our acquisition of lexical items as an ongoing effort.

Prior to tagging our initial set of MWEs for Freeling, a review process was carried out to ensure that they adhered to certain varietal and statistical criteria. Castilian Spanish was taken as the standard, and very rarely are other varieties accounted for.

The most time-consuming task was obviously identifying and marking up the components of the MWEs that can be inflected. This was a lengthy process, and the results had to be checked exhaustively, since a mistake could result in an MWE not being identified in any of its forms. This was performed manually, but aided by an interface that provided a set of templates with the most commonly used morphological structures, also reducing the possibility of typing mistakes. Next we added the morphological tags, a semiautomatic process that employed RE pattern matching and then a manual check.

[5] Interjections include idioms and other set phrases that have the form of a full sentence.

Valence assignment was a manual process in which lists of MWEs were rotated among team members, all native speakers of Spanish with training in Linguistics, to keep personal bias to a minimum, and hard cases were checked against corpora and decisions made on actual usage.[6] Agreement was usually high, since ambiguity and polysemy in MWEs is lower than that of individual words, especially in terms of polarity.

As mentioned in section 3.1 above, the valences assigned to the items in our database can range from -2 to 2. However, the results obtained from Sentitext's analyses can exceed these limits after the application of context rules. For example, the MWE *loco de atar* ("mad as a hatter") has a valence of -2. If we analyze the phrase *completamente loco de atar* with Sentitext, the analyzer will recognize the adjective phrase *loco de atar*, as well as the premodifying adverb *completamente*, which intensifies its valence by 2; this will result in a score of -4 for the entire phrase.

It is worth mentioning that MWEs do not require specific context rules –since their tags are the same as those used for individual words (AQ in this example), the rule that states that the adverb *completamente* to the right of an adjective intensifies its valence by 2 applies to both adjectives and MWEs tagged as such. This, which is a consequence of Freeling's annotation scheme, simplifies the acquisition and maintenance of context rules.

4.3 The role of MWEs in GSV calculation

As Table 3 shows, more than half of the MWEs in our lexicon are neutral, but this does not mean that they have no effect on the overall emotional content of texts. Neutral MWEs can be modified by words or other MWEs through the application of context rules in such a way that their polarity and/or valence is altered.

MWE Polarity	Number	Proportion
Neutral	10,823	56%
Negative	5,578	30%
Positive	2,586	14%

Table 3: Distribution of MWEs polarity in the Sentitext lexicon

For comparison's sake, our single words lexicon contains 9,404 words, all of them polarity-carrying, of which 6,907 (73%) are negative and 2,497 (27%) are positive. This is very similar to the distribution of sentiment-laden MWEs, with negative items being much more frequent than positive ones.

It is also important to note that, even when MWEs are neutral, their identification is necessary to produce the right number of lexical segments, which is taken into account in obtaining the GSV for the text.

There is yet another crucial way in which failing to identify a MWE will interfere with calculation of our GSV: if a sentiment-carrying word is part of a MWE, and that MWE is not accounted for by the *mwords* dictionary, the individual word (whose valence may or may not be correct or relevant) will be incorrectly tagged for valence.

This is particularly true of non-compositional MWEs, where the valence of the MWE cannot be deduced or calculated from the valences of the individual words that it comprises. By maintaining the MWE in the database, we eliminate the problem of having Sentitext identify parts of a MWE as individual words.

For example, the word "honor" tends to have a positive polarity, but it is also a word that frequently appears in neutral, negative and positive MWEs:

- Positive: *palabra de honor* (word of honor)
- Neutral: *dama de honor* (bridesmaid).
- Negative: *delito contra el honor* (offense against honor).

Examples of neutral individual words that appear in polarity-carrying MWEs are the following:[7]

- *darse a la bebida* (take to drink) [-2]
- *números rojos* (in the red) [-2]
- *alzamiento de bienes* (concealment of assets) [-2]
- *apaga y vámonos* (it can't be helped) [-2]
- quedarse a cuadros (be astonished) [-2]
- haber química (get on well) [2]
- ir como la seda (go smoothly) [2]

[6] The corpora used were the COE (*Corpus de Opinión del Español*), a collection of product reviews and opinion texts, compiled by our research team, and the *Corpus del Español*, a 100 million words reference corpus compiled by Mark Davies freely available for research purposes at http://www.corpusdelespanol.org.

[7] The number in square brackets marks the valence that the MWE has in our lexicon.

In all these cases no individual word that is part of the MWEs shows any polarity whatsoever, while the MWEs themselves clearly do.

It is also common to find cases in which polarity-carrying individual words are part of MWEs that have the opposite polarity:

- *amor egoísta* (selfish love) [-2]: *amor* has valence [2] as an individual word.
- ¡a buenas horas, mangas verdes! (about time, too!) [-1]: *bueno* has valence [1].
- (querer) con locura (madly in love) [2]: *locura*" has valence [-2].
- *libre de obstáculos* (free of obstacles) [2]: *obstáculo* has valence [-1].
- morir de gusto (die of pleasure) [2]: *morir* has valence [-2].

In all these cases, not being able to account for the MWEs, would have even a stronger negative effect on the overall result.

5 Conclusion

We have shown several significant ways in which MWEs contribute to the semantic orientation of the text as a whole.

First, MWEs show a much higher proportion of polarity items (44% in our lexicon) than single lexical items do. The distribution of polarity MWEs is also very relevant. Negative MWEs make up for more than double of positive ones (30% vs. 14%), which means that the higher the proportion of MWEs there are in a text, the more likely it is for it to be negative overall.

Second, the number of lexical units they contain would alter the global calculation of semantic orientation. And, finally, the polarity of those lexical items, if computed individually, often interferes with that of the MWE as a unit. Of particular importance is the case of non-compositional MWEs, where the valence of the MWE cannot be deduced or calculated from the valences of the individual words that it comprises. This is not only a question of neutral words acquiring a certain polarity when they appear in a MWE: as we have shown, some words may also reverse their polarity from positive to negative or the other way around.

As a result, we believe that proper management and extensive coverage of MWEs in lexicon-based Sentiment Analysis systems is critical to successfully analyzing input texts.

References

Andreevskaia, A. and S. Bergler. 2007. CLaC and CLaC-NB: knowledge-based and corpus-based approaches to sentiment tagging. *Proceedings of the 4th International Workshop on Semantic Evaluation* (pp. 117–120). ACL, Prague, Czech Republic.

Atserias, J., B. Casas, E. Cornelles, M. González, L. Padró, and M. Padró. 2006. FreeLing 1.3: Syntactic and semantic services in an open-source NLP library. *Proceedings of the 5th ELREC International Conference*. ELRA, Genoa.

Aue, A. and M. Gamon. 2005. Customizing sentiment classifiers to new domains: A case study. *Proceedings of RANLP 2005.* Borovets, Bulgaria.

Balahur, A., Z. Kozareva, and A. Montoyo. 2009. Determining the polarity and source of opinions expressed in political debates. *Proceedings of the 10th International Conference on Computational Linguistics and Intelligent Text Processing* (pp. 468–480). Springer-Verlag, Berlin, Heidelberg.

Baldwin, T. and S. Kim. 2010. Multiword expressions. *Handbook of Natural Language Processing, 2nd edition.* N. Indurkhya and F. J. Damerau (eds.) (pp. 267–292). CRC Press, Boca Raton.

Boldrini, E., A. Balahur, P. Martínez-Barco, and A. Montoyo. 2009. EmotiBlog: an annotation scheme for emotion detection and analysis in non-traditional textual genres. *Proceedings of the 2009 International Conference on Data Mining* (pp. 491–497). CSREA Press, Las Vegas, USA.

Brooke, J., M. Tofiloski, and M. Taboada. 2009. Cross-Linguistic Sentiment Analysis: From English to Spanish. *Proceedings of RANLP 2009,* (pp. 50–54). Borovets, Bulgaria.

Cruz, F., J.A. Troyano, F. Enriquez, and J. Ortega. (2008). Clasificación de documentos basada en la opinión: experimentos con un corpus de críticas de cine en español. *Procesamiento del Lenguaje Natural*, 41: 73–80.

EAGLES. 1996. Recommendations for the Morphosyntactic Annotation of Corpora (EAG--TCWG--MAC/R).

Erman, B. and B. Warren. 2000. The Idiom Principle and the Open Choice Principle. *Text*, *20*(1): 29–62.

Goldberg, A. B. and X. Zhu. (2006). Seeing stars when there aren't many stars: graph-based semi-supervised learning for sentiment categorization. *Proceedings of the 1st Workshop on Graph Based Methods for NLP* (pp. 45–52). ACL, Stroudsburg, PA, USA.

Gupta, N., G. Di Fabbrizio, and P. Haffner. 2010. Capturing the stars: predicting ratings for service and product reviews. *Proceedings of the NAACL HLT 2010 Workshop on Semantic Search* (pp. 36–43). ACL, Stroudsburg, PA, USA.

Hatzivassiloglou, V. and J. Wiebe. 2000. Effects of adjective orientation and gradability on sentence sub-

jectivity. *18th International Conference on Computational Linguistics* (pp. 299–305). ACL.
Jackendoff, R. 1997. *The Architecture of the Language Faculty*. MIT, Massachusetts.
Kennedy, A. and D. Inkpen. 2006. Sentiment classification of movie reviews using contextual valence shifters. *Computational Intelligence*, *22*(2): 110–125.
Moreno-Ortiz, A., F. Pineda, and R. Hidalgo. 2010. Análisis de valoraciones de usuario de hoteles con Sentitext: un sistema de análisis de sentimiento independiente del dominio. *Procesamiento de Lenguaje Natural*, 45: 31–39.
Moreno-Ortiz, A., C. Pérez, and R. Hidalgo. 2011. Domain-neutral, linguistically-motivated Sentiment Analysis: a performance evaluation. *Actas del XXVII Congreso de la SEPLN* (pp. 847–856). Huelva, Spain.
Moreno-Ortiz, A. and C. Pérez-Hernández. (2013). Lexicon-based Sentiment Analysis of Twitter messages in Spanish. *Procesamiento de Lenguaje Natural*, 50: 93–100.
Padró, L. 2011. Analizadores multilingües en FreeLing. *Linguamatica*, *3*(2): 13–20.
Pang, B., L. Lee, and S. Vaithyanathan. 2002. Thumbs up?: sentiment classification using machine learning techniques. *Proceedings of the ACL-02 Conference on Empirical Methods in NLP - Volume 10* (pp. 79–86).
Pang, B. and L. Lee. 2005. Seeing stars: Exploiting class relationships for sentiment categorization with respect to rating scales. *Proceedings of ACL 2005* (pp. 115–124). ACL.
Pang, B. and L. Lee. 2008. Opinion Mining and Sentiment Analysis. *Foundations and Trends in Information Retreival*, *2*(1-2): 1–135.
Polanyi, L. A. and Zaenen. 2006. Contextual valence shifters. *Computing Attitude and Affect in Text: Theory and Applications* (pp. 1–10). Springer, Dordrecht.
Riloff, E. J. and J. Wiebe. 2003. Learning extraction patterns for subjective expressions. *Proceedings of the 2003 Conference on Empirical Methods in NLP* (pp. 105–112). ACL, Stroudsburg, PA, USA.
Riloff, E., J. Wiebe, and T. Wilson. 2003. Learning subjective nouns using extraction pattern bootstrapping. *Proceedings of the 7th Conference on Natural Language Learning at HLT-NAACL 2003 - Volume 4* (pp. 25–32). ACL, Stroudsburg, PA, USA.
Taboada, M., J. Brooks, M. Tofiloski, K. Voll, and M. Stede. 2011. Lexicon-based methods for Sentiment Analysis. *Computational Linguistics*, *37*(2): 267–307.
Turney, P. D. 2002. Thumbs up or Thumbs down? Semantic orientation applied to unsupervised classification of reviews. *Proceedings of the 40th Annual Meeting of the ACL* (pp. 417–424). ACL, Philadelphia, USA.
Villena-Román, J., J. García, C. Moreno, L. Ferrer, S. Lana, J. González, and A. Westerski. (2013). TASS-Workshop on sentiment analysis at SEPLN. *Procesamiento de Lenguaje Natural*, 50: 37-44.

Introducing *PersPred*, a Syntactic and Semantic Database for Persian Complex Predicates

Pollet Samvelian and **Pegah Faghiri**
Université Sorbonne Nouvelle & CNRS
18, rue des Bernardins
75005, Paris, France
{pollet.samvelian, pegah.faghiri}@univ-paris3.fr

Abstract

This paper introduces *PersPred*, the first manually elaborated syntactic and semantic database for Persian Complex Predicates (CPs). Beside their theoretical interest, Persian CPs constitute an important challenge in Persian lexicography and for NLP. The first delivery, *PersPred 1*[1], contains 700 CPs, for which 22 fields of lexical, syntactic and semantic information are encoded. The semantic classification *PersPred* provides allows to account for the productivity of these combinations in a way which does justice to their compositionality without overlooking their idiomaticity.

1 Introduction

Persian has only around 250 simplex verbs, half of which are currently used by the speech community[2]. The morphological lexeme formation process outputting verbs from nouns (e.g. *xâb* 'sleep' > *xâb-idan* 'to sleep'; *raqs* 'dance' > *raqs-idan* 'to dance'), though available, is not productive. The verbal lexicon is mainly formed by syntactic combinations, including a verb and a non-verbal element, which can be a noun, e.g. *harf zadan* 'to talk' (Lit. 'talk hit'), an adjective, e.g. *bâz kardan* 'to open' (Lit. 'open do'), a particle, e.g. *bar dâštan* 'to take' (Lit. 'PARTICLE have'), or a prepositional phrase, e.g. *be kâr bordan* 'to use' (Lit. 'to work take'). These combinations are generally referred to as Complex Predicates (CPs), Compound Verbs or Light Verb Constructions (LVCs).

New "verbal concepts" are regularly coined as complex predicates (CPs) rather than simplex verbs, for instance *yonize kardan* 'to ionize' (Lit. 'ionized do') instead of *yon-idan*[3].

Several studies have focused on the dual nature of Persian CPs, which exhibit both lexical and phrasal properties (Goldberg, 2003; Vahedi-Langrudi, 1996; Karimi, 1997; Karimi-Doostan, 1997; Megerdoomian, 2002, among others). Indeed, these combinations display all properties of syntactic combinations, including some degree of semantic compositionality, which makes it impossible to establish a clearcut distinction between them and "ordinary" verb-object combinations for instance (cf. 2.1). On the other hand, these sequences also have word-like properties, since CP formation has all the hallmarks of a lexeme formation process, such as lexicalization (cf. 2.2). Thus, in the same way as the verbal lexicon of English includes all its simplex verbs, the inventory of the verbal lexicon in Persian, and consequently dictionaries, must include these com-

[1] *PersPred 1* is freely available under the LGPL-LR license, http://www.iran-inde.cnrs.fr/ (Language Resources for Persian).

[2] Sadeghi (1993) gives the estimation of 252 verbs, 115 of which are commonly used. Khanlari (1986) provides a list of 279 simplex verbs. The Bijankhan corpus contains 228 lemmas.

[3] In reality, there are verbs formed from nouns or adjectives, but they are mainly created by the Academy of Persian Language and Literature, who suggests and approves equivalents for the foreign general or technical terms. The verb *râyidan* 'to compute', for instance, is a recent creation by the Academy. However, it should be noted that these creations, which are far less numerous than spontaneous creations, are not easily adopted by native speakers, who almost systematically prefer using the CP counterpart, e.g. *kampyut kardan* (Lit. 'computation do') instead of *râyidan*.

binations. However, despite several attempts, this task has not been carried out in a systematic way and such a resource is cruelly missing. Although dictionaries mention some of the lexicalized combinations, either under the entry associated to the verb, or to the non verbal element, the underlying criteria in the choice of combinations is far from being clear and the resulting list significantly varies from one dictionary to another.

Computational studies have also mentioned the lack of large-scale lexical resources for Persian and have developed probabilistic measures to determine the acceptability of the combination of a verb and a noun as a CP (Taslimipoor et al., 2012).

PersPred is a syntactic and semantic database, which aims to contribute to fill this gap by proposing a framework for the storage and the description of Persian CPs. Its first delivery, *PersPred 1.*, contains more than 700 combinations of the verb *zadan* 'hit' with a noun, presented in a spreadsheet.

PersPred is not only a lexicographic resource, it is also the implementation of a theoretical view on Persian CPs. Adopting a Construction-based approach (cf. 4), *PersPred* sheds a new light on some crucial and closely related issues in CP formation:

- The way the productivity of these combinations can be accounted for despite their idiomaticity and the link generally established between compositionality and productivity (cf. 3).

- The relation between "lexical" and "light" verbs and the validity of such a distinction for a great number of Persian verbs.

The fact that Persian has *only* around 250 simplex verbs has a very obvious consequence which has generally been overlooked by theoretical studies: Almost *all* Persian verbs are light verbs, or, more precisely, are simultaneously light and lexical verbs. In other words, if one establishes a scale of specificity in the verbal meaning (Ritter and Rosen, 1996) going from highly specific verbs (e.g. *google*, *milk*) to lowly specific ones (e.g. *do*, *make*), most Persian verbs are located somewhere in the middle of the scale. Consequently, in many CPs, the verb has a lexical semantic content and cannot be considered as a light verb *sensu stricto*. This also entails that Persian CPs are not always as idiomatic as English LVCs, for instance, and that many aspects of their formation can be accounted for via compositionality. By providing a fine-grained semantic classification for Persian CPs, *PersPred* proposes a solution that does justice to the compositionality of these combinations, thus allowing to account for their productivity.

2 Persian CPs as Multiword Expressions

Several studies, including those in computational linguistics, treat Persian CPs like LVCs in languages such as English and French, and thus as MWEs (Fazly et al., 2007, among others). However, the fact that Persian CPs are generally formed by a "bare" (non-determined, non-referential) noun and a verb, in an adjacent position, makes them far more cohesive than English LVCs for instance, and leads some studies to treat these combination as *words* by default (Goldberg, 1996).

2.1 Phrasal Properties

It has been shown by several studies (Karimi-Doostan, 1997; Megerdoomian, 2002; Samvelian, 2012) that the two elements in a CP are clearly separate syntactic units: a) All inflection is prefixed or suffixed on the verb, as in (1), and never on the noun. b) The two elements can be separated by the pronominal clitics, (2), the future auxiliary, (3), or even by clearly syntactic constituents, (4). c) Both the noun and the verb can be coordinated, (5) and (6) respectively. d) The noun can be extracted, (7). e) CPs can be passivized, (8). In this case, the nominal element of the CP can become the subject of the passive construction, as does the Direct Object of a transitive construction. f) Finally, the noun can head a complex NP, (9).

(1) Maryam bâ Omid harf **ne-mi**-zan-**ad**
Maryam with Omid talk NEG-IPFV-hit-3S
'Maryam does not talk to Omid.'[4]

(2) Dust=**aš** dâr-am
friend=3S have-1S
'I like her/him/it.'

[4] DDO = definite direct object marker; EZ = *Ezafe* particle; IPFV = imperfective, NEG = negation, PP = past participle.

(3) Maryam Omid=râ dust **xâh-ad** dâšt
Maryam Omid=DDO friend AUX-3S had
'Maryam will like Omid.'

(4) Dast **be begol-hâ** na-zan
hand to flower-PL NEG-hit
'Don't touch the flowers.'

(5) Mu-hâ=yaš=râ **boros** yâ **šâne** zad
hair-PL=3S=DDO brush or comb hit
'(S)he brushed or combed her hair.'

(6) Omid sili **zad** va **xord**
Omid slap hit and strike
'Omid gave and received slaps.'

(7) **Dast** goft-am be gol-hâ ___ na-zan
hand said-1S to flower-PL ___ NEG-hit
'I told you not to touch the flowers.'

(8) a. Maryam be Omid tohmat zad
Maryam to Omid slander hit
'Maryam slandered Omid.'

b. Be Omid tohmat zade šod
to Omid slander hit.PP become
'Omid was slandered.'

(9) [In **xabar**=e mohem]=râ be mâ **dâd**
this news=EZ important=DDO to us gave
'(S)he gave us this important news.'

These observations show that the syntactic properties of CPs are comparable to regular Object-Verb combinations. While the noun in a CP is more cohesive with the verb than a bare direct object (in terms of word order, differential object marking, pronominal affix placement), it is impossible to draw a categorical syntactic distinction between the two types of combinations.

2.2 Lexical and Idiomatic Properties

While clearly being syntactic combinations, Persian CPs display several lexeme like properties (Bonami and Samvelian, 2010). From a semantic point of view, their meaning can be unpredictable (i.e. conventional). From a morphological point of view, the whole sequence behaves like a word in the sense that it feeds lexical formation rules. Finally, the association of a given noun and a given verb is more or less idiomatic.

CPs are lexicalized. In many cases, the meaning of a CP is not fully predictable from the meaning of its components. N-V combinations are subject to various levels of lexicalization.

In some cases, the CP meaning is a **specialization** of the predictable meaning of the combination. For instance *čâqu zadan* 'to stab' (Lit. 'knife hit') is not only to hit somebody with a knife; *dast dâdan* 'to shake hands' (Lit. 'hand give') does not only imply that you give your hand to somebody; *âb dâdan*, 'to water' (Lit. 'water give') is not just pouring water on something; šir dâdan 'to breastfeed' (Lit. 'milk give') is not just the action of giving milk to somebody. These particular specializations have to be learned, in the same way as one has to learn the meaning of the verbs such as *water* or *towel* in English.

In other examples **semantic drift** has taken place, either by metaphor or by metonymy. The link between the compositional meaning and the lexicalized meaning is sometimes still recoverable synchronically. For instance, the lexicalized meaning of *guš kardan* 'to listen' (Lit. 'ear do') can be recovered via metonymy. The CP designates the prototypical action done by ears. Likewise, in *zanjir zadan* 'to flagellate' (Lit. 'chain hit'), the elliptical element of the meaning, *pošt* 'shoulder', can also be recovered. The CP comes in fact from *bâ zanjir (be) pošt zadan* 'to hit one's shoulders with chains'.

However, in numerous other cases, the initial link is no more perceivable by speakers. For instance, *ru gereftan* 'to become cheeky' (Lit. 'face take') and *dast andâxtan* 'to mock' (Lit. 'hand throw') constitute opaque sequences in synchrony.

CPs feed lexeme formation rules. The fact that N-V combinations serve as inputs to further lexeme formation rules has been noted in several studies (cf. Introduction) and has been considered by some of them as an argument to support the "wordhood" of these sequences. For instance, the suffix *-i* forms abilitative adjectives from verbs, e.g. *xordan* 'eat' > *xordani* 'edible' (and by further conversion > *xordani* 'food'). This suffix combines with CPs, independently of whether they are compositional or not: *dust daštan* 'to love' > *dustdaštani* 'lovely'; *xat xordan* 'to be scratched' > *xatxordani* 'scratchable'; *juš xordan* 'to bind' > *jušxordani* 'linkable'.

(Non-)predictibility of the verb. Finally, the combination of a particular verb with a particular noun is idiosyncratic in the sense that there is sometimes no semantic justification for the choice of a particular verb. Thus, two semantically close or even synonymous nouns can be combined with two different verbs to give rise to almost synonymous CPs: *hesâdat kardan* (Lit. 'jealousy do') vs. *rašk bordan* (Lit. 'jealousy take') both mean 'to envy', 'to be jealous'; *sohbat kardan* (Lit. 'talk do') vs. *harf zadan* (Lit. 'talk hit') both mean 'to talk', 'to speak'.

3 Productivity of Persian CPs

Although Persian CPs are idiomatic, they are also highly productive. Several theoretical studies have suggested that compositionality is the key to this productivity and put forward hypotheses on how the contribution of the verb and the noun must be combined to obtain the meaning of the predicate (Folli et al., 2005; Megerdoomian, 2012). However, as (Samvelian, 2012) extensively argues, these "radical compositional" accounts are doomed, because they wrongly assume that a given verb and a given noun each have a consistent contribution through all their combinations to form a CP. In this study, we assume that:

1. Persian CPs do not constitute a homogenous class, ranging from fully compositional combinations to fully idiomatic phrases.
2. Compositionality and productivity constitute two distinct dimensions and thus productivity does not necessarily follow from compositionality.
3. A part of Persian CPs can receive a compositional account, provided compositonality is defined *a posteriori*. For these cases, compositionality does account for productivity.
4. For some other cases, analogical extension on the basis of the properties of the whole CP is responsible for productivity.

3.1 Compositionality-Based Productivity

With respect to their compositionality, Persian CPs are comparable to Idiomatically Combining Expressions (Nunberg et al., 1994), idioms whose parts carry identifiable parts of their idiomatic meanings (p. 496). In other words, the verb and the non-verbal element of a CP can be assigned a meaning in the context of their combination. Thus, the CP is compositional (or decompositional), in the sense that the meaning of the CP can be distributed to its components, and yet it is idiomatic, in the sense that the contribution of each member cannot be determined out of the context of its combination with the other one. This is the line of argumentation used by (Nunberg et al., 1994) to support a compositional view of expressions such as *spill the beans*.

Table 1 below illustrates this point. Each line contains a set of CPs formed with *kešidan* 'to pull', where the verb can be assigned a meaning comparable to that of a lexical verb in English.

Examples of CPs with *Kešidan*	
divâr – 'to build a wall', *jâdde* – 'to build a road', *pol* – 'to build a bridge'	> 'build'
lule – 'to set up pipes', *sim* – 'to install cables', *narde* – 'to set up a fence'	> 'set up'
sigâr – 'to smoke a cigarette', *pip* – 'to smoke a pipe', *taryâk* – 'to smoke opium'	>'smoke'
čâqu – 'to brandish a knife', *haftir* – 'to brandish a revolver', *šamšir* – 'to brandish a sword'	>'brandish'
ranj – 'to suffer', *dard* – 'to suffer from pain', *bixâbi* – 'to suffer from insomnia', *setam* – 'to suffer from injustice'	>'suffer from'
dâd – 'to scream', *faryâd* – 'to scream', *arbade* – 'to yell'	>'emit'
harf – 'to extort information', *e'terâf* – 'to extort a confession', *eqrâr* – 'to extort a confession'	>'extort'

Table 1: Meanings of *kešidan* in the context of its CPs

Given that *kešidan* alone cannot convey any of these meanings, these combinations can be considered as ICEs. On the basis of the meaning assigned to *kešidan* and the meaning of the CP as a whole, new combinations can be produced and interpreted. For instance, the newly coined *šabake kešidan* 'to install a network' can be interpreted given the CP *kâbl kešidan* 'to install cables' in Table 1.

3.2 Analogical Productivity

CPs such as *šâne kešidan* 'to comb', *kise kešidan* 'to rub with an exfoliating glove', *jâru kešidan* 'to broom' and *bros kešidan* 'to brush' constitute a rather coherent paradigm. They all denote an action carried out using an instrument in its conventional way. However, it is impossible to assign a lexical meaning to *kešidan*. Indeed, *kešidan* does not mean 'to use', but to use in a specific manner, which cannot be defined without resorting to the noun *kešidan* combines with. Nevertheless, the fact that these instrumental CPs exist enables speakers to create CPs such as *sešuâr kešidan* 'to do a brushing' (Lit. 'hairdryer pull') on an analogical basis.

In the same way, CPs such as *telefon zadan* 'to phone' (Lit. 'phone hit'), *telegrâf zadan* 'to send a telegraph' (Lit. 'telegraph hit'), *bisim zadan* 'to walkie-talkie', 'to communicate by means of a walkie-talkie' (Lit. 'walkie-talkie hit') constitute a rather coherent paradigm. However, it is impossible to assign a meaning to *zadan* in these combinations. Nevertheless recent combinations such as *imeyl zadan* 'to email' or *esemes zadan* 'to text, to sms' have been created by analogical extension.

4 A Construction-Based Approach

Building on the conclusions presented in the previous section, Samvelian (2012) proposes a Construction-based approach of Persian CPs. A Construction, in the sense of Goldberg (1995) and Kay and Fillmore (1999), is a conventional association between a form and a meaning. Given that Persian CPs are MWEs, they each correspond to a Construction. Constructions can be of various levels of abstractness and can be organized hierarchically, going from the most specific ones (in our case a given CP, *jâru zadan* 'to broom') to more abstract ones (e.g. Instrumental CPs).

Samvelian (2012) applies this Contruction-based perspective to the CPs formed with *zadan* 'to hit' and provides a set of abstract Constructions grouping these CPs on the basis of their semantic and syntactic similarities.

Although *zadan* is not the most frequent verb[5] in the formation of CPs compared to *kardan* 'to do' or *šodan* 'to become', it is nevertheless a productive one, in the sense that it regularly forms new CPs: *imeyl zadan* 'to email', *lâyk zadan* 'to like (on Facebook)', *tredmil zadan* 'to run on a treadmill', *epileydi zadan* 'to use an epilator'. Besides, *zadan* has a more consistent semantic content than *kardan* 'to do' or *šodan* 'to become', which function more or less like verbalizers with no real semantic contribution, similarly to conversion or derivation. *Zadan*, on the contrary, can convey several lexical meanings, such as 'hit', 'beat', 'cut', 'put', 'apply'... Consequently, CPs formed with *zadan* provide an interesting case study to highlight the continuum going from lexical verbs to light verbs (or from free syntactic combinations to idiomatic combinations), as well as the way new combinations are coined on the basis of semantic groupings.

Each class is represented by a partially fixed Construction. Here are two examples of Constructions:

(10) **Instrumental-*zadan* Construction**

N0	(*be*) N1	N	*zadan*
Agent	Patient	Instrument	

'N0 accomplishes the typical action for which N is used (on N1)'

N *zadan*: *bil* – 'to shovel', *boros* – 'to brush', *jâru* – 'to broom', *mesvâk* – 'to brush one's teeth', *otu* – 'to iron', *šâne* – 'to comb', *sohân* – 'to file', *suzan* – 'to sew', *qeyči* – 'to cut with scissors'...

(11) **Forming-*zadan* Construction**

N0	N	*zadan*
Location/Theme	Theme	

'N is formed on N0'/ 'N0 is changed into N'

N *zadan*: *javâne* – 'to bud', *juš* – 'to sprout', *kapak* – 'to go moldy', *šabnam* – 'to dew', *šokufe* – 'to bloom', *tabxâl* – 'to develop coldsore', *tâval* – 'to

[5]To give a rough approximation, the most frequent verb in the Bijankhan corpus (see section 5.1) is *kardan* with 30k occurrences, *zadan* stands in 21st place with 1k occurrences

blister', *yax* – 'to freeze', *zang* – 'to rust', *pine* – 'to become calloused', *nam* – 'to dampen'...

Note that these semantic groupings do not exclusively lie on the semantic relatedness of the nouns occurring in the CPs, but involve the Construction as a whole. While semantic relatedness of the nouns is indeed a good cue for grouping CPs, it does not always allow to account for the relatedness of otherwise clearly related CPs. For instance, *kapak zadan* 'go moldy' (Lit. 'mold hit'), *javâne zadan* 'bud' (Lit. 'bud hit'), *juš zadan* 'sprout' (Lit. 'spot hit'), *šabnam zadan* 'dew' (Lit. 'dew hit'), *zang zadan* 'rust' (Lit. 'rust hit') can be grouped together (see 11 above) on the basis of the fact that they all denote a change of state generally resulting in the formation, development or outbreak of an entity (denoted by the nominal element of the CP) on another entity (denoted by the grammatical subject of the CP). However *mold, bud, spot, dew* and *rust, ice, dampness* and *blister* do not form a natural class.

Constructions can be structured in networks, reflecting different relationships such as hyponymy/hyperonymy (subtypes vs supertypes), synonymy, valency alternations.

Semantic Subtypes and Supertypes. Some semantic classes can be grouped together into a more abstract class. In this case, the Construction that is associated to them is the subtype of a less specific Construction. For instance the CPs associated to the *Spreading-zadan Construction*, e.g. *rang zadan* 'to paint' (Lit. 'paint hit'), can be considered as *Locatum* (or *Figure*) CPs. *Locatum* verbs, e.g. *paint, salt* (Clark and Clark, 1979), incorporate a Figure (i.e. the noun to which the verb is morphologically related) and have a Ground argument realized as an NP or a PP: 'to paint sth' = 'to put paint (= Figure) on sth (= Ground). In the case of Persian *Locatum* CPs, the Figure is the nominal element of the CP.

Apart from the *Spreading-zadan Construction, Locatum-zadan Construction* has several other subtypes: *Incorporation-zadan Construction*, e.g. *namak zadan* 'to salt' (Lit. 'salt hit'), *Putting-zadan Construction*, e.g. *dastband zadan* 'to put handcuffs' (Lit. 'handcuff hit') and *Wearing-zadan Construction*, e.g. *eynak zadan* 'to wear glasses' (Lit. 'glasses hit').

Synonymous constructions. The same Construction can be realized by different verbs, e.g. *kardan* 'to do' and *kešidan* 'to pull' also form Instrumental predicates, e.g. *jâru kardan* and *jâru kešidan* 'to broom'. So, along with *Instrumental-zadan Construction*, there is also an *Instrumental-kešidan Construction* and an *Instrumental-kardan Construction*. These three partially fixed Constructions are subtypes of a more abstract Construction, with no lexically fixed element, namely *Instrumental Construction*. Synonymy rises when the same noun occurs in the same Construction realized by different verbs.

Valency alternating Constructions. The same Construction can display valency alternations. For instance, in an *Instrumental Construction*, the Agent argument can be mapped to the grammatical subject and the Patient to the grammatical object, in which case we obtain an "Active" *Instrumental Construction*, or the Patient can be mapped to the grammatical subject, which gives rise to a "Passive" *Instrumental Construction*. This valency alternation is often realized by a verb alternation in the CP: *otu zadan* 'to iron' vs. *otu xordan* 'to be ironed (Lit. 'iron collide'); *âtaš zadan* 'to set fire' vs. *âtaš gereftan* 'to take fire' (Lit. 'fire take').

For a detailed description of Constructions and their hierarchical organization see Samvelian (2012) and Samvelian and Faghiri (to appear).

5 PersPred's Database Conception

Building on Samvelian (2012), *PersPred 1* inventories the CPs formed with *zadan* and a nominal element. Its first delivery includes around 700 combinations grouped in 52 classes and 9 super classes. 22 fields are annotated for each combination.

5.1 Input Data

As Samvelian (2012) extensively argues, the decision whether a given Noun-Verb combination in Persian must be considered as a CP (or LVC) or a free Object-Verb is not straightforward and this opposition is better conceived of in terms of a continuum with a great number of verbs functioning as semi-lexical or semi-light verbs. Consequently, a combination such as *namak zadan* 'to salt' (Lit. 'salt hit') can be viewed either as a CP or as the combination of a lexical verb – *zadan* meaning 'to put', 'to add' or 'to incorporate' – and its object. Hence, the existence of *felfel zadan* 'to pepper', *zarčube zadan* 'to add tumeric' and many others, which constitute an open class. So, our main concern in the elaboration of *PersPred* is not to solve this insolvable problem. We rather intend to provide a sufficiently rich description of the totally idiomatic combinations as well as semi-productive and even totally productive ones, allowing a precise characterization of the lexical semantics of the simplex verbs in Persian. We thus aim to ultimately elaborate a comprehensive verbal lexicon for Persian.

PersPred is built up, and continues to be enriched, from different types of resources and through complementary methods, in a permanent back-and-forth movement.

1) A first list was established on the basis of Samvelian (2012), which proposes a manually extracted list of CPs from various lexicographic resources, literature, media and the Web, along with their semantic classification.

2) This initial list was enriched in two ways, automatic extraction from the Bijankhan corpus[6] and by manually adding semantically related combinations.

Automatic extraction. We used the Bijankhan corpus (Bijankhan, 2004), a freely available corpus of 2.6m tokens, from journalistic texts, annotated for POS. We first lemmatized the verbs (228 types, 185k tokens)[7] and then extracted CP candidates according to the following pattern : N-V or P-N-V, since, as also mentioned by Tamsilipoor et al. (2012), the N-V pattern can be considered to be the prototypical pattern of the CP construction in Persian. Additionally, in order to include prepositional CPs, e.g. *dar nazar gereftan* 'take into account' (Lit. in view take) or *be zamin zadan* 'make fall' (Lit. to ground hit), we also took into account the noun's preceding element if it was a preposition. In total, we extracted a set of 150k combinations (37k types) regardless of the verbal lemma with, as expected, a large number of hapaxes (25k). For *zadan*, we have 1056 combinations of 386 types with 267 hapaxes. It should be noted that low frequency does not imply the irrelevance of the combination since the frequency is corpus-dependent, for instance well established CPs such as *pelk zadan* 'blink', *neq zadan* 'nag', *havâr zadan* 'scream' or *neyrang zadan* 'deceive' have only one occurrence in the corpus. Hence, the manual validation of all the extracted combination types is necessary. To do so, we stored all the candidates in a spreadsheet sorted by descending order of type frequency and manually filtered out irrelevant sequences.

Manual enrichment. Given the existing classes, we considered a set of new candidates to expand each class on the basis of semantic relatedness. We used a simple heuristic – based on Google search results for the exact expression formed by the noun and the verb in its infinitive form – combined with our native speaker intuition to decide whether a candidate should be retained or not. For instance, given the existence of the class labeled `Communicating` with members such as *telefon zadan* 'to phone' or *faks zadan* 'to fax', we considered combinations such as *imeyl zadan* 'to email' and *esemes zadan* 'to SMS', 'to text'.

Note that for totally productive classes (e.g. *Incoporating* class with members such *namak zadan* 'salt' (see above), listing all potential combinations was useless, since the verb selects the noun it combines with in the same way as a lexical verb selects its complements, i.e. via restricting its conceptual class. So, the actual size of a class in *PersPred 1* does not necessarily reflect its real extension.

5.2 Encoded Information

PersPred 1 contains 22 different fields which are conceived to capture different types of lexical, syntactic and semantic information. Tables 2, 3 and 4 below illustrate these fields via the example of the CP *âb zadan* 'wet'. Note that 2 extra fields provide (at least) one attested example in Persian script and its phonetic transcription.

Lemma information. 9 fields provide information on the lemma of the CP and its combining parts, including French and English translations of the Noun, the Verb and the CP.

`CP-Lemma` indicates the lexical identity of the CP. Consequently there are as many lemmas asso-

[6] http://ece.ut.ac.ir/dbrg/bijankhan/

[7] We took the verbal periphrasis into account in the way that a complex conjugation of, for example, three tokens such as *xânde xâhad šod* 'will be read' or two tokens such as *zade ast* 'have hit', are lemmatized and counted as one verb.

Field	Example
Verb	(V in Persian script)
Noun	(N in Persian script)
N-transcription	âb
V-transcription	zadan
CP-lemma	âb-zadan0
N-FR-translation	eau
N-EN-translation	water
CP-FR-translation	mouiller
CP-EN-translation	to wet

Table 2: Lemma fields for *âb zadan* 'to wet'

ciated to the same combination as meanings. Thus CP-Lemma allows to distinguish homonymous CPs on the one hand and to group polysemous and syntactically alternating CPs on the other hand. The notation used is as follows: The CP-lemma is encoded by the concatenation of the nominal and the verbal element, linked by a hyphen and followed by a number, beginning from 0. Homonymous CPs are formed with the same components but refer to clearly different events or situations. For instance, *suzan zadan* (Lit. needle hit) means either to sew or to give an injection. A different lemma is associated to each meaning in this case, suzan-zadan0 and suzan-zadan1. We have adopted an approach favoring grouping of polysemous CPs, by assigning the same lemma to polysemous CPs. Polysemy is hence accounted for by creating multiple lexical entries.

Subcategorization and syntactic information. 8 fields represent the syntactic construction of the CP and its English equivalent through an abstract syntactic template inspired, as mentioned above, by Gross (1975). Valency alternations and synonymy are also represented through 3 fields, Intransitive, Transitive and Synonymous Variants.

The subcatgorization frame is provided by Synt-Construction combined with PRED-N, Prep-Form-N1, Prep-Form-N2, where N stands for a bare noun or a nominal projection (i.e. NP) and the number following N indicates the obliqueness hierarchy among nominal elements: N0 is the 1st argument (subject); N1 the direct object; Prep N1 the prepositional object and so on.

The nominal element of the CP, indicated by PRED-N, is also assigned a number. Even though, this element does not display the typical semantic properties of an argument, from a syntactic point of view it can undergo different operations, which means that it has a syntactic function and must thus be taken into account in the obliqueness hierarchy. PRED-N specifies which constituent in Synt-Construction is the nominal element of the CP (i.e. forms a CP with the verb), and thus takes as its value either N0, N1, N2 or N3 or Prep Nx, in case the nominal of the CP is introduced by a preposition. Prep-Form-N1 and Prep-Form-N2 indicate either the lemma of the preposition which introduces N1 and N2, in case the preposition is lexically fixed, or its semantic value:

Field	Example
Synt-Construction	N0 Prep N1 N2 V
PRED-N	N2
Prep-N1	be
Prep-N2	NONE
Construction-trans-En	N0 wets N2
Intrans-Var	xordan
Trans-Var	NONE
Syn-Var	NONE

Table 3: Syntactic fields for *âb zadan* 'to wet'

Alternations in the argument realization (i.e. direct *vs* prepositional) give rise to several entries. For instance, the second argument of *âb zadan* 'to wet', can either be realized as an NP or a PP (i.e. Dative shift alternation). Consequently, *âb zadan* has two entries which differ with respect to their Synt-Construction feature value: N0 Prep N1 N2 V vs N0 N1 N2 V. Note that these two entries are considered to be two different realizations of the same lemma (i.e. they have the same value for CP-Lemma).

Construction-EN-Trans simultaneously provides the English translation of the CP and the way the arguments of the Persian CP (as encoded in Synt-Construction) are mapped with the grammatical functions in the English translation.

Intrans-Variant, Trans-Variant and Syn-Variant provide information about valency alternations and synonymy. The value of these features is either a verbal lemma or NONE, if there is no attested variant. `Intrans-Variant` provides the lemma of one or several verbs that can be used to produce a CP where the Patient (N1 or N2) argument is assigned the subject function, i.e. becomes N0. This alternation is somehow comparable to the passive alternation. `Trans-Variant` gives the lemma of the verb(s) used to add an extra argument (or participant) to the CP. This external participant generally has a Cause interpretation and is realized as the subject of the "transitive/Causative" CP. The first argument of the initial CP is mapped in this case onto the Object function. `Syn-Variant` gives the lemma of the set of verbs forming a synonymous predicate with the same noun.

Semantic information. 5 fields are dedicated to semantic information, e.g. the semantic subtype and supertype and the type of meaning extension (metaphor, metonymy, synecdoche), if applicable.

Field	Example
`Sem-Class`	Spreading
`Sem-Super-Class`	Locatum
`Constant-Sem`	Liquid
`Subject-Sem`	Human
`Meaning-Exension`	NONE

Table 4: Semantic fields for *âb zadan* 'to wet'

`Sem-Class` and `Sem-Super-Class` give the semantic classification of the CP, i.e. the semantic class and the semantic superclass which the CP is a member of (cf. Section 4 for a detailed explanation). The value of `Sem-Class` corresponds to the most specific partially fixed Construction of which the CP is an instance. The value of `Sem-Super-Class` is the less specific Construction of which the CP is an instance. These feature allow for a hierarchical organization of CPs in classes and super-classes, implementing the Construction networks mentioned in Section 4. CPs which do not pertain to any of the classes are nevertheless considered as the only member of the class they represent. All these singleton classes are assigned the value "isolated" for `Sem-Super-Class`.

`Subject-Sem` and `Constant-Sem` give the semantic class of the subject and the nominal element of the CP. Our classification is more fine-grained than the one adopted in Wordnet, but it can easily be converted into a Wordnet-type classification.

`Meaning-Extension` indicates if a CP has undergone semantic drift, mainly metaphor, metonymy or synecdoche. In the case of a metaphoric extension, the concerned CP is linked to the CP from which it is metaphorically driven.

The integration of a given CP into a given class has been decided on the basis of its most salient semantic properties or some of its meaning components. It should be noted that some meaning components cut across the classes identified in *PersPred 1* and consequently, the CPs that display these meaning components can be cross-classified in different classes[8]. At this stage, only one specific class (i.e. Construction) is mentioned for each CP. One of the future developments of *PersPred* will be to include multiple class memberships.

6 Conclusion

In this paper, we presented *PersPred 1*, which inaugurates the elaboration of a large-scale syntactic and semantic database for Persian CPs. *PersPred 1* is dedicated to CPs formed with *zadan* 'to hit'. We plan to extend its coverage by integrating CPs formed with *dâdan* 'to give', *gereftan* 'to take' and *xordan* 'to collide' shortly. Bearing in mind that integrating new verbs will have an impact on the semantic classes and their networks, and given the fact that our main difficulties so far have been the semantic classification and the time-consuming task of manual annotation, we are currently elaborating semi-automatic annotating methods in order to achieve a satisfactory pace in the future development of *PersPred*.

Acknowledgments

This work was supported by the bilateral project *PerGram*, funded by the ANR (France) and the DGfS (Germany) [grant no. MU 2822/3-I] and is related to the work package LR4.1 of the Labex EFL (funded by the ANR/CGI). We would like to thank Gwendoline Fox and the anonymous reviewers for their helpful comments.

[8]See (Levin, 1993) for similar remarks on English verb classes.

References

Mohammad Bijankhan. 2004. The role of the corpus in writing a grammar : An introduction to a software. *Iranian Journal of Linguistics*, 10(2).

Olivier Bonami and Pollet Samvelian. 2010. Persian complex predicates: Lexeme formation by itself. Paper presented at Septièmes Décembrettes Morphology Conference, Toulouse, December 3.

Eve V. Clark and Herbert H. Clark. 1979. When nouns surface as verbs. *Language*, 55(4):767–811.

Afsaneh Fazly, Suzanne Stevenson, and Ryan North. 2007. Automatically learning semantic knowledge about multiword predicates. *Language Resources and Evaluation*, 41:61–89.

Raffaella Folli, Heidi Harley, and Simin Karimi. 2005. Determinants of event type in Persian complex predicates. *Lingua*, 115:1365–1401.

Adele E. Goldberg. 1995. *A Construction Grammar Approach to Argument Structure*. University of Chicago Press, Chicago.

Adele E. Goldberg. 1996. Words by default: Optimizing constraints and the Persian complex predicate. In *Annual Proceedings of the Berkeley Linguistic Society 22*, pages 132–146. Berkeley.

Adele E. Goldberg. 2003. Words by default: The Persian complex predicate construction. In E. Francis and L. Michaelis, editors, *Mismatch: Form-Function Incongruity and the Architecture of Grammar*, pages 117–146. CSLI Publications, Stanford.

Maurice Gross. 1975. *Méthodes en syntaxe : régime des constructions complétives*. Hermann, Paris.

Gholamhossein Karimi-Doostan. 1997. *Light Verb Constructions in Persian*. Ph.D. thesis, University of Essex.

Simin Karimi. 1997. Persian complex verbs: Idiomatic or compositional. *Lexicology*, 3:273–318.

Paul Kay and Charles J. Fillmore. 1999. Grammatical constructions and linguistic generalizations: The *What's X doing Y?* construction. *Language*, 75(1–33).

Parviz Khanlari. 1986. *Tarix-e zabân-e farsi (A History of the Persian Language)*. Editions Nashr-e Now.

Beth Levin. 1993. *English Verb Classes and Alternations*. The University of Chicago Press, Chicago.

Karine Megerdoomian. 2002. *Beyond Words and Phrases: A Unified Theory of Predicate Composition*. Ph.D. thesis, University of Southern California.

Karine Megerdoomian. 2012. The status of the nominal in persian complex predicates. *Natural Language and Linguistic Theory*, 30(1):179–216.

Geoffrey Nunberg, Ivan A. Sag, and Thomas Wasow. 1994. Idioms. *Language*, 70:491–538.

Elizabeth Ritter and Sara Rosen. 1996. Strong and weak predicates: Reducing the lexical burden. *Linguistic Analysis*, 26:1–34.

Ali Ashraf Sadeghi. 1993. On denominative verbs in Persian. In *Farsi Language and the Language of Science*, pages 236–246. University Press, Tehran.

Pollet Samvelian and Pegah Faghiri. to appear. Rethinking compositionality in persian complex predicats. In *Proceedings of the 39th Berkeley Linguistics Society*. Linguistic Society of America, Berkeley.

Pollet Samvelian. 2012. *Grammaire des prédicats complexes. Les constructions nom-verbe*. Lavoisier.

Shiva Taslimipoor, Afsaneh Fazly, and Ali Hamzeh. 2012. Using noun similarity to adapt an acceptability measure for persian light verb constructions. In *Language Resources and Evaluation Conference (LREC 2012)*, Istanbul.

Mohammad-Mehdi Vahedi-Langrudi. 1996. *The syntax, Semantics and Argument Structure of Complex Predicates in Modern Farsi*. Ph.D. thesis, University of Ottawa.

Improving Word Translation Disambiguation by Capturing Multiword Expressions with Dictionaries

Lars Bungum, Björn Gambäck, André Lynum, Erwin Marsi
Norwegian University of Science and Technology
Sem Sælands vei 7–9; NO—7491 Trondheim, Norway
{bungum,gamback,andrely,emarsi}@idi.ntnu.no

Abstract

The paper describes a method for identifying and translating multiword expressions using a bi-directional dictionary. While a dictionary-based approach suffers from limited recall, precision is high; hence it is best employed alongside an approach with complementing properties, such as an n-gram language model.

We evaluate the method on data from the English-German translation part of the cross-lingual word sense disambiguation task in the 2010 semantic evaluation exercise (SemEval). The output of a baseline disambiguation system based on n-grams was substantially improved by matching the target words and their immediate contexts against compound and collocational words in a dictionary.

1 Introduction

Multiword expressions (MWEs) cause particular lexical choice problems in machine translation (MT), but can also be seen as an opportunity to both generalize outside the bilingual corpora often used as training data in statistical machine translation approaches and as a method to adapt to specific domains. The identification of MWEs is in general important for many language processing tasks (Sag et al., 2002), but can be crucial in MT: since the semantics of many MWEs are non-compositional, a suitable translation cannot be constructed by translating the words in isolation. Identifying MWEs can help to identify idiomatic or otherwise fixed language usage, leading to more fluent translations, and potentially reduce the amount of lexical choice an MT system faces during target language generation.

In any translation effort, automatic or otherwise, the selection of target language lexical items to include in the translation is a crucial part of the final translation quality. In rule-based systems lexical choice is derived from the semantics of the source words, a process which often involves complex semantic composition. Data-driven systems on the other hand commonly base their translations nearly exclusively on cooccurrences of bare words or phrases in bilingual corpora, leaving the responsibility of selecting lexical items in the translation entirely to the local context found in phrase translation tables and language models with no explicit notion of the source or target language semantics. Still, systems of this type have been shown to produce reasonable translation quality without explicitly considering word translation disambiguation.

Bilingual corpora are scarce, however, and unavailable for most language pairs and target domains. An alternative approach is to build systems based on large monolingual knowledge sources and bilingual lexica, as in the hybrid MT system PRESEMT (Sofianopoulos et al., 2012). Since such a system explicitly uses a translation dictionary, it must at some point in the translation process decide which lexical entries to use; thus a separate word translation disambiguation module needs to be incorporated. To research available methods in such a module we have identified a task where we can use public datasets for measuring how well a method is able to select the optimal of many translation choices from a source language sentence.

In phrase-based statistical MT systems, the translation of multiword expressions can be a notable source of errors, despite the fact that those systems explicitly recognize and use alignments of sequential chunks of words. Several researchers have approached this problem by adding MWE translation tables to the systems, either through expanding the phrase tables (Ren et al., 2009) or by injecting the MWE translations into the decoder (Bai et al., 2009). Furthermore, there has been some interest in automatic mining of MWE pairs from bilingual corpora as a task in itself: Caseli et al. (2010) used a dictionary for evaluation of an automatic MWE extraction procedure using bilingual corpora. They also argued for the filtering of stopwords, similarly to the procedure described in the present paper. Sharoff et al. (2006) showed how MWE pairs can be extracted from comparable monolingual corpora instead of from a parallel bilingual corpus.

The methodology introduced in this paper employs bilingual dictionaries as a source of multiword expressions. Relationships are induced between the source sentence and candidate translation lexical items based on their correspondence in the dictionary. Specifically, we use a deterministic multiword expression disambiguation procedure based on translation dictionaries in both directions (from source to target language and vice versa), and a baseline system that ranks target lexical items based on their immediate context and an n-gram language model. The n-gram model represents a high-coverage, low-precision companion to the dictionary approach (i.e., it has complementary properties). Results show that the MWE dictionary information substantially improves the baseline system.

The 2010 Semantic Evaluation exercise (SemEval'10) featured a shared task on Cross-Lingual Word Sense Disambiguation (CL-WSD), where the focus was on disambiguating the translation of a single noun in a sentence. The participating systems were given an English word in its context and asked to produce appropriate substitutes in another language (Lefever and Hoste, 2010b). The CL-WSD data covers Dutch, French, Spanish, Italian and German; however, since the purpose of the experiments in this paper just was to assess our method's ability to choose the right translation of a word given its context, we used the English-to-German part only.

The next section details the employed disambiguation methodology and describes the data sets used in the experiments. Section 3 then reports on the results of experiments applying the methodology to the SemEval datasets, particularly addressing the impact of the dictionary MWE correspondences. Finally, Section 4 sums up the discussion and points to issues that can be investigated further.

2 Methodology

The core of the disambiguation model introduced in this paper is dictionary-based multiword extraction. Multiword extraction is done in both a direct and indirect manner: *Direct extraction* uses adjacent words in the source language in combination with the word to be translated, if the combination has an entry in the source-to-target language (SL–TL) dictionary. *Indirect extraction* works in the reverse direction, by searching the target-to-source (TL–SL) dictionary and looking up translation candidates for the combined words. Using a dictionary to identify multiword expressions after translation has a low recall of target language MWEs, since often there either are no multiword expressions to be discovered, or the dictionary method is unable to find a translation for an MWE. Nevertheless, when an MWE really is identified by means of the dictionary-based method, the precision is high.

Due to the low recall, relying on multiword expressions from dictionaries would, however, not be sufficient. Hence this method is combined with an n-gram language model (LM) based on a large target language corpus. The LM is used to rank translation candidates according to the probability of the n-gram best matching the context around the translation candidate. This is a more robust but less precise approach, which servers as the foundation for the high-precision but low-recall dictionary approach.

In the actual implementation, the n-gram method thus first provides a list of its best suggestions (currently top-5), and the dictionary method then prepends its candidates to the top of this list. Consequently, n-gram matching is described before dictionary-based multiword extraction in the following section. First, however, we introduce the data sets used in the experiments.

*(a) AGREEMENT in the form of an exchange of letters between the European Economic Community and the **Bank** for International Settlements concerning the mobilization of claims held by the Member States under the medium-term financial assistance arrangements* {bank 4; bankengesellschaft 1; kreditinstitut 1; zentralbank 1; finanzinstitut 1}
(b) The Office shall maintain an electronic data bank with the particulars of applications for registration of trade marks and entries in the Register. The Office may also make available the contents of this data **bank** *on CD-ROM or in any other machine-readable form.* {datenbank 4; bank 3; datenbanksystem 1; daten 1}
*(c) established as a band of 1 km in width from the **banks** of a river or the shores of a lake or coast for a length of at least 3 km.* {ufer 4; flussufer 3}

Table 1: Examples of contexts for the English word *bank* with possible German translations

2.1 The CL-WSD Datasets

The data sets used for the SemEval'10 Cross-Lingual Word Sense Disambiguation task were constructed by making a 'sense inventory' of all possible target language translations of a given source language word based on word-alignments in Europarl (Koehn, 2005), with alignments involving the relevant source words being manually checked. The retrieved target words were manually lemmatised and clustered into translations with a similar sense; see Lefever and Hoste (2010a) for details.

Trial and test instances were extracted from two other corpora, JRC-Acquis (Steinberger et al., 2006) and BNC (Burnard, 2007). The trial data for each language consists of five nouns (with 20 sentence contexts per noun), and the test data of twenty nouns (50 contexts each, so 1000 in total per language, with the CL-WSD data covering Dutch, French, Spanish, Italian and German). Table 1 provides examples from the trial data of contexts for the English word *bank* and its possible translations in German.

Gold standard translations were created by having four human translators picking the contextually appropriate sense for each source word, choosing 0–3 preferred target language translations for it. The translations are thus restricted to those appearing in Europarl, probably introducing a slight domain bias. Each translation has an associated count indicating how many annotators considered it to be among their top-3 preferred translations in the given context.

bank, bankanleihe, bankanstalt, bankdarlehen, bankengesellschaft, bankensektor, bankfeiertag, bankgesellschaft, bankinstitut, bankkonto, bankkredit, banknote, blutbank, daten, datenbank, datenbanksystem, euro-banknote, feiertag, finanzinstitut, flussufer, geheimkonto, geldschein, geschäftsbank, handelsbank, konto, kredit, kreditinstitut, nationalbank, notenbank, sparkasse, sparkassenverband, ufer, weltbank, weltbankgeber, west-bank, westbank, westjordanien, westjordanland, westjordanufer, westufer, zentralbank

Table 2: All German translation candidates for *bank* as extracted from the gold standard

In this way, for the English lemma *bank*, for example, the CL-WSD trial gold standard for German contains the word *Bank* itself, together with 40 other translation candidates, as shown in Table 2. Eight of those are related to river banks (*Ufer*, but also, e.g., *Westbank* and *Westjordanland*), three concern databases (*Datenbank*), and one is for blood banks. The rest are connected to different types of financial institutions (such as *Handelsbank* and *Finanzinstitut*, but also by association *Konto, Weldbankgeber, Banknote, Geldschein, Kredit*, etc.).

2.2 N-Gram Context Matching

N-gram matching is used to produce a ranked list of translation candidates and their contexts, both in order to provide robustness and to give a baseline performance. The n-gram models were built using the IRSTLM toolkit (Federico et al., 2008; Bungum and Gambäck, 2012) on the DeWaC corpus (Baroni and Kilgarriff, 2006), using the stopword list from NLTK (Loper and Bird, 2002). The n-gram matching procedure consists of two steps:

1. An nth order source context is extracted and the translations for each SL word in this context are retrieved from the dictionary. This includes stopword filtering of the context.

2. All relevant n-grams are inspected in order from left to right and from more specific (5-grams) to least specific (single words).

For each part of the context with matching n-grams in the target language model, the appropriate target translation candidates are extracted and ranked according to their language model probability. This results in an n-best list of translation candidates.

Since dictionary entries are lemma-based, lemmatization was necessary to use this approach in combination with the dictionary enhancements. The source context is formed by the lemmata in the sentence surrounding the focus word (the word to be disambiguated) by a window of up to four words in each direction, limited by a 5-gram maximum length. In order to extract the semantically most relevant content, stopwords are removed before constructing this source word window. For each of the 1–5 lemmata in the window, the relevant translation candidates are retrieved from the bilingual dictionary. The candidates form the ordered translation context for the source word window.

The following example illustrates how the translation context is created for the focus word 'bank'. First the relevant part of the source language sentence with the focus word in bold face:

(1) The BIS could conclude stand-by credit agreements with the creditor countries' central **bank** if they should so request.

For example, using a context of two words in front and two words after the focus word, the following source language context is obtained after a preprocessing involving lemmatization, stopword removal, and insertion of sentence start (<s>) and end markers (</s>):

(2) country central **bank** request </s>

From this the possible n-grams in the target side context are generated by assembling all ordered combinations of the translations of the source language words for each context length: the widest contexts (5-grams) are looked up first before moving on to narrower contexts, and ending up with looking up only the translation candidate in isolation.

Each of the n-grams is looked up in the language model and for each context part the n-grams are ordered according to their language model probability. Table 3 shows a few examples of such generated n-grams with their corresponding scores from the n-gram language model.[1] The target candidates (italics) are then extracted from the ordered list of target language n-grams. This gives an n-best list of translation candidates from which the top-1 or top-5 can be taken. Since multiple senses in the dictionary can render the same literal output, duplicate translation candidates are filtered out from the n-best list.

[1]There are no scores for 4- and 5-grams; as expected when using direct translation to generate target language n-grams.

n	n-gram	LM score
5	land mittig *bank* nachsuchen </s>	Not found
4	mittig *bank* nachsuchen </s>	Not found
3	mittig *bank* nachsuchen	Not found
3	*kredit* anfragen </s>	-0.266291
2	mittig *bank*	-3.382560
2	zentral *blutbank*	-5.144870
1	*bank*	-3.673000

Table 3: Target language n-gram examples from lookups of stopword-filtered lemmata *country central bank request* reported in log scores. The first 3 n-grams were not found in the language model.

2.3 Dictionary-Based Context Matching

After creating the n-gram based list of translation candidates, additional candidates are produced by looking at multiword entries in a bilingual dictionary. The existence of multiword entries in the dictionary corresponding to adjacent lemmata in the source context or translation candidates in the target context is taken as a clear indicator for the suitability of a particular translation candidate. Such entries are added to the top of the n-best list, which represents a strong preference in the disambiguation system.

Dictionaries are used in all experiments to look up translation candidates and target language translations of the words in the context, but this approach is mining the dictionaries by using lookups of greater length. Thus is, for example, the dictionary entry *Community Bank* translated to the translation candidate *Commerzbank*; this translation candidate would be put on top of the list of prioritized answers.

Two separate procedures are used to find such indicators, a direct procedure based on the source context and an indirect procedure based on the weaker target language context. These are detailed in pseudocode in Algorithms 1 and 2, and work as follows:

Source Language (SL) Method (Algorithm 1)
If there is a dictionary entry for the source word and one of its adjacent words, search the set of translations for any of the translation candidates for the word alone. Specifically, transla-

Algorithm 1 SL algorithm to rank translation candidates (tcands) for SL lemma b given list of $tcands$

```
procedure FindCand(list rlist, SL-lemma b, const tcands)              ▷ rlist is original ranking
    comblemmas ← list(previouslemma(b) + b, b + nextlemma(b))         ▷ Find adjacent lemmata
    for lem ∈ comblemmas do
        c ← sl-dictionary-lookup(lem)                                 ▷ Look up lemma in SL→TL dict.
        if c ∈ tcands then rlist ← list(c + rlist)                    ▷ Push lookup result c onto rlist if in tcands
        end if
    end for
    return rlist                  ▷ Return new list with lemmata whose translations were in tcands on top
end procedure
```

Algorithm 2 TL algorithm to rank translation candidates (tcands) for SL lemma b given list of $tcands$

[The ready-made TL $tcands$ from the dataset are looked up in TL-SL direction. It is necessary to keep a list of the reverse-translation of the individual $tcand$ as well as the original $tcand$ itself, in order to monitor which $tcand$ it was. If the SL context is found in either of these reverse lookups the matching $tcand$ is ranked high.]

```
procedure FindCand(list rlist, SL-lemma b, const tcands)              ▷ rlist is original ranking
    for cand ∈ tcands do                                              ▷ Assemble list of TL translations
        translist ← list(cand, tl-dictionary-lookup(cand)) + translist
                                          ▷ Append TL→SL lookup results of tcands with cand as id
    end for
    for cand, trans ∈ translist do
        if previouslemma(b)||nextlemma(b) ∈ trans then                ▷ If trans contains either SL lemma
            rlist ← list(cand) + rlist                                ▷ append this cand onto rlist
        end if
    end for
    return rlist
        ▷ Return tcands list; top-ranking tcands whose SL-neighbours were found in TL→SL lookup
end procedure
```

tions of the combination of the source word and an adjacent word in the context are matched against translation candidates for the word.

Target Language (TL) Method (Algorithm 2) If a translation candidate looked up in the reverse direction matches the source word along with one or more adjacent words, it is a good translation candidate. TL candidates are looked up in a TL–SL dictionary and multiword results are matched against SL combinations of disambiguation words and their immediate contexts.

For both methods the dictionary entry for the target word or translation candidate is matched against the immediate context. Thus both methods result in two different lookups for each focus word, combining it with the previous and next terms, respectively. This is done exhaustively for all combinations of translations of the words in the context window. Only one adjacent word was used, since very few of the candidates were able to match the context even with one word. Hence, virtually none would be found with more context, making it very unlikely that larger contexts would contribute to the disambiguation procedure, as wider matches would also match the one-word contexts.

Also for both methods, translation candidates are only added once, in case the same translation candidate generates hits with either (or both) of the methods. Looking at the running example, stopword filtered and with lemmatized context:

(3) country central **bank** request

This example generates two source language multiword expressions, *central bank* and *bank request*. In the source language method, these word combinations are looked up in the dictionary where the *zentralbank* entry is found for *central bank*, which is also found as a translation candidate for *bank*.

The target language method works in the reverse order, looking up the translation candidates in the TL–SL direction and checking if the combined lemmata are among the candidates' translations into the source language. In the example, the entry *zentralbank:central bank* is found in the dictionary, matching the source language context, so *zentralbank* is assumed to be a correct translation.

2.4 Dictionaries

Two English-German dictionaries were used in the experiments, both with close to 1 million entries (translations). One is a free on-line resource, while the other was obtained by reversing an existing proprietary German-English dictionary made available to the authors by its owners:

- The GFAI dictionary (called 'D1' in Section 3 below) is a proprietary and substantially extended version of the Chemnitz dictionary, with 549k EN entries including 433k MWEs, and 552k DE entries (79k MWEs). The Chemnitz electronic German-English dictionary[2] itself contains over 470,000 word translations and is available under a GPL license.

- The freely available CC dictionary[3] ('D2' below) is an internet-based German-English and English-German dictionary built through user generated word definitions. It has 565k/440k (total/MWE) EN and 548k/210k DE entries.

Note that the actual dictionaries are irrelevant to the discussion at hand, and that we do not aim to point out strengths or weaknesses of either dictionary, nor to indicate a bias towards a specific resource.

3 Results

Experiments were carried out both on the trial and test data described in Section 2.1 (5 trial and 20 test words; with 20 resp. 50 instances for each word; in total 1100 instances in need of disambiguation). The results show that the dictionaries yield answers with high precision, although they are robust enough to solve the SemEval WSD challenge on their own.

For measuring the success rate of the developed models, we adopt the 'Out-Of-Five' (OOF) score (Lefever and Hoste, 2010b) from the SemEval'10 Cross-Lingual Word Sense Disambiguation task. The Out-Of-Five criterion measures how well the top five candidates from the system match the top five translations in the gold standard:

$$OOF(i) = \frac{\sum_{a \in A_i} freq_i(a)}{|H_i|}$$

where H_i denotes the multiset of translations proposed by humans for the focus word in each source sentence s_i ($1 \leq i \leq N$, N being the number of test items). A_i is the set of translations produced by the system for source term i. Since each translation has an associated count of how many annotators chose it, there is for each s_i a function $freq_i$ returning this count for each term in H_i (0 for all other terms), and $max\ freq_i$ gives the maximal count for any term in H_i. For the first example in Table 1:

$$\begin{cases} H_1 = \{\text{bank, bank, bank, bank, zentralbank,} \\ \qquad \text{bankengesellschaft, kreditinstitut, finanzinstitut}\} \\ freq_1(\text{bank}) = 4 \\ \ldots \\ freq_1(\text{finanzinstitut}) = 1 \\ maxfreq_1 = 4 \end{cases}$$

and the cardinality of the multiset is: $|H_1| = 8$. This equates to the sum of all top-3 preferences given to the translation candidates by all annotators.

For the Out-Of-Five evaluation, the CL-WSD systems were allowed to submit up to five candidates of equal rank. OOF is a recall-oriented measure with no additional penalty for precision errors, so there is no benefit in outputting less than five candidates. With respect to the previous example from Table 1, the maximum score is obtained by system output $A_1 = \{$bank, bankengesellschaft, kreditinstitut, zentralbank, finanzinstitut$\}$, which gives $OOF(1) = (4+1+1+1+1)/8 = 1$, whereas $A_2 = \{$bank, bankengesellschaft, nationalbank, notenbank, sparkasse$\}$ would give $OOF(1) = (4+1)/8 = 0.625$.[4]

[2] http://dict.tu-chemnitz.de/

[3] http://www.dict.cc/

[4] Note that the maximum OOF score is not always 1 (i.e., it is not normalized), since the gold standard sometimes contains more than five translation alternatives.

Dictionary	Source language D1	Source language D2	Source language comb	Target language D1	Target language D2	Target language comb	All comb
Top	*8.89*	6.99	*8.89*	22.71	24.43	***25.34***	24.67
Low	0.00	0.00	0.00	0.00	0.00	0.00	0.00
Mean	2.71	0.99	*3.04*	8.35	7.10	*9.24*	**10.13**

Table 4: F_1-score results for individual dictionaries

Dictionary	Source language D1	Source language D2	Source language comb	Target language D1	Target language D2	Target language comb	All comb
coach	1.00	0.00	1.00	0.21	0.00	0.21	0.21
education	0.83	0.67	0.83	0.47	0.62	0.54	0.53
execution	0.00	0.00	0.00	0.17	0.22	0.17	0.17
figure	1.00	0.00	1.00	0.51	0.57	0.55	0.55
job	0.88	0.80	0.94	0.45	0.78	0.46	0.44
letter	1.00	0.00	1.00	0.66	0.75	0.62	0.66
match	1.00	1.00	1.00	0.80	0.50	0.80	0.80
mission	0.71	0.33	0.71	0.46	0.37	0.36	0.36
mood	0.00	0.00	0.00	0.00	0.00	0.00	0.00
paper	0.68	0.17	0.68	0.53	0.35	0.55	0.55
post	1.00	1.00	1.00	0.39	0.48	0.45	0.48
pot	0.00	0.00	0.00	1.00	1.00	1.00	1.00
range	1.00	1.00	1.00	0.28	0.37	0.30	0.30
rest	1.00	0.67	1.00	0.60	0.56	0.56	0.58
ring	0.09	0.00	0.09	0.37	0.93	0.38	0.38
scene	1.00	0.00	1.00	0.50	0.42	0.44	0.50
side	1.00	0.00	1.00	0.21	0.16	0.23	0.27
soil	1.00	0.00	1.00	0.72	0.58	0.66	0.69
strain	0.00	0.00	0.00	0.51	0.88	0.55	0.55
test	1.00	1.00	1.00	0.62	0.52	0.57	0.61
Mean	0.84	0.74	0.84	0.50	0.56	0.49	0.51

Table 5: Precision scores for all terms filtering out those instances for which no candidates were suggested

For assessing overall system performance in the experiments, we take the best ('Top'), worst ('Low'), and average ('Mean') of the OOF scores for all the SL focus words, with F_1-score reported as the harmonic mean of the precision and recall of the OOF scores. Table 4 shows results for each dictionary approach on the test set, with 'D1' being the GFAI dictionary, 'D2' the CC dictionary, and 'comb' the combination of both. Target language look-up contributes more to providing good translation candidates than the source language methodology, and also outperforms a strategy combining all dictionaries in both directions ('All comb').

Filtering out the instances for which no candidate translation was produced, and taking the average precision scores only over these, gives the results shown in Table 5. Markedly different precision scores can be noticed, but the source language method again has higher precision on the suggestions it makes than the target language counterpart.

Dictionary	Source language D1	Source language D2	Target language D1	Target language D2
Mean	*3.25*	1.5	**12.65**	11.45
Total	223	256	**1,164**	880

Table 6: Number of instances with a translation candidate ('Mean') and the total number of suggested candidates

	Most Freq	Most Freq Aligned	5-gram	5-gram + Dict	All Dict Comb	VSM Model
Top	51.77	68.71	52.02	52.74	24.67	**55.92**
Low	1.76	9.93	14.09	**15.40**	0.00	10.73
Mean	21.18	34.61	30.36	**36.38**	10.13	30.30

Table 7: Overview of results (F_1-scores) on SemEval data

As shown in Table 6, this higher precision is offset by lower coverage, with far fewer instances actually producing a translation candidate with the dictionary lookup methods. There is a notable difference in the precision of the SL and TL approaches, coinciding with more candidates produced by the latter. Several words in Table 5 give 100% precision scores for at least one dictionary, while a few give 0% precision for some dictionaries. The word 'mood' even has 0% precision for both dictionaries in both directions.

Table 7 gives an overview of different approaches to word translation disambiguation on the dataset. For each method, the three lines again give both the best and worst scoring terms, and the mean value for all test words. The maximum attainable score for each of those would be 99.28, 90.48 and 95.47, respectively, but those are perfect scores not reachable for all items, as described above (OOF-scoring). Instead the columns *Most Freq* and *Most Freq aligned* give the baseline scores for the SemEval dataset: the translation most frequently seen in the corpus and the translation most frequently aligned in a word-aligned parallel corpus (Europarl), respectively. Then follows the results when using only a stopword-filtered *5-gram* model built with the IRSTLM language modeling kit (Federico and Cettolo, 2007), and when combining the 5-gram model with the dictionary approach (*5-gram + Dict*).

The next column (*All Dict Comb*) shows how the dictionary methods fared on their own. The combined dictionary approach has low recall (see Table 6) and does not alone provide a good solution to the overall problem. Due to high precision, however, the approach is able to enhance the n-gram method that already produces acceptable results. Finally, the column *VSM Model* as comparison gives the results obtained when using a Vector Space Model for word translation disambiguation (Marsi et al., 2011).

Comparing the dictionary approach to state-of-the-art monolingual solutions to the WTD problem on this dataset shows that the approach performs better for the Lowest and Mean scores of the terms, but not for the Top scores (Lynum et al., 2012). As can be seen in Table 7, the vector space model produced the overall best score for a single term. However, the method combining a 5-gram language model with the dictionary approach was best both at avoiding really low scores for any single term and when comparing the mean scores for all the terms.

4 Discussion and Conclusion

The paper has presented a method for using dictionary lookups based on the adjacent words in both the source language text and target language candidate translation texts to disambiguate word translation candidates. By composing lookup words by using both neighbouring words, improved disambiguation performance was obtained on the data from the SemEval'10 English-German Cross-Lingual Word Sense Disambiguation task. The extended use of dictionaries proves a valuable source of information for disambiguation, and can introduce low-cost phrase-level translation to quantitative Word Sense Disambiguation approaches such as N-gram or Vector Space Model methods, often lacking the phrases-based dimension.

The results show clear differences between the source and target language methods of using dictionary lookups, where the former has very high precision (0.84) but low coverage, while the TL method compensates lower precision (0.51) with markedly better coverage. The SL dictionary method provided answers to only between 1.5 and 3.25 of 50 instances per word on average, depending on the dictionary. This owes largely to the differences in algorithms, where the TL method matches any adjacent lemma to the focus word with the translation of the pre-defined translation candidates, whereas the SL method matches dictionaries of the combined lemmata of the focus word and its adjacent words to the same list of translation candidates. False positives are expected with lower constraints such as these. On the SemEval data, the contribution of the dictionary methods to the n-grams is mostly in improving the average score.

The idea of acquiring lexical information from corpora is of course not new in itself. So did, e.g., Rapp (1999) use vector-space models for the purpose of extracting ranked lists of translation candidates for extending a dictionary for word translation disambiguation. Chiao and Zweigenbaum (2002) tried to identify translational equivalences by investigating the relations between target and source language word distributions in a restricted domain, and also applied reverse-translation filtering for improved performance, while Sadat et al. (2003) utilised non-aligned, comparable corpora to induce a bilingual lexicon, using a bidirectional method (SL→TL, TL→SL, and a combination of both).

Extending the method to use an arbitrary size window around all words in the context of each focus word (not just the word itself) could identify more multiword expressions and generate a more accurate bag-of-words for a data-driven approach. Differences between dictionaries could also be explored, giving more weight to translations found in two or more dictionaries. Furthermore, the differences between the SL and TL methods could explored further, investigating in detail the consequences of using a symmetrical dictionary, in order to study the effect that increased coverage has on results. Testing the idea on more languages will help verify the validity of these findings.

Acknowledgements

This research has received funding from NTNU and from the European Community's 7th Framework Programme under contract nr 248307 (PRESEMT). Thanks to the other project participants and the anonymous reviewers for several very useful comments.

References

Bai, M.-H., You, J.-M., Chen, K.-J., and Chang, J. S. (2009). Acquiring translation equivalences of multiword expressions by normalized correlation frequencies. In *Proceedings of the 2009 Conference on Empirical Methods in Natural Language Processing*, pages 478–486, Singapore. ACL.

Baroni, M. and Kilgarriff, A. (2006). Large linguistically-processed web corpora for multiple languages. In *Proceedings of the 11th Conference of the European Chapter of the Association for Computational Linguistics*, pages 87–90, Trento, Italy. ACL.

Bungum, L. and Gambäck, B. (2012). Efficient n-gram language modeling for billion word web-corpora. In *Proceedings of the 8th International Conference on Language Resources and Evaluation*, pages 6–12, Istanbul, Turkey. ELRA. Workshop on Challenges in the Management of Large Corpora.

Burnard, L., editor (2007). *Reference Guide for the British National Corpus (XML Edition)*. BNC Consortium, Oxford, England. http://www.natcorp.ox.ac.uk/XMLedition/URG.

Caseli, H. d. M., Ramisch, C., das Graças Volpe Nunes, M., and Villavicencio, A. (2010). Alignment-based extraction of multiword expressions. *Language Resources and Evaluation*, 44(1-2):59–77. Special Issue on Multiword expression: hard going or plain sailing.

Chiao, Y.-C. and Zweigenbaum, P. (2002). Looking for candidate translational equivalents in specialized comparable corpora. In *Proceedings of the 40th Annual Meeting of the Association for Computational Linguistics*, volume 2, pages 1–5, Philadelphia, Pennsylvania. ACL. Also published in *AMIA Annual Symposium 2002*, pp. 150–154.

Federico, M., Bertoldi, N., and Cettolo, M. (2008). Irstlm: an open source toolkit for handling large scale language models. In *INTERSPEECH*, pages 1618–1621. ISCA.

Federico, M. and Cettolo, M. (2007). Efficient handling of n-gram language models for statistical machine translation. In *Proceedings of the 45th Annual Meeting of the Association for Computational Linguistics*, pages 88–95, Prague, Czech Republic. ACL. 2nd Workshop on Statistical Machine Translation.

Koehn, P. (2005). Europarl: A parallel corpus for statistical machine translation. In *Proceedings of the 10th Machine Translation Summit*, pages 79–86, Phuket, Thailand.

Lefever, E. and Hoste, V. (2010a). Construction of a benchmark data set for cross-lingual word sense disambiguation. In *Proceedings of the 7th International Conference on Language Resources and Evaluation*, pages 1584–1590, Valetta, Malta. ELRA.

Lefever, E. and Hoste, V. (2010b). SemEval-2010 Task 3: Cross-lingual word sense disambiguation. In *Proceedings of the 48th Annual Meeting of the Association for Computational Linguistics*, pages 15–20, Uppsala, Sweden. ACL. 5th International Workshop on Semantic Evaluation.

Loper, E. and Bird, S. (2002). NLTK: the natural language toolkit. In *Proceedings of the ACL-02 Workshop on Effective tools and methodologies for teaching natural language processing and computational linguistics - Volume 1*, ETMTNLP '02, pages 63–70, Stroudsburg, PA, USA. Association for Computational Linguistics.

LREC06 (2006). *Proceedings of the 5th International Conference on Language Resources and Evaluation*, Genova, Italy. ELRA.

Lynum, A., Marsi, E., Bungum, L., and Gambäck, B. (2012). Disambiguating word translations with target language models. In *Proceedings of the 15th International Conference on Text, Speech and Dialogue*, pages 378–385, Brno, Czech Republic. Springer.

Marsi, E., Lynum, A., Bungum, L., and Gambäck, B. (2011). Word translation disambiguation without parallel texts. In *Proceedings of the International Workshop on Using Linguistic Information for Hybrid Machine Translation*, pages 66–74, Barcelona, Spain.

Rapp, R. (1999). Automatic identification of word translations from unrelated English and German corpora. In *Proceedings of the 37th Annual Meeting of the Association for Computational Linguistics*, pages 519–526, Madrid, Spain. ACL.

Ren, Z., Lü, Y., Cao, J., Liu, Q., and Huang, Y. (2009). Improving statistical machine translation using domain bilingual multiword expressions. In *Proceedings of the 47th Annual Meeting of the Association for Computational Linguistics*, pages 47–54, Singapore. ACL. Workshop on Multiword Expressions: Identification, Interpretation, Disambiguation and Applications.

Sadat, F., Yoshikawa, M., and Uemura, S. (2003). Learning bilingual translations from comparable corpora to cross-language information retrieval: Hybrid statistics-based and linguistics-based approach. In *Proceedings of the 41th Annual Meeting of the Association for Computational Linguistics*, pages 57–64, Sapporo, Japan. ACL. 6th International Workshop on Information Retrieval with Asian languages; a shorter version published in *ACL Annual Meeting 2003*, pp. 141–144.

Sag, I., Baldwin, T., Bond, F., Copestake, A., and Flickinger, D. (2002). Multiword expressions: A pain in the neck for NLP. In Gelbukh, A., editor, *Computational Linguistics and Intelligent Text Processing: Proceedings of the 3rd International Conference*, number 2276 in Lecture Notes in Computer Science, pages 189–206, Mexico City, Mexico. Springer-Verlag.

Sharoff, S., Babych, B., and Hartley, A. (2006). Using collocations from comparable corpora to find translation equivalents. In LREC06 (2006), pages 465–470.

Sofianopoulos, S., Vassiliou, M., and Tambouratzis, G. (2012). Implementing a language-independent MT methodology. In *Proceedings of the 50th Annual Meeting of the Association for Computational Linguistics*, pages 1–10, Jeju, Korea. ACL. First Workshop on Multilingual Modeling.

Steinberger, R., Pouliquen, B., Widiger, A., Ignat, C., Erjavec, T., Tufiş, D., and Varga, D. (2006). The JRC-Acquis: A multilingual aligned parallel corpus with 20+ languages. In LREC06 (2006), pages 2142–2147.

Complex Predicates are Multi-word Expressions

Martha Palmer
Department of Linguistics
University of Colorado at Boulder
295 UCB
Boulder, Colorado 80309-029, USA
Martha.Palmer@colorado.edu

Abstract

Practitioners of English Natural Language Processing often feel fortunate because their tokens are clearly marked by spaces on either side. However, the spaces can be quite deceptive, since they ignore the boundaries of multi-word expressions, such as noun-noun compounds, verb particle constructions, light verb constructions and constructions from Construction Grammar, e.g., caused-motion constructions and resultatives. Correctly identifying and handling these types of expressions can be quite challenging, even from the viewpoint of manual annotation. This talk will review the pervasive nature of these constructions, touching on Arabic and Hindi as well as English. Using several illustrative examples from newswire and medical informatics, current best practices for annotation and automatic identification will be described, with an emphasis on contributions from predicate argument structures.

About the Speaker

Martha Palmer is a Professor of Linguistics and Computer Science, and a Fellow of the Institute of Cognitive Science at the University of Colorado. Her current research is aimed at building domain-independent and language independent techniques for semantic interpretation based on linguistically annotated data, such as Proposition Banks. She has been the PI on NSF, NIH and DARPA projects for linguistic annotation (syntax, semantics and pragmatics) of English, Chinese, Korean, Arabic and Hindi. She has been a member of the Advisory Committee for the DARPA TIDES program, Chair of SIGLEX, Chair of SIGHAN, a past President of the Association for Computational Linguistics, and is a Co-Editor of JNLE and of LiLT and is on the CL Editorial Board. She received her Ph.D. in Artificial Intelligence from the University of Edinburgh in 1985.

The (Un)expected Effects of Applying Standard Cleansing Models to Human Ratings on Compositionality

Stephen Roller[†‡] **Sabine Schulte im Walde** [‡] **Silke Scheible** [†]

[†]Department of Computer Science
The University of Texas at Austin
roller@cs.utexas.edu

[‡]Institut für Maschinelle Sprachverarbeitung
Universität Stuttgart
{schulte,scheible}@ims.uni-stuttgart.de

Abstract

Human ratings are an important source for evaluating computational models that predict compositionality, but like many data sets of human semantic judgements, are often fraught with uncertainty and noise. However, despite their importance, to our knowledge there has been no extensive look at the effects of cleansing methods on human rating data. This paper assesses two standard cleansing approaches on two sets of compositionality ratings for German noun-noun compounds, in their ability to produce compositionality ratings of higher consistency, while reducing data quantity. We find (i) that our ratings are highly robust against aggressive filtering; (ii) Z-score filtering fails to detect unreliable item ratings; and (iii) Minimum Subject Agreement is highly effective at detecting unreliable subjects.

1 Introduction

Compounds have long been a reoccurring focus of attention within theoretical, cognitive, and computational linguistics. Recent manifestations of interest in compounds include the Handbook of Compounding (Lieber and Stekauer, 2009) on theoretical perspectives, and a series of workshops[1] and special journal issues with respect to the computational perspective (Journal of Computer Speech and Language, 2005; Language Resources and Evaluation, 2010; ACM Transactions on Speech and Language Processing, to appear). Some work has focused on modeling meaning and compositionality for specific classes, such as particle verbs (McCarthy et al., 2003; Bannard, 2005; Cook and Stevenson, 2006); adjective-noun combinations (Baroni and Zamparelli, 2010; Boleda et al., 2013); and noun-noun compounds (Reddy et al., 2011b; Reddy et al., 2011a). Others have aimed at predicting the compositionality of phrases and sentences of arbitrary type and length, either by focusing on the learning approach (Socher et al., 2011); by integrating symbolic models into distributional models (Coecke et al., 2011; Grefenstette et al., 2013); or by exploring the arithmetic operations to predict compositionality by the meaning of the parts (Widdows, 2008; Mitchell and Lapata, 2010).

An important resource in evaluating compositionality has been *human compositionality ratings*, in which human subjects are asked to rate the degree to which a compound is *transparent* or *opaque*. Transparent compounds, such as *raincoat*, have a meaning which is an obvious combination of its constituents, e.g., a raincoat is a coat against the rain. Opaque compounds, such as *hot dog*, have little or no relation to one or more of their constituents: a hot dog need not be hot, nor is it (hopefully) made of dog. Other words, such as *ladybug*, are transparent with respect to just one constituent. As many words do not fall clearly into one category or the other, subjects are typically asked to rate the compositionality of words or phrases on a scale, and the mean of several judgements is taken as the gold standard.

Like many data sets of human judgements, compositionality ratings can be fraught with large quantities of uncertainty and noise. For example, participants typically agree on items that are clearly transparent or opaque, but will often disagree about the

[1] www.multiword.sourceforge.net

gray areas in between. Such uncertainty represents an inherent part of the semantic task and is the major reason for using the mean ratings of many subjects.

Other types of noise, however, are undesirable, and should be eliminated. In particular, we wish to examine two types of potential noise in our data. The first type of noise (**Type I noise: *uncertainty***), comes from when a subject is unfamiliar or uncertain about particular words, resulting in sporadically poor judgements. The second type of noise (**Type II noise: *unreliability***), occurs when a subject is consistently unreliable or uncooperative. This may happen if the subject misunderstands the task, or if a subject simply wishes to complete the task as quickly as possible. Judgements collected via crowdsourcing are especially prone to this second kind of noise, when compared to traditional pen-and-paper experiments, since participants aim to maximize their hourly wage.[2]

In this paper, we apply two standard cleansing methods (Ben-Gal, 2005; Maletic and Marcus, 2010), that have been used on similar rating data before (Reddy et al., 2011b), on two data sets of compositionality ratings of German noun-noun compounds. We aim to address two main points. The first is to assess the cleansing approaches in their ability to produce compositionality ratings of higher quality and consistency, while facing a reduction of data mass in the cleansing process. In particular, we look at the effects of removing outlier judgements resulting from uncertainty (Type I noise) and dropping unreliable subjects (Type II noise). The second issue is to assess the overall reliability of our two rating data sets: Are they clean enough to be used as gold standard models in computational linguistics approaches?

2 Compositionality Ratings

Our focus of interest is on German noun-noun compounds (see Fleischer and Barz (2012) for a detailed overview), such as *Ahornblatt* 'maple leaf' and *Feuerwerk* 'fireworks', and *Obstkuchen* 'fruit cake' where both the head and the modifier are nouns. We rely on a subset of 244 noun-noun compounds collected by von der Heide and Borgwaldt (2009), who created a set of 450 concrete, depictable German noun compounds according to four compositionality classes (transparent+transparent, transparent+opaque, opaque+transparent, opaque+opaque).

We are interested in the degrees of compositionality of the German noun-noun compounds, i.e., the relation between the meaning of the whole compound (e.g., *Feuerwerk*) and the meaning of its constituents (e.g., *Feuer* 'fire' and *Werk* 'opus'). We work with two data sets of compositionality ratings for the compounds. The first data set, the **individual compositionality ratings**, consists of participants rating the compositionality of a compound with respect to each of the individual constituents. These judgements were collected within a traditional controlled, pen-and-paper setting. For each compound-constituent pair, 30 native German speakers rated the compositionality of the compound with respect to its constituent on a scale from 1 (opaque/non-compositional) to 7 (transparent/compositional). The subjects were allowed to omit ratings for unfamiliar words, but very few did; of the 14,640 possible ratings judgements, only 111 were left blank. Table 1 gives several examples of such ratings. We can see that *Fliegenpilz* 'toadstool' is an example of a very opaque (non-compositional) word with respect to *Fliege* 'housefly/bow tie'; it has little to do with either houseflies or bow ties. On the other hand *Teetasse* 'teacup' is highly compositional: it is a *Tasse* 'cup' intended for *Tee* 'tea'.

The second data set, the **whole compositionality ratings** consists of participants giving a single rating for the entire compound. These ratings, previously unpublished, reflect a very different view of the same compounds. Rather than rating compounds with respect to their constituents, subjects were asked to give a *single rating for the entire compound* using the same 1-7 scale as before. The ratings were collected via Amazon Mechanical Turk (AMT). The data was controlled for spammers by removing subjects who failed to identify a number of fake words. Subjects who rated less than 10 compounds or had a low AMT reputation were also removed. The resulting data represents 150 different subjects with roughly 30 ratings per compound. Most participants rated only a few dozen items. We can see examples of these ratings in Table 2.

[2]See Callison-Burch and Dredze (2010) for a collection of papers on data collected with AMT. While the individual approaches deal with noise in individual ways, there is no general approach to clean crowdsourcing data.

Compound	W.R.T.	Subject 1	Subject 2	Subject 3	Subject 4	Mean	Comb.
Fliegenpilz 'toadstool'	*Fliege* 'housefly/bow tie'	3	1	1	2	1.75	3.37
Fliegenpilz 'toadstool'	*Pilz* 'mushroom'	5	7	7	7	6.50	
Sonnenblume 'sunflower'	*Sonne* 'sun'	4	3	1	2	2.50	4.11
Sonnenblume 'sunflower'	*Blume* 'flower'	7	7	7	6	6.75	
Teetasse 'teacup'	*Tee* 'tea'	6	6	4	2	4.50	4.50
Teetasse 'teacup'	*Tasse* 'cup'	7	6	4	1	4.50	

Table 1: Sample compositionality ratings for three compounds with respect to their constituents. We list the mean rating for only these 4 subjects to facilitate examples. The Combined column is the geometric mean of both constituents.

Compound	Subject 1	Subject 2	Subject 3	Subject 4	Mean
Fliegenpilz 'toadstool'	-	2	1	2	2.67
Sonnenblume 'sunflower'	3	3	1	2	2.75
Teetasse 'teacup'	7	7	7	6	6.75

Table 2: Example whole compositionality ratings for three compounds. Note that Subject 1 chose not to rate *Fliegenpilz*, so the mean is computed using only the three available judgements.

3 Methodology

In order to check on the reliability of compositionality judgements in general terms as well as with regard to our two specific collections, we applied two standard cleansing approaches[3] to our rating data: *Z-score filtering* is a method for filtering Type I noise, such as random guesses made by individuals when a word is unfamiliar. *Minimum Subject Agreement* is a method for filtering out Type II noise, such as subjects who seem to misunderstand the rating task or rarely agree with the rest of the population. We then evaluated the original vs. cleaned data by one intrinsic and one extrinsic task. Section 3.1 presents the two evaluations and the unadulterated, baseline measures for our experiments. Sections 3.2.1 and 3.2.2 describe the cleansing experiments and results.

3.1 Evaluations and Baselines

For evaluating the cleansing methods, we propose two metrics, an intrinsic and an extrinsic measure.

3.1.1 Intrinsic Evaluation: Consistency between Rating Data Sets

The intrinsic evaluation measures the consistency between our two ratings sets *individual* and *whole*. Assuming that the compositionality ratings for a compound depend heavily on both constituents, we expect a strong correlation between the two data sets. For a compound to be rated transparent as a whole, it should be transparent with respect to both of its constituents. Compounds which are highly transparent with respect to only one of their constituents should be penalized appropriately.

In order to compute a correlation between the whole ratings (which consist of one average rating per compound) and the individual ratings (which consist of two average ratings per compound, one for each constituent), we need to combine the individual ratings to arrive at a single value. We use the geometric mean to combine the ratings, which is effectively identical to the multiplicative methods in Widdows (2008), Mitchell and Lapata (2010) and Reddy et al. (2011b). [4] For example, using our means listed in Table 1, we may compute the combined rating for *Sonnenblume* as $\sqrt{6.75 * 2.50} \approx 4.11$. These combined ratings are computed for all compounds, as listed in the "Comb." column of Table 1. We then compute our consistency measure as the Spearman's ρ rank correlation between these combined individual ratings with the whole ratings ("Mean" in Table 2). The original, unadulterated data sets have a consistency measure of 0.786, indicating that, despite the very different collection methodologies, the two ratings sets largely agree.

3.1.2 Extrinsic Evaluation: Correlation with Association Norms

The extrinsic evaluation compares the consistency

[3]See Ben-Gal (2005) or Maletic and Marcus (2010) for overviews of standard cleansing approaches.

[4]We also tried the arithmetic mean, but the multiplicative method always performs better.

Word	Example Associations
Fliegenpilz 'toadstool'	*giftig* 'poisonous', *rot* 'red', *Wald* 'forest'
Fliege 'housefly/bow tie'	*nervig* 'annoying', *summen* 'to buzz', *Insekt* 'insect'
Pilz 'mushroom'	*Wald* 'forest', *giftig* 'poisonous', *sammeln* 'to gather'
Sonnenblume 'sunflower'	*gelb* 'yellow', *Sommer* 'summer', *Kerne* 'seeds'
Sonne 'sun'	*Sommer* 'summer', *warm* 'warm', *hell* 'bright'
Blume 'flower'	*Wiese* 'meadow', *Duft* 'smell', *Rose* 'rose'

Table 3: Example association norms for two German compounds and their constituents.

between our two rating sets *individual* and *whole* with evidence from a large collection of association norms. Association norms have a long tradition in psycholinguistic research to investigate semantic memory, making use of the implicit notion that associates reflect meaning components of words (Deese, 1965; Miller, 1969; Clark, 1971; Nelson et al., 1998; Nelson et al., 2000; McNamara, 2005; de Deyne and Storms, 2008). They are collected by presenting a *stimulus word* to a subject and collecting the first words that come to mind.

We rely on association norms that were collected for our compounds and constituents via both a large scale web experiment and Amazon Mechanical Turk (Schulte im Walde et al., 2012) (unpublished). The resulting combined data set contains 85,049/34,560 stimulus-association tokens/types for the compound and constituent stimuli. Table 3 gives examples of associations from the data set for some stimuli.

The guiding intuition behind comparing our rating data sets with association norms is that a compound which is compositional with respect to a constituent should have similar associations as its constituent (Schulte im Walde et al., 2012).

To measure the correlation of the rating data with the association norms, we first compute the *Jaccard similarity* that measures the overlap in two sets, ranging from 0 (perfectly dissimilar) to 1 (perfectly similar). The Jaccard is defined for two sets, A and B, as

$$J(A, B) = \frac{|A \cap B|}{|A \cup B|}.$$

For example, we can use Table 3 to compute the Jaccard similarity between *Sonnenblume* and *Sonne*:

$$\frac{|\{Sommer\}|}{|\{gelb, Sommer, Kerne, warm, hell\}|} = 0.20.$$

After computing the Jaccard similarity between all compounds and constituents across the association norms, we correlate this association overlap with the average individual ratings (i.e., column "Mean" in Table 1) using Spearman's ρ. This correlation "Assoc Norm (Indiv)" reaches $\rho = 0.638$ for our original data. We also compute a combined Jaccard similarity using the geometric mean, e.g.

$$\sqrt{J(Fliegenpilz, Fliege) * J(Fliegenpilz, Pilz)},$$

and calculate Spearman's ρ with the whole ratings (i.e., column "Mean" in Table 2). This correlation "Assoc Norm (Whole)" reaches $\rho = 0.469$ for our original data.

3.2 Data Cleansing

We applied the two standard cleansing approaches, *Z-score Filtering* and *Minimum Subject Agreement*, to our rating data, and evaluated the results.

3.2.1 Z-score Filtering

Z-score filtering is a method to filter out Type I noise, such as random guesses made by individuals when a word is unfamiliar. It makes the simple assumption that each item's ratings should be roughly normally distributed around the "true" rating of the item, and throws out all outliers which are more than z^* standard deviations from the item's mean. With regard to our compositionality ratings, for each item i (i.e., a compound in the *whole* data, or a compound–constituent pair in the *individual* data) we compute the mean $\bar{x}_i$ and standard deviation σ_i of the ratings for the given item. We then remove all values from x_i where

$$|x_i - \bar{x}_i| > \sigma_i z^*,$$

with the parameter z^* indicating the *maximum allowed Z-score* of the item's ratings. For example, if a particular item has ratings of $x_i = (1, 2, 1, 6, 1, 1)$, then the mean $\bar{x}_i = 2$ and the standard deviation

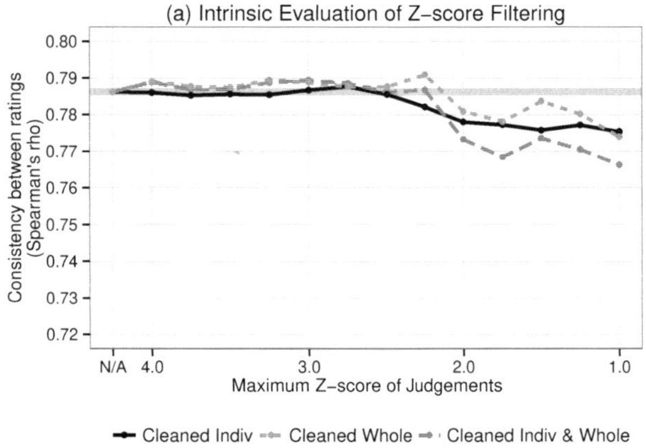

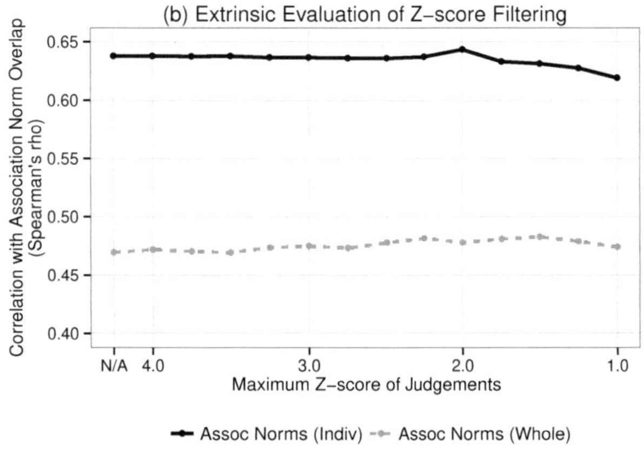

Figure 1: Intrinsic and Extrinsic evaluation of Z-score filtering. We see that Z-score filtering makes a minimal difference when filtering is strict, and is slightly detrimental with more aggressive filtering.

$\sigma_i = 2$. If we use a z^* of 1, then we would filter ratings outside of the range $[2 - 1 * 2, 2 + 1 * 2]$. Thus, the resulting new x_i would be $(1, 2, 1, 1, 1)$ and the new mean $\bar{x}_i$ would be 1.2.

Filtering Outliers Figure 1a shows the results for the intrinsic evaluation of Z-score filtering. The solid black line represents the consistency of the filtered individual ratings with the unadulterated whole ratings. The dotted orange line shows the consistency of the filtered whole ratings with the unadulterated individual ratings, and the dashed purple line shows the consistency between the data sets when both are filtered. In comparison, the consistency between the unadulterated data sets is provided by the horizontal gray line. We see that Z-score filtering overall has a minimal effect on the consistency of the two data sets. It provides very small improvements with high Z-scores, but is slightly detrimental at more aggressive levels.

Figure 1b shows the effects of Z-score filtering with our extrinsic evaluation of correlation with association norms. At all levels of filtering, we see that correlation with association norms remains mostly independent of the level of filtering.

An important factor to consider when evaluating these results is the amount of data dropped at each of the filtering levels. Figure 2 shows the data retention rate for the different data sets and levels. As expected, more aggressive filtering results in a substantially lower data retention rate. Comparing this curve to the consistency ratings gives a clear picture: the decrease in consistency is probably mostly due to the decrease in available data but not due to filtering outliers. As such, we believe that Z-score filtering does not substantially improve data quality, but may be safely applied with a conservative maximum allowed Z-score.

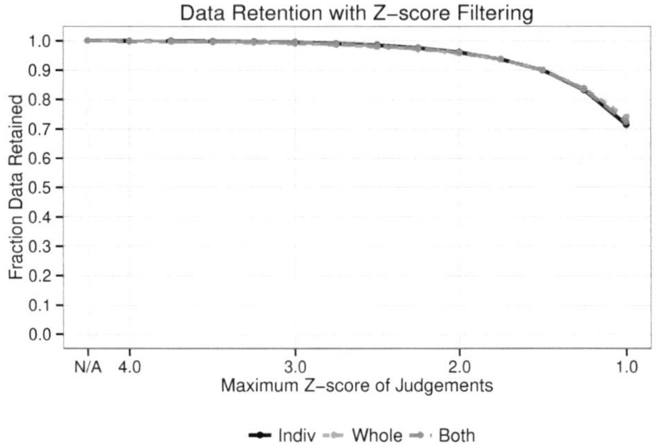

Figure 2: The data retention rate of Z-score filtering. Data retention drops rapidly with aggressive filtering.

Filtering Artificial Noise Z-score filtering has little impact on the consistency of the data, but we would like to determine whether this is due because our data being very clean, so the filtering does not apply, or Z-score filtering not being able to detect the Type I noise. To test these two possibilities, we artificially introduce noise into our data sets: we create 100 variations of the original ratings matrices, where with 0.25 probability, each entry in the matrix was

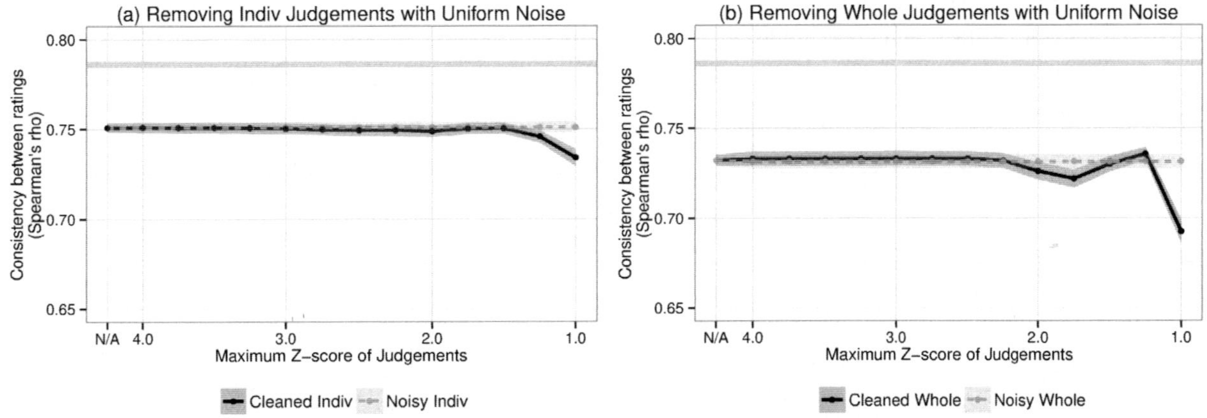

Figure 3: Ability of Z-score filtering at removing artificial noise added in the (a) individual and (b) whole judgements. The orange lines represent the consistency of the data with the noise, but no filtering, while the black lines indicate the consistency after Z-score filtering. Z-score filtering appears to be unable to find uniform random noise in either situation.

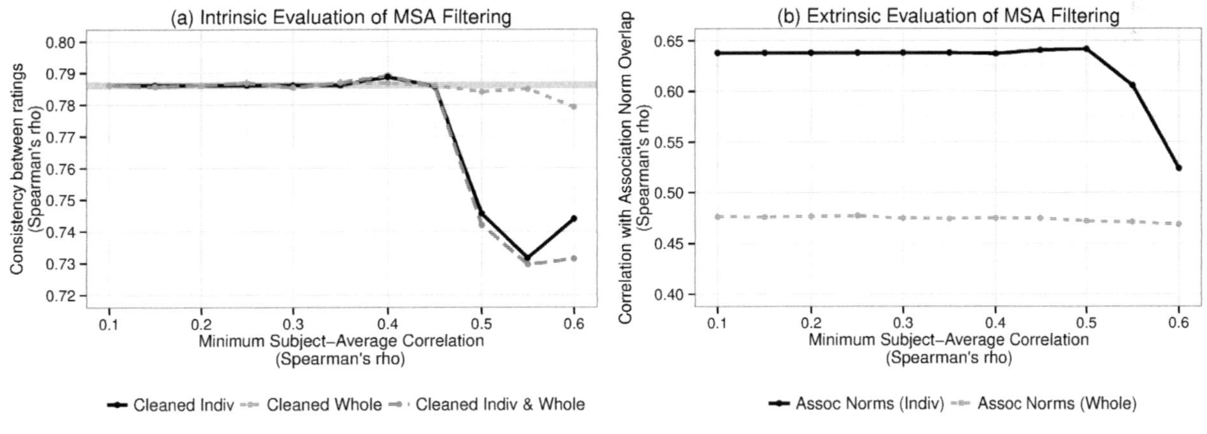

Figure 4: Intrinsic and Extrinsic evaluation of Minimum Subject Agreement filtering. We see virtually no gains using subject filtering, and the individual judgements are quite hindered by aggressive filtering.

replaced with a uniform random integer between 1 and 7. That is, roughly 1 in 4 of the entries in the original matrix were replaced with random, uniform noise. We then apply Z-score filtering on each of these noisy matrices and report their average consistency with its companion, unadulterated matrix. That is, we add noise to the individual ratings matrix, and then compare its consistency with the original whole ratings matrix, and vice versa. Thus if we are able to detect and remove the artificial noise, we should see higher consistencies in the filtered matrix over the noisy matrix.

Figure 3 shows the results of adding noise to the original data sets. The lines indicate the averages over all 100 matrix variations, while the shaded areas represent the 95% confidence intervals. Surprisingly, even though 1/4 entries in the matrix were replaced with random values, the decrease in consistency is relatively low in both settings. This likely indicates our data already has high variance. Furthermore, in both settings, we do not see any increase in consistency from Z-score filtering. We must conclude that Z-score appears ineffective at removing Type I noise in compositionality ratings.

We also tried introducing artificial noise in a second way, where judgements were not replaced with a uniformly random value, but a fixed offset of either +3 or -3, e.g., 4's became either 1's or 7's. Again, the values were changed with probability of 0.25. The results were remarkably similar, so we do not include them here.

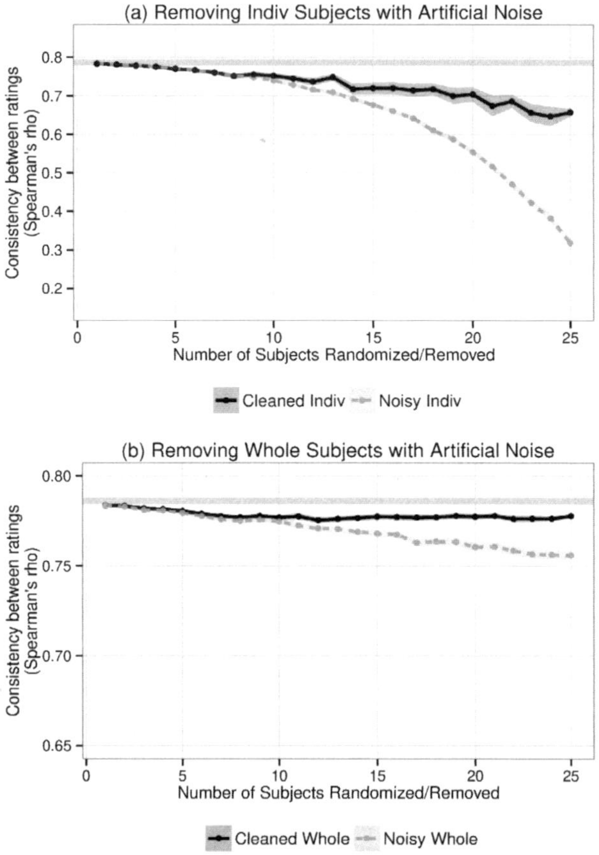

Figure 5: Ability of subject filtering at detecting highly deviant subjects. We see that artificial noise strongly hurts the quality of the individual judgements, while having a much weaker effect on the whole judgements. The process is effective at identifying deviants in both settings.

3.2.2 Minimum Subject Agreement

Minimum Subject Agreement is a method for filtering out subjects who seem to misunderstand the rating task or rarely agree with the rest of the population. For each subject in our data, we compute the average ratings for each item *excluding the subject*. The subject's *rank agreement* with the exclusive averages is computed using Spearman's ρ. We can then remove subjects whose rank agreement is below a threshold, or remove the n subjects with the lowest rank agreement.

Filtering Unreliable Subjects Figure 4 shows the effect of subject filtering on our intrinsic and extrinsic evaluations. We can see that mandating minimum subject agreement has a strong, negative impact on the individual ratings after a certain threshold is reached, but virtually no effect on the whole ratings. When we consider the corresponding data retention curve in Figure 6, the result is not surprising: the dip in performance for the individual ratings comes with a data retention rate of roughly 25%. In this way, it's actually surprising that it does so well: with only 25% of the original data, consistency is only 5 points lower. The effects are more dramatic in the extrinsic evaluation.

On the other hand, subject filtering has almost no effect on the whole ratings. This is not surprising, as most subjects have only rated at most a few dozen items, so removing subjects corresponds to a smaller reduction in data, as seen in Figure 6. Furthermore, the subjects with the highest deviations tend to be

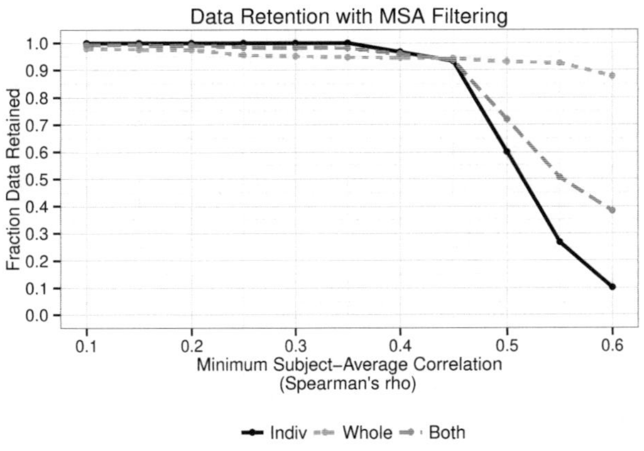

Figure 6: Data retention rates for various levels of minimum subject agreement. The whole ratings remain relatively untouched by mandating high levels of agreement, but individual ratings are aggressively filtered after a single breaking point.

the subjects who rated the fewest items since their agreement is more sensitive to small changes. As such, the subjects removed tend to be the subjects with the least influence on the data set.

Removing Artificial Subject-level Noise To test the hypothesis that minimum subject agreement filtering is effective at removing Type II noise, we introduce artificial noise at the subject level. For these experiments, we create 100 variations of our matrices where n subjects have all of their ratings replaced with random, uniform ratings. We then apply subject-level filtering where we remove the n subjects who agree least with the overall averages.

Figure 5a shows the ability of detecting Type II noise in the individual ratings. The results are unsurprising, but encouraging. We see that increasing the number of randomized subjects rapidly lowers the consistency with the whole ratings. However, the cleaned whole ratings matrix maintains a fairly high consistency, indicating that we are doing a nearly perfect job at identifying the noisy individuals.

Figure 5b shows the ability of detecting Type II noise in the whole ratings. Again, we see that the cleaned noisy ratings have a higher consistency than the noisy ratings, indicating the efficacy of subject agreement filtering at detecting unreliable subjects. The effect is less pronounced in the whole ratings than the individual ratings due to the lower proportion of subjects being randomized.

Identification of Spammers Removing subjects with the least agreement lends itself to another sort of evaluation: predicting subjects rejected during data collection. As discussed in Section 2, subjects who failed to identify the fake words or had an overall low reputability were filtered from the data before any analysis. To test the quality of minimum subject agreement, we reconstructed the data set where these previously rejected users were included, rather than removed. Subjects who rated fewer than 10 items were still excluded.

The resulting data set had a total of 242 users: 150 (62.0%) which were included in the original data, and 92 (38.0%) which were originally rejected. After constructing the modified data set, we sorted the subjects by their agreement. Of the 92 subjects with the lowest agreement, 75 of them were rejected in the original data set (81.5%). Of the 150 subjects with the highest agreement, only 17 of them were rejected from the original data set (11.3%). The typical precision-recall tradeoff obviously applies.

Curiously, we note that the minimum subject agreement at this 92nd subject was 0.457. Comparing with the curves for the *individual ratings* in Figures 4a and 6, we see this is the point where intrinsic consistency and data retention both begin dropping rapidly. While this may be a happy coincidence, it does seem to suggest that the ideal minimum subject agreement is roughly where the data retention rate starts rapidly turning.

Regardless, we can definitely say that minimum subject agreement is a highly effective way of rooting out spammers and unreliable participants.

4 Conclusion

In this paper, we have performed a thorough analysis of two sets of compositionality ratings to German noun-noun compounds, and assessed their reliability from several perspectives. We conclude that asking for ratings of compositionality of compound words is reasonable and that such judgements are notably reliable and robust. Even when compositionality ratings are collected in two very different settings (laboratory vs. AMT) and with different dynamics, the produced ratings are highly consistent. This is shown by the high initial correlation of the two sets of compositionality ratings. We believe this provides strong evidence that human judgements of compositionality, or at least these particular data sets, are reasonable as gold standards for other computational linguistic tasks.

We also find that such ratings can be highly robust against large amounts of data loss, as in the case of aggressive Z-score and minimum subject agreement filtering: despite data retention rates of 10-70%, consistency between our data sets never dropped more than 6 points. In addition, we find that the correlation between compositionality ratings and association norms is substantial, but generally much lower and less sensitive than internal consistency.

We generally find Type I noise to be very difficult to detect, and Z-score filtering is mostly ineffective at eliminating unreliable item ratings. This is confirmed by both our natural and artificial experiments. At the same time, Z-score filtering seems fairly harmless at conservative levels, and probably can be safely applied in moderation with discretion.

On the other hand, we have confirmed that minimum subject agreement is highly effective at filtering out incompetent and unreliable subjects, as evidenced by both our artificial and spammer detection experiments. We conclude that, as we have defined it, Type II noise is easily detected, and removing this noise produces much higher quality data. We recommend using subject agreement as a first-pass identifier of likely unreliable subjects in need of manual review.

We would also like to explore other types of compounds, such as adjective-noun compounds (e.g. *Großeltern* 'grandparents'), and compounds with more than two constituents (e.g. *Bleistiftspitzmachine* 'automatic pencil sharpener').

Acknowledgments

We thank the SemRel group, Alexander Fraser, and the reviewers for helpful comments and feedback. The authors acknowledge the Texas Advanced Computing Center (TACC) for providing grid resources that have contributed to these results.[5]

[5] `http://www.tacc.utexas.edu`

References

Collin Bannard. 2005. Learning about the Meaning of Verb–Particle Constructions from Corpora. *Computer Speech and Language*, 19:467–478.

Marco Baroni and Roberto Zamparelli. 2010. Nouns are vectors, adjectives are matrices: Representing adjective-noun constructions in semantic space. In *Proceedings of the 2010 Conference on Empirical Methods in Natural Language Processing*, pages 1183–1193, Cambridge, MA, October.

Irad Ben-Gal. 2005. Outlier detection. In O. Maimon and L. Rockach, editors, *Data Mining and Knowledge Discobery Handbook: A Complete Guide for Practitioners and Researchers*. Kluwer Academic Publishers.

Gemma Boleda, Marco Baroni, Nghia The Pham, and Louise McNally. 2013. On adjective-noun composition in distributional semantics. In *Proceedings of the 10th International Conference on Computational Semantics*, Potsdam, Germany.

Chris Callison-Burch and Mark Dredze, editors. 2010. *Proceedings of the NAACL/HLT Workshop on Creating Speech and Language Data with Amazon's Mechanical Turk*, Los Angeles, California.

Herbert H. Clark. 1971. Word Associations and Linguistic Theory. In John Lyons, editor, *New Horizon in Linguistics*, chapter 15, pages 271–286. Penguin.

Bob Coecke, Mehrnoosh Sadrzadeh, and Stephen Clark. 2011. Mathematical foundations for a compositional distributional model of meaning. *Linguistic Analysis*, 36(1-4):345–384.

Paul Cook and Suzanne Stevenson. 2006. Classifying Particle Semantics in English Verb-Particle Constructions. In *Proceedings of the ACL/COLING Workshop on Multiword Expressions: Identifying and Exploiting Underlying Properties*, Sydney, Australia.

Simon de Deyne and Gert Storms. 2008. Word associations: Norms for 1,424 dutch words in a continuous task. *Behavior Research Methods*, 40(1):198–205.

James Deese. 1965. *The Structure of Associations in Language and Thought*. The John Hopkins Press, Baltimore, MD.

Wolfgang Fleischer and Irmhild Barz. 2012. *Wortbildung der deutschen Gegenwartssprache*. de Gruyter.

Edward Grefenstette, G. Dinu, Y. Zhang, Meernoosh Sadrzadeh, and Marco Baroni. 2013. Multi-step regression learning for compositional distributional semantics. In *Proceedings of the 10th International Conference on Computational Semantics*, Potsdam, Germany.

Rochelle Lieber and Pavol Stekauer, editors. 2009. *The Oxford Handbook of Compounding*. Oxford University Press.

Jonathan I. Maletic and Adrian Marcus. 2010. Data cleansing: A prelude to knowledge discovery. In O. Maimon and L. Rokach, editors, *Data Mining and Knowledge Discovery Handbook*. Springer Science and Business Media, 2 edition.

Diana McCarthy, Bill Keller, and John Carroll. 2003. Detecting a Continuum of Compositionality in Phrasal Verbs. In *Proceedings of the ACL-SIGLEX Workshop on Multiword Expressions: Analysis, Acquisition and Treatment*, Sapporo, Japan.

Timothy P. McNamara. 2005. *Semantic Priming: Perspectives from Memory and Word Recognition*. Psychology Press, New York.

George Miller. 1969. The Organization of Lexical Memory: Are Word Associations sufficient? In George A. Talland and Nancy C. Waugh, editors, *The Pathology of Memory*, pages 223–237. Academic Press, New York.

Jeff Mitchell and Mirella Lapata. 2010. Composition in Distributional Models of Semantics. *Cognitive Science*, 34:1388–1429.

Douglas L. Nelson, Cathy L. McEvoy, and Thomas A. Schreiber. 1998. The University of South Florida Word Association, Rhyme, and Word Fragment Norms.

Douglas L. Nelson, Cathy L. McEvoy, and Simon Dennis. 2000. What is Free Association and What does it Measure? *Memory and Cognition*, 28:887–899.

Siva Reddy, Ioannis P. Klapaftis, Diana McCarthy, and Suresh Manandhar. 2011a. Dynamic and Static Prototype Vectors for Semantic Composition. In *Proceedings of the 5th International Joint Conference on Natural Language Processing*, pages 705–713, Chiang Mai, Thailand.

Siva Reddy, Diana McCarthy, and Suresh Manandhar. 2011b. An Empirical Study on Compositionality in Compound Nouns. In *Proceedings of the 5th International Joint Conference on Natural Language Processing*, pages 210–218, Chiang Mai, Thailand.

Sabine Schulte im Walde, Susanne Borgwaldt, and Ronny Jauch. 2012. Association Norms of German Noun Compounds. In *Proceedings of the 8th International Conference on Language Resources and Evaluation*, pages 632–639, Istanbul, Turkey.

Richard Socher, Eric H. Huang, Jeffrey Pennington, Andrew Y. Ng, and Christopher D. Manning. 2011. Dynamic Pooling and Unfolding Recursive Autoencoders for Paraphrase Detection. In *Advances in Neural Information Processing Systems 24*.

Claudia von der Heide and Susanne Borgwaldt. 2009. Assoziationen zu Unter-, Basis- und Oberbegriffen. Eine explorative Studie. In *Proceedings of the 9th Norddeutsches Linguistisches Kolloquium*, pages 51–74.

Dominic Widdows. 2008. Semantic Vector Products: Some Initial Investigations. In *Proceedings of the 2nd Conference on Quantum Interaction*, Oxford, UK.

Determining Compositionality of Word Expressions Using Word Space Models

Lubomír Krčmář, Karel Ježek
University of West Bohemia
Faculty of Applied Sciences
Department of Computer Science and Engineering
Pilsen, Czech Republic
{lkrcmar, jezek_ka}@kiv.zcu.cz

Pavel Pecina
Charles University in Prague
Faculty of Mathematics and Physics
Institute of Formal and Applied Linguistics
Prague, Czech Republic
pecina@ufal.mff.cuni.cz

Abstract

This research focuses on determining semantic compositionality of word expressions using word space models (WSMs). We discuss previous works employing WSMs and present differences in the proposed approaches which include types of WSMs, corpora, preprocessing techniques, methods for determining compositionality, and evaluation testbeds.

We also present results of our own approach for determining the semantic compositionality based on comparing distributional vectors of expressions and their components. The vectors were obtained by Latent Semantic Analysis (LSA) applied to the ukWaC corpus. Our results outperform those of all the participants in the Distributional Semantics and Compositionality (DISCO) 2011 shared task.

1 Introduction

A word expression is semantically compositional if its meaning can be understood from the literal meaning of its components. Therefore, semantically compositional expressions involve e.g. "small island" or "hot water"; on the other hand, semantically non-compositional expressions are e.g. "red tape" or "kick the bucket".

The notion of compositionality is closely related to idiomacy – the higher the compositionality the lower the idiomacy and vice versa (Sag et al., 2002; Baldwin and Kim, 2010).

Non-compositional expressions are often referred to as Multiword Expressions (MWEs). Baldwin and Kim (2010) differentiate the following sub-types of compositionality: lexical, syntactic, semantic, pragmatic, and statistical. This paper is concerned with semantic compositionality.

Compositionality as a feature of word expressions is not discrete. Instead, expressions populate a continuum between two extremes: idioms and free word combinations (McCarthy et al., 2003; Bannard et al., 2003; Katz, 2006; Fazly, 2007; Baldwin and Kim, 2010; Biemann and Giesbrecht, 2011). Typical examples of expressions between the two extremes are "zebra crossing" or "blind alley".

Our research in compositionality is motivated by the hypothesis that a special treatment of semantically non-compositional expressions can improve results in various Natural Language Processing (NPL) tasks, as shown for example by Acosta et al. (2011), who utilized MWEs in Information Retrieval (IR). Besides that, there are other NLP applications that can benefit from knowing the degree of compositionality of expressions such as machine translation (Carpuat and Diab, 2010), lexicography (Church and Hanks, 1990), word sense disambiguation (Finlayson and Kulkarni, 2011), part-of-speech (POS) tagging and parsing (Seretan, 2008) as listed in Ramisch (2012).

The main goal of this paper is to present an analysis of previous approaches using WSMs for determining the semantic compositionality of expressions. The analysis can be found in Section 2. A special attention is paid to the evaluation of the proposed models that is described in Section 3. Section 4 presents our first intuitive experimental setup and results of LSA applied to the DISCO 2011 task. Section 5 concludes the paper.

2 Semantic Compositionality of Word Expressions Determined by WSMs

Several recent works, including Lin (1999), Schone and Jurafsky (2001), Baldwin et al. (2003), McCarthy et al. (2003), Katz (2006), Johannsen et al. (2011), Reddy et al. (2011a), and Krčmář et al. (2012), show the ability of methods based on WSMs to capture the degree of semantic compositionality of word expressions. We analyse the proposed methods and discuss their differences. As further described in detail and summarized in Table 1, the approaches differ in the type of WSMs, corpora, preprocessing techniques, methods for determining the compositionality, datasets for evaluation, and methods of evaluation itself.

Our understanding of WSM is in agreement with Sahlgren (2006): "The word space model is a computational model of word meaning that utilizes the distributional patterns of words collected over large text data to represent semantic similarity between words in terms of spatial proximity". For more information on WSMs, see e.g. Turney and Pantel (2010), Jurgens and Stevens (2010), or Sahlgren (2006).

WSMs and their parameters WSMs can be built by different algorithms including LSA (Landauer and Dumais, 1997), Hyperspace Analogue to Language (HAL) (Lund and Burgess, 1996), Random Indexing (RI) (Sahlgren, 2005), and Correlated Occurrence Analogue to Lexical Semantics (COALS) (Rohde et al., 2005). Every algorithm has its own specifics and can be configured in different ways. The configuration usually involves e.g. the choice of context size, weighting functions, or normalizing functions. While Schone and Jurafsky (2001), Baldwin et al. (2003), and Katz (2006) addopted LSA-based approaches, Johannsen et al. (2011) and Krčmář et al. (2012) employ COALS; the others use their own specific WSMs.

Corpora and text preprocessing Using different corpora and their preprocessing naturally leads to different WSMs. The preprocessing can differ e.g. in the choice of used word forms or in removal/retaining of low-frequency words. For example, while Lin (1999) employs a 125-million-word newspaper corpus, Schone and Jurafsky (2001) use a 6.7-million-word subset of the TREC databases, Baldwin et al. (2003) base their experiments on 90 million words from the British National Corpus (Burnard, 2000). Krčmář et al. (2012), Johannsen et al. (2011), and Reddy et al. (2011a) use the ukWaC corpus, consisting of 1.9 billion words from web texts (Baroni et al., 2009). As for preprocessing, Lin (1999) extracts triples with dependency relationships, Baldwin et al. (2003), Reddy et al. (2011a), and Krčmář et al. (2012) concatenate word lemmas with their POS categories. Johannsen et al. (2011) use word lemmas and remove low-frequency words while Reddy et al. (2011a), for example, keep only frequent content words.

Methods We have identified three basic methods for determining semantic compositionality:

1) The substitutability-based methods exploit the fact that replacing components of non-compositional expressions by words which are similar leads to anti-collocations (Pearce, 2002). Then, frequency or mutual information of such expressions (anti-collocations) is compared with the frequency or mutual information of the original expressions. For example, consider expected occurrence counts of "hot dog" and its anti-collocations such as "warm dog" or "hot terrier".

2) The component-based methods, utilized for example by Baldwin et al. (2003) or Johannsen et al. (2011), compare the distributional characteristics of expressions and their components. The context vectors expected to be different from each other are e.g. the vector representing the expression "hot dog" and the vector representing the word "dog".

3) The compositionality-based methods compare two vectors of each analysed expression: the true co-occurrence vector of an expression and the vector obtained from vectors corresponding to the components of the expression using a compositionality function (Reddy et al., 2011a). The most common compositionality functions are vector addition or pointwise vector multiplication (Mitchell and Lapata, 2008). For example, the vectors for "hot dog" and "hot"$\oplus$"dog" are supposed to be different.

Evaluation datasets There is still no consensus on how to evaluate models determining semantic compositionality. However, by examining the discussed papers, we have observed an increasing ten-

Paper	Corpora	WSMs	Methods	Data (types)	Evaluation
Lin (1999)	125m, triples	own	SY	NVAA c.	dicts., P/R
Schone+Jurafsky(2001)	6.7m TREC	LSA	SY, CY	all types	WN, P/Rc
Baldwin et al. (2003)	BNC+POS	LSA	CT	NN, VP	WN, PC
McCarthy et al. (2003)	BNC+GR	own	CTn	PV	MA, WN, dicts., S
Katz (2006)	GNC	LSA	CY	PNV	MA, P/R, Fm
Krčmář et al. (2012)	ukWaC+POS	COALS	SY	AN, VO, SV	MA, CR, APD, CL
Johannsen et al. (2011)	ukWaC	COALS	SY, CT	AN, VO, SV	MA, CR, APD, CL
Reddy et al. (2011a)	ukWaC+POS	own	CT, CY	NN	MA, S, R2

Table 1: Overview of experiments applying WSMs to determine semantic compositionality of word expressions. BNC - British National Corpus, GR - grammatical relations, GNC - German newspaper corpus, TREC - TREC corpus; SY - substitutability-based methods, CT - component-based methods, CTn - component-based methods comparing WSM neighbors of expressions and their components, CY - compositionality-based methods; NVAP c. - noun, verb, adjective, adverb combinations, NN - noun-noun, VP - verb-particles, AN - adjective-noun, VO - verb-object, SV - subject-verb, PV - phrasal-verb, PNV - preposition-noun-verb; dicts. - dictionaries of idioms, WN - Wordnet, MA - use of manually annotated data, S - Spearman correlation, PC - Pearson correlation, CR - Spearman and Kendall correlations, APD - average point difference, CL - classification, P/R - Precision/Recall, P/Rc - Precision/Recall curves, Fm - F measure, R2 - goodness.

dency to exploit manually annotated data from a specific corpus, ranging from semantically compositional to non-compositional expressions (McCarthy et al., 2003; Katz, 2006; Johannsen et al., 2011; Reddy et al., 2011a; Krčmář et al., 2012).

This approach, as opposed to the methods based on dictionaries of MWEs (idioms) or Wordnet (Miller, 1995), has the following advantages: Firstly, the classification of a manually annotated data is not binary but finer-grained, enabling the evaluation to be more detailed. Secondly, the low-coverage problem of dictionaries, which originates for example due to the facts that new MWEs still arise or are domain specific, is avoided.[1] For example, Lin (1999), Schone and Jurafsky (2001), Baldwin et al. (2003) used Wordnet or other dictionary-type resources.

3 Evaluation Methods

This section discusses evaluation methods including average point difference (APD), Spearman and Kendall correlations, and precision of classification (PoC) suggested by Biemann and Giesbrecht (2011); Precision/nBest, Recall/nBest and Precision/Recall curves proposed by Evert (2005); and Average Precision used by Pecina (2009). Our evaluation is based on the English part of the manually annotated datasets DISCO 2011 (Biemann and Giesbrecht, 2011), further referred to as DISCO-En-Gold.

Disco-En-Gold consists of 349 expressions divided into training (TrainD), validation (ValD), and test data (TestD) manually assigned scores from 0 to 100, indicating the level of compositionality (the lower the score the lower the compositionality and vice versa). The expressions are of the following types: adjective-noun (AN), verb-object (VO), and subject-verb (SV). Based on the numerical scores, the expressions are also classified into three disjoint classes (coarse scores): low, medium, and high compositional.[2] A sample of the Disco-En-Gold data is presented in Table 2.

Comparison of evaluation methods The purpose of the DISCO workshop was to find the best methods for determining semantic compositionality. The participants were asked to create systems capable of assigning the numerical values closest to the ones assigned by the annotators (Gold values). The proposed APD evaluation measure is calculated as the mean difference between the particular systems' val-

[1]The consequence of using a low-coverage dictionary can cause underestimation of the used method since the dictionary does not have to contain MWEs correctly found by that method.

[2]Several expressions with the numerical scores close to the specified thresholds were not classified into any class.

Type	Expression	Ns	Cs
EN_ADJ_NN	blue chip	11	low
EN_V_OBJ	buck trend	14	low
EN_ADJ_NN	open source	49	medium
EN_V_OBJ	take advantage	57	medium
EN_ADJ_NN	red squirrel	90	high
EN_V_SUBJ	student learn	98	high

Table 2: A sample of manually annotated expressions from Disco-En-Gold with their numerical scores (Ns) and coarse scores (Cs).

ues and the Gold values assigned to the same expressions. PoC is defined as the ratio of correct coarse predictions to the number of all the predictions.

Following Krčmář et al. (2012), we argue that for the purpose of comparison of the methods, the values assigned to a set of expressions by a certain model are not as important as is the ranking of the expressions (which is not sensitive to the original distribution of compositionality values). Similarly as Evert (2005), Pecina (2009), and Krčmář et al. (2012) we adopt evaluation based on ranking (although the measures such as PoC or APD might provide useful information too).

Evaluation based on ranking can be realized by measuring ranked correlations (Spearman and Kendall) or Precision/Recall scores and curves commonly used e.g. in IR (Manning et al., 2008). In IR, Precision is defined as the ratio of found relevant documents to all the retrieved documents with regards to a user's query. Recall is defined as the ratio of found relevant documents to all the relevant documents in a test set to the user's query. The Precision/Recall curve is a curve depicting the dependency of Precision upon Recall. Analogously, the scheme can be used for evaluation of the methods finding semantically non-compositional expressions. However, estimation of Recall is not possible without knowledge of the correct class[3] for every expression in a corpus. To bypass this, Evert (2005) calculates Recall with respect to the set of annotated data divided into non-compositional and compositional classes. The Precision/nBest, Recall/nBest, and Precision/Recall curves for the LSA experiment described in the following section are depicted in Figures 1 and 2.

Evert's (2005) curves allow us to visually compare the results of the methods in more detail. To facilitate comparison of several methods, we also suggest using average precision (AP) adopted from Pecina (2009), which reduces information provided by a single Precision/Recall curve to one value. AP is defined as a mean Precision at all the values of Recall different from zero.

4 LSA experiment

LSA is WSM based on the Singular Value Decomposition (SVD) factorization (Deerwester et al., 1990) applied to the co-occurrence matrix. In the matrix, the numbers of word occurrences in specified contexts[4] are stored. The row vectors of the matrix capture the word meanings.[5] The idea of using SVD is to project vectors corresponding to the words into a lower-dimensional space and thus bring the vectors of words with similar meaning near to each other.

We built LSA WSM and applied the component-based method to Disco-En-Gold. We used our own modification of the LSA algorithm originally implemented in the S-Space package (Jurgens and Stevens, 2010). The modification lies in treating expressions and handling stopwords. Specifically, we added vectors for the examined expressions to WSM in such a way that the original vectors for words were preserved. This differentiates our approach e.g. from Baldwin et al. (2003) or Johannsen et al. (2011) who label the expressions ahead of time and build WSMs treating them as single words. Treating the expressions as the single words affects the WSM vectors of their constituents. As an example, consider the replacement of occurrences of "short distance" by e.g. the EXP#123 label. This affects the WSM vectors of "short" and "distance" since the numbers of their occurrences and the numbers of contexts they occur in drops. Consequently, this also affects the methods for determining the compositionality which are based upon using the vectors of

[3]A semantically non-compositional expression or a semantically compositional expressions

[4]The commonly used contexts for words are documents or the preceding and following words in a specified window.

[5]WSMs exploit Harris' distributional hypothesis (Harris, 1954), which states that semantically similar words tend to appear in similar contexts.

expressions' constituents.

As for treating stopwords, we mapped the trigram expressions containing the determiners "the", "a", or "an" as the middle word to the corresponding bigram expressions without the determiners. The intuition is to extract more precise co-occurrence vectors for the VO expressions often containing some intervening determiner. As an example, compare the occurrences of "reinvent wheel" and "reinvent (determiner) wheel" in the ukWaC corpus which are 27 and 623, respectively, or the occurrences of "cross bridge" and "cross (determiner) bridge" being 50 and 1050, respectively.[6]

We built LSA WSM from the whole ukWaC POS-tagged corpus for all the word lemmas concatenated with their POS tags excluding stopwords. We treated the following strings as stopwords: the lemmas with frequency below 50 (omitting low-frequency words), the strings containing two adjacent non-letter characters (omitting strings such as web addresses and sequences of e.g. star symbols), and lemmas with a different POS tag from noun, proper noun, adjective, verb, and adverb (omitting closed-class words). As contexts, the entire documents were used.

The co-occurrence matrix for words was normalized by applying the log-entropy transformation and reduced to 300 dimensions. Using these settings, Landauer and Dumais (1997) obtained the best results. Finally, the co-occurrence vectors of expressions were expressed in the lower-dimensional space of words in a manner analogous to how a user's query is being expressed in lower-dimensional space of documents in IR (Berry et al., 1995). The Disco-En-Gold expressions were sorted in ascending order by the average cosine similarity between the vectors corresponding to the expressions and the vectors corresponding to their components.

Evaluation We have not tried to find the optimal parameter settings for the LSA-based model yet. Therefore, we present the results on the concatenation of TrainD with ValD giving us TrainValD and on TestD. The expressions "leading edge" and "broken link" were removed from TestD because they occur in the ukWaC corpus assigned with the required POS tags less than 50 times. APs with the Spearman and Kendall correlations between the compositionality values assigned by the LSA-based model and the Gold values are depicted in Table 3. The Spearman correlations of the LSA model applied to the whole TrainValD and TestD are highly significant with p-values < 0.001. For the AP evaluation, the expressions with numerical values less or equal to 50 were classified as non-compositional[7], giving us the ratio of non-compositional expressions in TrainValD and TestD equal to 0.26 and 0.20, respectively. The Precision/nBest and Recall/nBest graphs corresponding to the LSA-based model applied to TestD are depicted in Figure 1. The Precision/Recall graphs corresponding to the LSA-based model applied to TrainD and TestD are depicted in Figure 2.

For comparison, the graphs in Figures 1 and 2 also show the curves corresponding to the evaluation of Pointwise Mutual Information (PMI).[8] The co-occurrence statistics of the expressions in Disco-En-Gold was extracted from the window of size three, sliding through the whole lemmatized ukWaC corpus.

Discussion As suggested in Section 3, we compare the results of the methods using Spearman and Kendall correlations, AP, and Everts' curves. We present the results of the LSA and PMI models alongside the results of the best performing models participating in the DISCO task. Namely, Table 3 presents the correlation values of our models, the best performing WSM-based model (Reddy et al., 2011b), the best performing model based upon association measures (Chakraborty et al., 2011), and random baseline models.

The poor results achieved by employing PMI are similar to the results of random baselines and in accordance with those of participants of the DISCO workshop (Chakraborty et al., 2011). We hypothesize that the PMI-based model incorrectly assigns low values of semantic compositionality (high val-

[6]More precisely, the occurrences were calculated from the POS-tagged parallels of the expressions.

[7]Choice of this value can affect the results. The value of 50 was chosen since it is the middle value between the manually assigned scores ranging from 0 to 100.

[8]PMI is an association measure used to determine the strength of association between two or more words based on their occurrences and co-occurrences in a corpus (Pecina, 2009).

Model	Dataset	ρ-All	ρ-AN	ρ-VO	ρ-SV	τ-All	τ-AN	τ-VO	τ-SV	AP-All
LSA	TrainValD	0.47	0.54	0.36	0.57	0.32	0.38	0.24	0.44	0.61
PMI	TrainValD	0.02	-0.25	0.29	0.14	0.01	-0.18	0.20	0.10	0.28
baseline	TrainValD	0.00	0.00	0.00	0.00	0.00	0.00	0.00	0.00	0.26
LSA	TestD	0.50	0.50	0.56	0.41	0.35	0.36	0.39	0.30	0.53
Reddy-WSM	TestD	0.35	-	-	-	0.24	-	-	-	-
StatMix	TestD	0.33	-	-	-	0.23	-	-	-	-
PMI	TestD	-0.08	-0.07	0.13	-0.08	-0.06	-0.04	0.08	-0.07	0.21
baseline	TestD	0.00	0.00	0.00	0.00	0.00	0.00	0.00	0.00	0.20

Table 3: The values of AP, Spearman (ρ) and Kendall (τ) correlations between the LSA-based and PMI-based model respectively and the Gold data with regards to the expression type. Every zero value in the table corresponds to the theoretically achieved mean value of correlation calculated from the infinite number of correlation values between the ranking of scores assigned by the annotators and the rankings of scores being obtained by a random number genarator. Reddy-WSM stands for the best performing WSM in the DISCO task (Reddy et al., 2011b). StatMix stands for the best performing system based upon association measures (Chakraborty et al., 2011). Only ρ-All and τ-All are available for the models explored by Reddy et al. (2011b) and Chakraborty et al. (2011).

ues of PMI) to frequently occurring fixed expressions. For example, we observed that the calculated values of PMI for "international airport" and "religious belief" were high.

To the contrary, our results achieved by employing the LSA model are statistically significant and better than those of all the participants of the DISCO workshop. However, the data set is probably not large enough to provide statistically reliable comparison of the methods and it is not clear how reliable the dataset itself is (the interannotator agreement was not analyzed) and therefore we can not make any hard conclusions.

5 Conclusion

We analysed the previous works applying WSMs for determining the semantic compositionality of expressions. We discussed and summarized the majority of techniques presented in the papers. Our analysis reveals a large diversity of approaches which leads to incomparable results (Table 1). Since it has been shown that WSMs can serve as good predictors of semantic compositionality, we aim to create a comparative study of the approaches.

Our analysis implies to evaluate the proposed approaches using human annotated data and evaluation techniques based on ranking. Namely, we suggest using Spearman and Kendall correlations, Precision/nBest, Recall/nBest, Precision/Recall curves, and AP.

Using the suggested evaluation techniques, we present the results of our first experiments exploiting LSA (Figures 1, 2 and Table 3). The results of the LSA-based model, compared with random baselines, PMI-based model, and all the WSM-based and statistical-based models proposed by the participants of the DISCO task, are very promising.

Acknowledgments

We thank to Vít Suchomel for providing the ukWaC corpus and the anonymous reviewers for their helpful comments and suggestions. The research is supported by Advanced Computing and Information Systems (grant no. SGS-2013-029) and by the Czech Science Foundation (grant no. P103/12/G084). Also, the access to the CERIT-SC computing facilities provided under the programme Center CERIT Scientific Cloud, part of the Operational Program Research and Development for Innovations, reg. no. CZ. 1.05/3.2.00/08.0144 is highly appreciated.

References

Otavio Costa Acosta, Aline Villavicencio, and Viviane P. Moreira. 2011. Identification and treatment of multiword expressions applied to information retrieval. In *Proceedings of the Workshop on Multiword Expressions: from Parsing and Generation to the Real World*, MWE '11, pages 101–109, Stroudsburg, PA, USA.

Timothy Baldwin and Su Nam Kim. 2010. Multiword expressions. In Nitin Indurkhya and Fred J. Damerau, editors, *Handbook of Natural Language Processing, Second Edition*. CRC Press, Taylor and Francis Group, Boca Raton, FL. ISBN 978-1420085921.

Timothy Baldwin, Colin Bannard, Takaaki Tanaka, and Dominic Widdows. 2003. An empirical model of multiword expression decomposability. *Proceedings of the ACL 2003 workshop on Multiword expressions analysis acquisition and treatment*, pages 89–96.

Colin Bannard, Timothy Baldwin, and Alex Lascarides. 2003. A statistical approach to the semantics of verb-particles. In *Proceedings of the ACL 2003 workshop on Multiword expressions: analysis, acquisition and treatment*, volume 18 of *MWE '03*, pages 65–72, Stroudsburg, PA, USA.

Marco Baroni, Silvia Bernardini, Adriano Ferraresi, and Eros Zanchetta. 2009. The WaCky wide web: a collection of very large linguistically processed web-crawled corpora. *Journal of Language Resources And Evaluation*, 43(3):209–226.

Michael W. Berry, Susan T. Dumais, and Gavin W. O'Brien. 1995. Using linear algebra for intelligent information retrieval. *SIAM Rev.*, 37(4):573–595.

Chris Biemann and Eugenie Giesbrecht. 2011. Distributional semantics and compositionality 2011: shared task description and results. In *Proceedings of the Workshop on Distributional Semantics and Compositionality*, DiSCo '11, pages 21–28.

Lou Burnard. 2000. User reference guide for the British National Corpus. Technical report, Oxford University Computing Services.

Marine Carpuat and Mona Diab. 2010. Task-based evaluation of multiword expressions: a pilot study in statistical machine translation. In *Human Language Technologies: The 2010 Annual Conference of the North American Chapter of the Association for Computational Linguistics*, HLT '10, pages 242–245, Stroudsburg, PA, USA.

Tanmoy Chakraborty, Santanu Pal, Tapabrata Mondal, Tanik Saikh, and Sivaju Bandyopadhyay. 2011. Shared task system description: Measuring the compositionality of bigrams using statistical methodologies. In *Proceedings of the Workshop on Distributional Semantics and Compositionality*, pages 38–42, Portland, Oregon, USA.

Kenneth Ward Church and Patrick Hanks. 1990. Word association norms, mutual information, and lexicography. *Comput. Linguist.*, 16(1):22–29.

Scott C. Deerwester, Susan T. Dumais, Thomas K. Landauer, George W. Furnas, and Richard A. Harshman. 1990. Indexing by latent semantic analysis. *Journal of the American Society of Information Science*, 41(6):391–407.

Stefan Evert. 2005. *The statistics of word cooccurrences: word pairs and collocations*. Ph.D. thesis, Universität Stuttgart, Holzgartenstr. 16, 70174 Stuttgart.

Afsaneh Fazly. 2007. *Automatic Acquisition of Lexical Knowledge about Multiword Predicates*. Ph.D. thesis, University of Toronto.

Mark Alan Finlayson and Nidhi Kulkarni. 2011. Detecting multi-word expressions improves word sense disambiguation. In *Proceedings of the Workshop on Multiword Expressions: from Parsing and Generation to the Real World*, MWE '11, pages 20–24, Stroudsburg, PA, USA.

Zellig Harris. 1954. Distributional structure. *Word*, 10(23):146–162.

Anders Johannsen, Hector Martinez Alonso, Christian Rishøj, and Anders Søgaard. 2011. Shared task system description: frustratingly hard compositionality prediction. In *Proceedings of the Workshop on Distributional Semantics and Compositionality*, DiSCo '11, pages 29–32, Stroudsburg, PA, USA.

David Jurgens and Keith Stevens. 2010. The s-space package: an open source package for word space models. In *Proceedings of the ACL 2010 System Demonstrations*, ACLDemos '10, pages 30–35, Stroudsburg, PA, USA.

Graham Katz. 2006. Automatic identification of non-compositional multi-word expressions using latent semantic analysis. In *In Proceedings of the ACL/COLING-06 Workshop on Multiword Expressions: Identifying and Exploiting Underlying Properties*, pages 12–19.

Lubomír Krčmář, Karel Ježek, and Massimo Poesio. 2012. Detection of semantic compositionality using semantic spaces. *Lecture Notes in Computer Science*, 7499 LNAI:353–361.

Thomas K. Landauer and Susan T. Dumais. 1997. A solution to Plato's problem: The latent semantic analysis theory of acquisition, induction, and representation of knowledge. *Psychological Review*, 104(2):211–240.

Dekang Lin. 1999. Automatic identification of non-compositional phrases. In *Proceedings of the 37th annual meeting of the Association for Computational Linguistics on Computational Linguistics*, ACL '99, pages 317–324, Stroudsburg, PA, USA.

Kevin Lund and Curt Burgess. 1996. Producing high-dimensional semantic spaces from lexical co-occurrence. *Behavior Research Methods*, 28(2):203–208.

Christopher D. Manning, Prabhakar Raghavan, and Hinrich Schütze. 2008. *Introduction to Information Retrieval*. Cambridge University Press, New York, NY, USA.

Diana McCarthy, Bill Keller, and John Carroll. 2003. Detecting a continuum of compositionality in phrasal verbs. In *Proceedings of the ACL 2003 workshop on Multiword expressions analysis acquisition and treatment*, volume 18 of *MWE '03*, pages 73–80.

George A. Miller. 1995. WordNet: A lexical database for English. *Communications of the ACM*, 38:39–41.

Jeff Mitchell and Mirella Lapata. 2008. Vector-based models of semantic composition. In *Proceedings of ACL-08: HLT*, pages 236–244, Columbus, Ohio.

Darren Pearce. 2002. A Comparative Evaluation of Collocation Extraction Techniques. In *Proceedings of the Third International Conference on Language Resources and Evaluation, LREC*.

Pavel Pecina. 2009. *Lexical Association Measures: Collocation Extraction*, volume 4 of *Studies in Computational and Theoretical Linguistics*. ÚFAL, Praha, Czechia.

Carlos Ramisch. 2012. A generic framework for multiword expressions treatment: from acquisition to applications. In *Proceedings of ACL 2012 Student Research Workshop*, ACL '12, pages 61–66, Stroudsburg, PA, USA.

Siva Reddy, Diana McCarthy, and Suresh Manandhar. 2011a. An empirical study on compositionality in compound nouns. In *Proceedings of 5th International Joint Conference on Natural Language Processing*, pages 210–218, Chiang Mai, Thailand.

Siva Reddy, Diana McCarthy, Suresh Manandhar, and Spandana Gella. 2011b. Exemplar-based word-space model for compositionality detection: Shared task system description. In *Proceedings of the Workshop on Distributional Semantics and Compositionality*, pages 54–60, Portland, Oregon, USA.

Douglas L. Rohde, Laura M. Gonnerman, and David C. Plaut. 2005. An improved model of semantic similarity based on lexical co-occurrence. *Unpublished manuscript*.

Ivan A. Sag, Timothy Baldwin, Francis Bond, Ann A. Copestake, and Dan Flickinger. 2002. Multiword expressions: A pain in the neck for nlp. In *Proceedings of the Third International Conference on Computational Linguistics and Intelligent Text Processing*, CICLing '02, pages 1–15, London, UK. Springer-Verlag.

Magnus Sahlgren. 2005. An introduction to random indexing. In *Methods and Applications of Semantic Indexing Workshop at the 7th International Conference on Terminology and Knowledge Engineering*, Leipzig, Germany.

Magnus Sahlgren. 2006. *The Word-Space Model: Using distributional analysis to represent syntagmatic and paradigmatic relations between words in high-dimensional vector spaces*. Ph.D. thesis, Stockholm University.

Patrick Schone and Daniel Jurafsky. 2001. Is knowledge-free induction of multiword unit dictionary headwords a solved problem? In *Proceedings of the 2001 Conference on Empirical Methods in Natural Language Processing*, pages 100–108.

Violeta Seretan. 2008. *Collocation extraction based on syntactic parsing*. Ph.D. thesis, University of Geneva.

Peter D. Turney and Patrick Pantel. 2010. From frequency to meaning: vector space models of semantics. *J. Artif. Int. Res.*, 37(1):141–188.

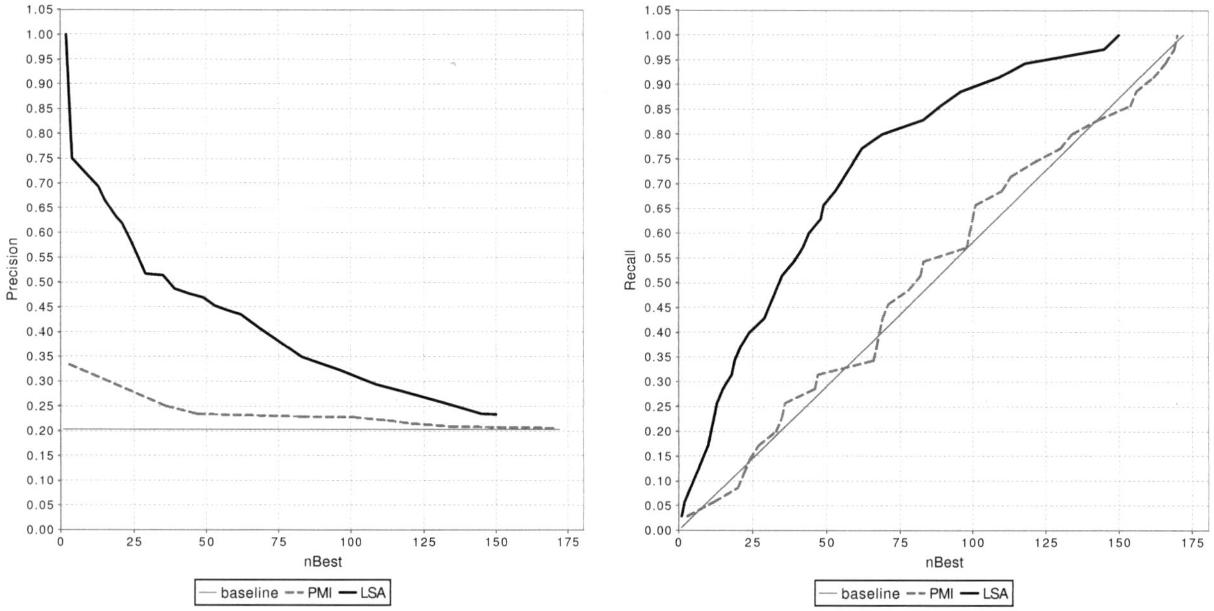

Figure 1: Smoothed graphs depicting the dependency of Precision (left) and Recall (right) upon the nBest selected non-compositional candidates from the ordered list of expressions in TestD created by the LSA and PMI-based models.

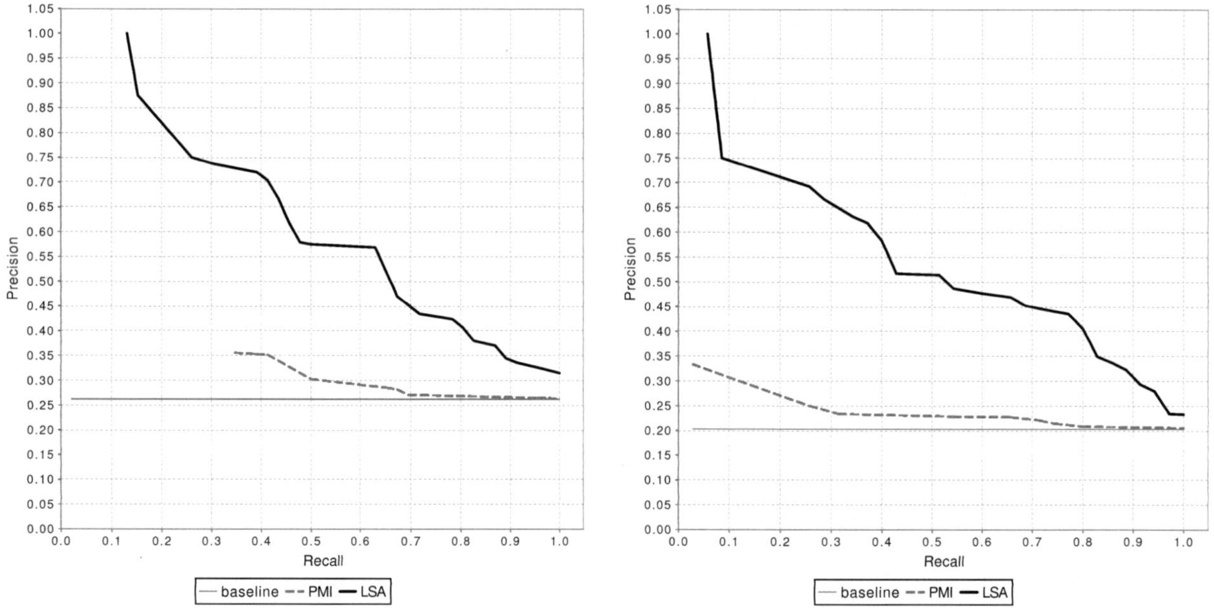

Figure 2: Smoothed graphs depicting the dependency of Precision upon Recall using the LSA and PMI-based models ordering the expressions in TrainValD (left) and TestD (right) according to their non-compositionality.

Modelling the internal variability of MWEs

Malvina Nissim
Department of Linguistics and Oriental Studies
University of Bologna
Via Zamboni 33, 40126 Bologna, Italy
malvina.nissim@unibo.it

Abstract

The issue of flexibility of multiword expressions (MWEs) is crucial towards their identification and extraction in running text, as well as their better understanding from a linguistic perspective. If we project a large MWE lexicon onto a corpus, projecting fixed forms suffers from low recall, while an unconstrained flexible search for lemmas yields a loss in precision. In this talk, I will describe a method aimed at maximising precision in the identification of MWEs in flexible mode, building on the idea that internal variability can be modelled via so-called variation patterns. I will discuss the advantages and limitations of using variation patterns, compare their performance to that of association measures, and explore their usability in MWE extraction, too.

About the Speaker

Malvina Nissim is a tenured researcher in computational linguistics at the University of Bologna. Her research focuses on the computational handling of several lexical semantics and discourse phenomena, such as the choice of referring expressions, semantic relations within compounds and in argument structure, multiword expressions, and, more recently, on the annotation and automatic detection of modality. She is also a co-founder and promoter of the Senso Comune project, devoted to the creation of a common knowledge base for Italian via crowdsourcing. She graduated in Linguistics from the University of Pisa, and obtained her PhD in Linguistics from the University of Pavia. Before joining the University of Bologna she was a post-doc at the University of Edinburgh and at the Institute for Cognitive Science and Technology in Rome.

Automatically Assessing Whether a Text Is Clichéd, with Applications to Literary Analysis

Paul Cook
Department of Computing and Information Systems
The University of Melbourne
Victoria 3010, Australia
paulcook@unimelb.edu.au

Graeme Hirst
Department of Computer Science
University of Toronto
Toronto, ON, Canada M5S 3G4
gh@cs.toronto.edu

Abstract

Clichés, as trite expressions, are predominantly multiword expressions, but not all MWEs are clichés. We conduct a preliminary examination of the problem of determining how clichéd a text is, taken as a whole, by comparing it to a reference text with respect to the proportion of more-frequent n-grams, as measured in an external corpus. We find that more-frequent n-grams are over-represented in clichéd text. We apply this finding to the "Eumaeus" episode of James Joyce's novel *Ulysses*, which literary scholars believe to be written in a deliberately clichéd style.

1 Clichés

In the broadest sense a cliché is a tired, overused, unoriginal idea, whether it be in music, in the visual arts, in the plot of a novel or drama, or in the language of literature, journalism, or rhetoric. Here, we are interested only in clichés of linguistic form. Clichés are overused, unoriginal expressions that appear in a context where something more novel might have reasonably been expected, or which masquerade as something more original, more novel, or more creative than they actually are. A cliché is a kind of ersatz novelty or creativity that is, *ipso facto*, unwelcome or deprecated by the reader. Clichés appear to be intuitively recognized by readers, but are difficult to define more formally.

Clichés are predominantly multiword expressions (MWEs) and are closely related to the idea of formulaic language, which for Wray (2002, 2008, summarized in 2009) is a psycholinguistic phenomenon: a formula is stored and retrieved as a single prefabricated unit, without deeper semantic analysis, even if it is made up of meaningful smaller units and regardless of whether it is or isn't semantically transparent. She demonstrates that formulaic language is a heterogeneous phenomenon, encompassing many types of MWEs including fixed expressions (Sag et al., 2002, e.g., *whys and wherefores*), semi-fixed expressions (e.g., *hoist with/by his own petard* 'injured by that with which he would injure others'), and syntactically-flexible expressions (e.g., sb_1 *haul* sb_2 *over the coals* 'reprimand severely', allowing also the passive sb_2 *was hauled over the coals (by* sb_1*)*). Formulaic language can exhibit any of the types of idiomaticity required by Baldwin and Kim (2010) for an expression to be considered an MWE, i.e., lexical (*de rigueur*), syntactic (*time and again*), semantic (*fly off the handle* 'lose one's temper'), pragmatic (*nice to see you*), and statistical idiomaticity (which many of the previous examples also exhibit).

Another theme relating formulaic language to MWEs is that of a common or preferred (though not necessarily invariable) way for native speakers to express an idea, i.e., institutionalization; for example, felicitations to someone having a birthday are usually expressed as *happy birthday* or (largely in British English) *many happy returns* rather than any of the many other semantically similar possibilities (*#merry birthday*; cf. *merry Christmas*).

However, formulaic language, including clichés, goes beyond the typical view of MWEs in that it has a cultural aspect as well as a purely linguistic aspect, as it includes catchphrases and allusions to language in popular culture, such as well-known lines from songs, jokes, advertisements, books, and movies (*curiouser and curiouser* from Lewis Carroll's *Alice's Adventures in Wonderland*; *go ahead, make my day* 'I dare you to attack me or do something bad, for if you do I will take great pleasure in defeating and punishing you' from the 1983 Clint Eastwood movie *Sudden Impact*).

Furthermore, not all formulaic language is clichéd; a weather forecast, for example, has no pretensions of being linguistically creative or original, but it would be a mistake to think of it as clichéd, no matter how formulaic it might be. Conversely, a cliché might not be formulaic from Wray's psycholinguistic perspective — stored and recognized as a single unit — even if its occurrence is at least frequent enough in relevant contexts for it to be recognized as familiar, trite, and unoriginal.

Finally, not all MWEs are clichés. Verb–particle constructions such as *look up* ('seek information in a resource') and *clear out* are common expressions, but aren't unoriginal in the sense of being tired and over-used. Moreover, they are not *attempts* at creativity. On the other hand, clichés are typically MWEs. Some particularly long clichés, however, are more prototypical of proverbs than MWEs (e.g., *the grass is always greener on the other side*). Single words can also be trite and over-used, although this tends to be strongly context dependent.

This paper identifies clichés as an under-studied problem closely related to many issues of interest to the MWE community. We propose a preliminary method for assessing the degree to which a text is clichéd, and then show how such a method can contribute to literary analysis. Specifically, we apply this approach to James Joyce's novel *Ulysses* to offer insight into the ongoing literary debate about the use of clichés in this work.

2 Related work

Little research in computational linguistics has specifically addressed clichés. The most relevant work is that of Smith et al. (2012) who propose a method for identifying clichés in song lyrics, and determining the extent to which a song is clichéd. Their method combines information about rhymes and the df-idf of trigrams (tf-idf, but using document frequency instead of term frequency) in song lyrics. However, this method isn't applicable for our goal of determining how clichéd an arbitrary text is with a focus on literary analysis, because in this case rhyming is not a typical feature of the texts. Moreover, repetition in song lyrics motivated their df-idf score, but this is not a salient feature of the texts we consider.

In his studies of clichés in *Ulysses*, Byrnes (2012) has drawn attention to the concept of the *cliché density* of a text, i.e., the number of clichés per unit of text (e.g., 1000 words). Byrnes manually identified clichés in *Ulysses*, but given a comprehensive cliché lexicon, automatically measuring cliché density appears to be a straightforward application of MWE identification — i.e., determining which tokens in a text are part of an MWE. Although much research on identification has focused on specific kinds of MWEs (Baldwin and Kim, 2010), whereas clichés are a mix of types, simple regular expressions could be used to identify many fixed and semi-fixed clichés. Nevertheless, an appropriate cliché lexicon would be required for this approach. Moreover, because of the relationship between clichés and culture, to be applicable to historical texts, such as for the literary analysis of interest to us, a lexicon for the appropriate time period would be required.

Techniques for MWE extraction could potentially be used to (semi-) automatically build a cliché lexicon. Much work in this area has again focused on specific types of MWEs — e.g., verb–particle constructions (Baldwin, 2005) or verb–noun combinations (Fazly et al., 2009) — but once more the heterogeneity of clichés limits the applicability of such approaches for extracting them. Methods based on strength of association — applied to *n*-grams or words co-occurring through some other relation such as syntactic dependency (see Evert, 2008, for an overview) — could be applied to extract a wider range of MWEs, although here most research has focused on two-word co-occurrences, with considerably less attention paid to longer MWEs. Even if general-purpose MWE extraction were a solved problem, methods would still be required to distinguish between MWEs that are and aren't clichés.

3 Cliché-density of known-clichéd text

Frequency per se is not a necessary or defining criterion of formulaic language. Wray (2002) points out that even in quite large corpora, many undoubted instances of formulaic language occur infrequently or not at all; for example, Moon (1998) found that formulae such as *kick the bucket* and *speak for yourself!* occurred zero times in her 18 million–word representative corpus of English. Nevertheless in a very large corpus we'd expect a formulaic expression to be more frequent than a more-creative expression suitable in the same context. Viewing clichés as a type of formulaic language, we hypothesized that a highly-clichéd text will tend to contain more n-grams whose frequency in an external corpus is medium or high than a less-clichéd text of the same size.

We compared a text known to contain many clichés to more-standard text. As a highly-clichéd text we created a document consisting solely of a sample of 1,988 clichés from a website (`clichesite.com`) that collects them.[1] For a reference "standard" text we used the written portion of the British National Corpus (BNC, Burnard, 2000). But because a longer text will tend to contain a greater proportion of low-frequency n-gram types (as measured in an external corpus) than a shorter text, it is therefore crucial to our analysis that we compare equal-size texts. We down-sampled our reference text to the same size as our highly-clichéd text, by randomly sampling sentences.

For each 1–5-gram type in each document (i.e., in the sample of clichés and in the sample of sentences from the BNC), we counted its frequency in an external corpus, the Web 1T 5-gram Corpus (Web 1T, Brants and Franz, 2006). Histograms for the frequencies are shown in Figure 1. The x-axis is the log of the frequency of the n-gram in the corpus, and the y-axis is the proportion of n-grams that had that frequency. The dark histogram is for the sample from the BNC, and the light histogram is for the clichés; the area where the two histograms overlap is medium grey. For 1-grams, the two histograms are quite similar; hence the following observations are not merely due to simple differences in word frequency. For the 3–5-grams, the light areas show that the clichés contain many more n-gram types with medium or high frequency in Web 1T than the sample of sentences from the BNC. For each of the 3–5-grams, the types in the sample of clichés are significantly more frequent than those in the BNC using a Wilcoxon rank sum test ($p \ll 0.001$). The histogram for the 2-grams, included for completeness, is beginning to show the trend observed for the 3–5-grams, but there is no significant difference in mean frequency in this case.

This finding supports our hypothesis that clichéd text contains more higher-frequency n-grams than standard text. In light of this finding, in the following section we apply this n-gram–based analysis to the study of clichés in *Ulysses*.

4 Assessing cliché-density for literary analysis

Ulysses, by James Joyce, first published in 1922, is generally regarded as one of the greatest English-language novels of the twentieth century. It is divided into 18 episodes written in widely varying styles and genres. For example, some episodes are, or contain, long passages of stream-of-consciousness thought of one of the characters; another is written in catechism-style question-and-answer form; some parts are relatively conventional.

Byrnes (2010, 2012) points out that it has long been recognized that, intuitively, some parts of the novel are written in deliberately formulaic, clichéd language, whereas some other parts use novel, creative language. However, this intuitive impression had not previously been empirically substantiated. Byrnes took the simple step of actually counting the clichés in four episodes of the book and confirmed the intuition. In particular, he found that the "Eumaeus" episode contained many more clichés than the other episodes considered. However, these results are based on a single annotator identifying the clichés — Byrnes himself — working with an informal definition of the concept, and possibly biased by expected outcomes. By automatically and objectively measuring the extent to which "Eumaeus" is clichéd, we can offer further evidence — of a very different type — to this debate.

[1]Because we don't know the coverage of this resource, it would not be appropriate to use it for an MWE-identification approach to measuring cliché-density.

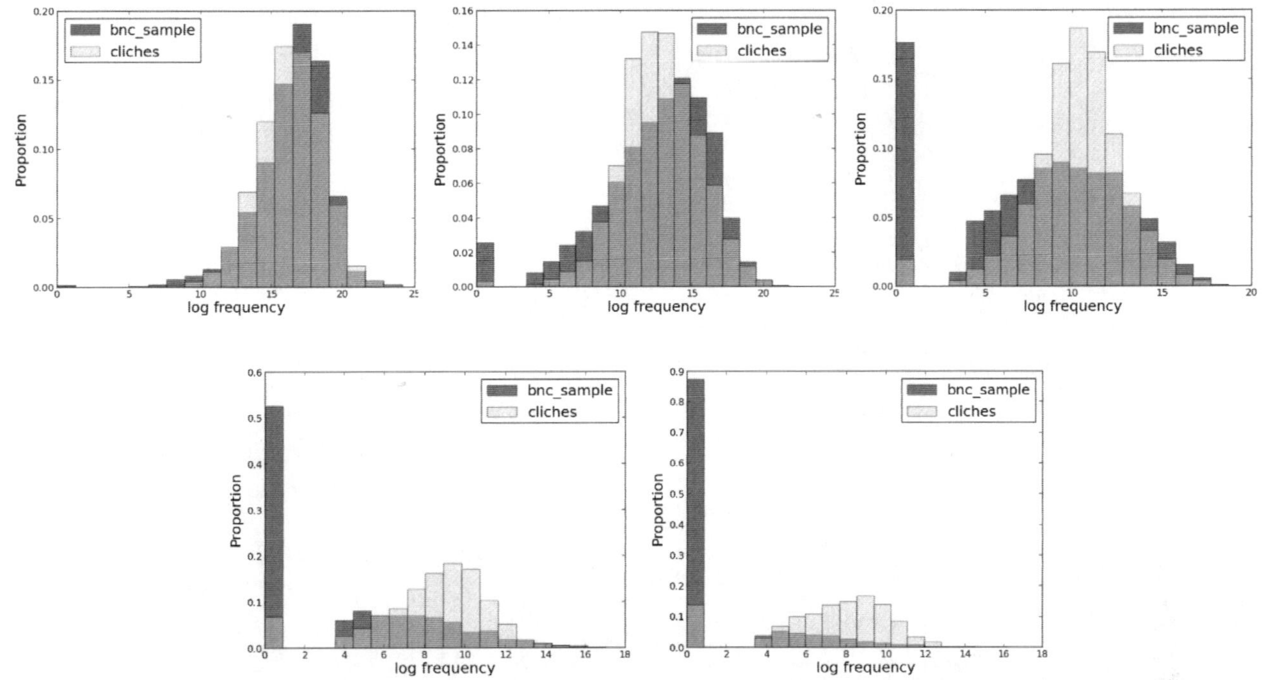

Figure 1: Histograms for the log frequency of n-grams in a sample of sentences from the BNC and a collection of known clichés. 1–5-grams are shown from left to right, top to bottom.

We compared "Eumaeus" to a background text consisting of episodes 1–2 and 4–10 of *Ulysses*, which are not thought to be written in a marked style. Because formulaic language could vary over time, we selected an external corpus from the time period leading up to the publication of *Ulysses* — the Google Books NGram Corpus (Michel et al., 2011) for the years 1850–1910 (specifically, the "English 2012" version of this corpus). We down-sampled each episode, by randomly sampling sentences, to the size of the smallest, to ensure that we compared equal-size texts.

Figures 2 and 3 show histograms for the frequencies in the external corpus of the 1–5-grams in "Eumaeus" and in the background episodes. If "Eumaeus" is more-clichéd than the background episodes, then, given our results in Section 3 above, we would expect it to contain more high-frequency higher-order n-grams. We indeed observe this in the histograms for the 3- and 4-grams. The differences for each of the 3–5-grams are again significant using Wilcoxon rank sum tests ($p \ll 0.001$ for 3- and 4-grams, $p < 0.005$ for 5-grams), although the effect is less visually striking than in the analysis in Section 3, particularly for the 5-grams. One possible reason for this difference is that in the analysis in Section 3 the known-clichéd text was artificial in the sense that it was a list of expressions, as opposed to natural text.

We further compared the mean frequency of the 3-, 4-, and 5-grams in "Eumaeus" to that of each individual background episode, again down-sampling by randomly sampling sentences, to ensure that equal-size texts are compared. In each case we find that the mean n-gram frequency is highest in "Eumaeus". These results are consistent with Byrnes's finding that "Eumaeus" is written in a clichéd style.

5 Conclusions

Clichés are an under-studied problem in computational linguistics that is closely related to issues of interest to the MWE community. In our preliminary analysis, we showed that a highly-clichéd text contains more higher-frequency n-gram types than a more-standard text. We then applied this approach to literary analysis, confirming beliefs about the use of clichés in the "Eumaeus" episode of *Ulysses*.

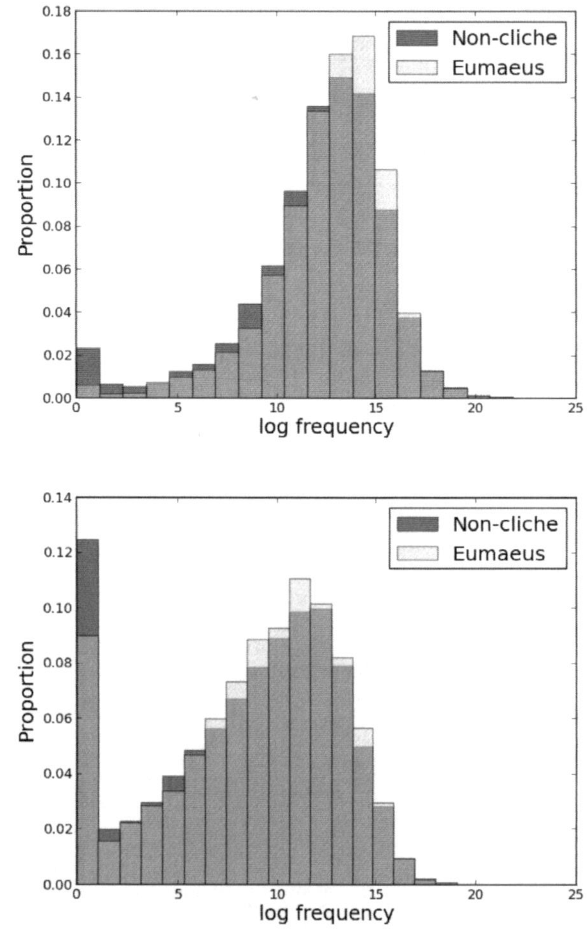

Figure 2: Histograms for the log frequency of n-grams in the "Eumaeus" episode of Ulysses and episodes known to be non-clichéd. 1-, and 2-grams are shown on the top and bottom, respectively.

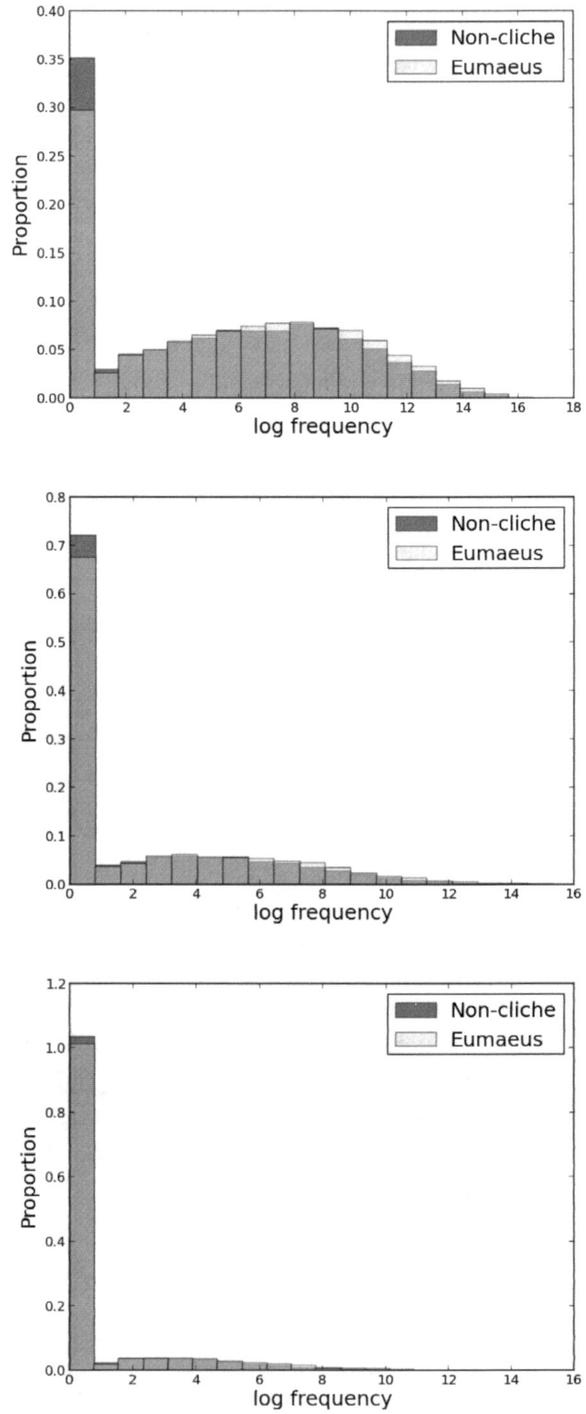

Figure 3: Histograms for the log frequency of n-grams in the "Eumaeus" episode of Ulysses and episodes known to be non-clichéd. 3-, 4-, and 5-grams are shown on the top, middle, and bottom, respectively.

Acknowledgments

We thank Timothy Baldwin and Bahar Salehi for their insightful comments on this work. This work was supported financially by the Natural Sciences and Engineering Research Council of Canada.

References

Timothy Baldwin. 2005. The deep lexical acquisition of English verb-particle constructions. *Computer Speech and Language, Special Issue on Multiword Expressions*, 19(4):398–414.

Timothy Baldwin and Su Nam Kim. 2010. Multiword expressions. In Nitin Indurkhya and Fred J.

Damerau, editors, *Handbook of Natural Language Processing, Second Edition*, pages 267–292. CRC Press, Boca Raton, USA.

Thorsten Brants and Alex Franz. 2006. Web 1T 5-gram Corpus version 1.1.

Lou Burnard. 2000. *The British National Corpus Users Reference Guide*. Oxford University Computing Services.

Robert Byrnes. 2010. A statistical analysis of the "Eumaeus" phrasemes in James Joyce's *Ulysses*. In *Actes des 10es Journées internationales d'Analyse statistique des Données Textuelles / Proceedings of the 10th International Conference on Textual Data Statistical Analysis*, pages 289–295. Rome, Italy.

Robert Byrnes. 2012. The stylometry of cliché density and character in James Joyce's *Ulysses*. In *Actes des 11es Journées internationales d'Analyse statistique des Données Textuelles / Proceedings of the 11th International Conference on Textual Data Statistical Analysis*, pages 239–246. Liège, Belgium.

Stefan Evert. 2008. Corpora and collocations. In *Corpus Linguistics. An International Handbook*. Article 58. Mouton de Gruyter, Berlin.

Afsaneh Fazly, Paul Cook, and Suzanne Stevenson. 2009. Unsupervised type and token identification of idiomatic expressions. *Computational Linguistics*, 35(1):61–103.

Jean-Baptiste Michel, Yuan Kui Shen, Aviva Presser Aiden, Adrian Veres, Matthew K. Gray, William Brockman, The Google Books Team, Joseph P. Pickett, Dale Hoiberg, Dan Clancy, Peter Norvig, Jon Orwant, Steven Pinker, Martin A. Nowak, and Erez Lieberman Aiden. 2011. Quantitative analysis of culture using millions of digitized books. *Science*, 331(6014):176–182.

Rosamund Moon. 1998. *Fixed Expressions and Idioms in English: A Corpus-Based Approach*. Clarendon Press.

Ivan A. Sag, Timothy Baldwin, Francis Bond, Ann Copestake, and Dan Flickinger. 2002. Multiword expressions: A pain in the neck for NLP. In *Proceedings of the Third International Conference on Intelligent Text Processing and Computational Linguistics (CICLING 2002)*, pages 1–15.

Alex G. Smith, Christopher X. S. Zee, and Alexandra L. Uitdenbogerd. 2012. In your eyes: Identifying clichés in song lyrics. In *Proceedings of the Australasian Language Technology Association Workshop 2012*, pages 88–96. Dunedin, New Zealand.

Alison Wray. 2002. *Formulaic Language and the Lexicon*. Cambridge University Press.

Alison Wray. 2008. *Formulaic Language: Pushing the Boundaries*. Oxford University Press.

An Analysis of Annotation of Verb-Noun Idiomatic Combinations in a Parallel Dependency Corpus[†]

Zdenka Uresova and **Jana Sindlerova** and **Eva Fucikova** and **Jan Hajic**
Charles University in Prague
Faculty of Mathematics and Physics
Institute of Formal and Applied Linguistics*
{uresova,sindlerova,fucikova,hajic}@ufal.mff.cuni.cz

Abstract

While working on valency lexicons for Czech and English, it was necessary to define treatment of multiword entities (MWEs) with the verb as the central lexical unit. Morphological, syntactic and semantic properties of such MWEs had to be formally specified in order to create lexicon entries and use them in treebank annotation. Such a formal specification has also been used for automated quality control of the annotation vs. the lexicon entries. We present a corpus-based study, concentrating on multilayer specification of verbal MWEs, their properties in Czech and English, and a comparison between the two languages using the parallel Czech-English Dependency Treebank (PCEDT). This comparison revealed interesting differences in the use of verbal MWEs in translation (discovering that such MWEs are actually rarely translated as MWEs, at least between Czech and English) as well as some inconsistencies in their annotation. Adding MWE-based checks should thus result in better quality control of future treebank/lexicon annotation. Since Czech and English are typologically different languages, we believe that our findings will also contribute to a better understanding of verbal MWEs and possibly their more unified treatment across languages.

[†] This work has been supported by the Grant No. GPP406/13/03351P of the Grant Agency of the Czech Republic. The data used have been provided by the LINDAT/Clarin infrastructural project LM2010013 supported by the MSMT CR (http://lindat.cz).

* Authors' full address: Institute of Formal and Applied Linguistics, Charles University in Prague, Faculty of Mathematics and Physics, Malostranske nam. 25, 11800 Prague 1, Czech Republic

1 Introduction: Valency and MWEs

Valency is a linguistic phenomenon which plays a crucial role in the majority of today's linguistic theories and may be considered a base for both lexicographical and grammatical work. After valency was first introduced into linguistics by L. Tesnière (1959), the study of valency was taken up by many scholars, with a wealth of material now available; cf. (Ágel et al., 2006). In the theoretical framework of Functional Generative Description (Sgall et al., 1986), the following researchers have substantially contributed to valency research: J. Panevová (1977; 1998); P. Sgall (1998), M. Lopatková (2010), V. Kettnerová (2012), Z. Urešová (2011a; 2011b).

In general, valency is understood as a specific ability of certain lexical units - primarily of verbs - to open "slots" to be filled in by other lexical units. By filling up these slots the core of the sentence structure is built. Valency is mostly approached syntactically, semantically or by combining these two perspectives. Valency terminology is not consistent (cf. valency, subcategorization, argument structure, etc.), however, valency as a verbal feature seems to be language universal (Goldberg, 1995).

MWEs are expressions which consist of more than a single word while having non-compositional meaning. They can be defined (Sag et al., 2002) as "idiosyncratic interpretations that cross word boundaries." As the MWE Workshop itself attests, MWEs form a complex issue, both theoretically and practically in various NLP tasks. Here, we will concentrate on certain types of verbal MWEs only.

Verbal MWEs can be divided into several groups

(cf. Sect. 1.3.2 in (Baldwin and Kim, 2010)):

- verb-particle constructions (VPCs), such as *take off*, *play around*, or *cut short*,
- prepositional verbs (PVs), such as *refer to*, *look for*, or *come across*,
- light-verb constructions (LVCs or verb-complement pairs or support verb constructions, see e.g. (Calzolari et al., 2002)), such as *give a kiss*, *have a drink*, or *make an offer*,
- verb-noun idiomatic combinations (VNICs or VP idioms), such as the (in)famous *kick the bucket*, *spill the beans*, or *make a face*.

While (Baldwin and Kim, 2010) define VNICs as being "composed of a verb and noun in direct object position,"[1] we found that their syntax can be more diverse and thus we will include also constructions like *be at odds* or *make a mountain out of a molehill* into this class. Our goal is to look mainly at the surface syntactic representation of MWEs, therefore, we will follow the above described typology even though the exact classification might be more complex.

2 Verbal Valency and MWEs in Dependency Treebanks

In the Prague Dependency Treebank family of projects (PDT(s)) annotated using the *Tectogrammatical Repesentation* of deep syntax and semantics (Böhmová et al., 2005), valency information is stored in valency lexicons. Each verb token in PDTs is marked by an ID (i.e., linked to) of the appropriate valency frame in the valency lexicon. For Czech, both the PDT (Hajič et al., 2012a) and the Czech part of the PCEDT 2.0 (Hajič et al., 2012b)[2] use PDT-Vallex[3]; for English (the English part of PCEDT, i.e. the texts from the Wall Street Journal portion of the Penn Treebank (WSJ/PTB), cf. (Marcus et al., 1993)) we use EngVallex,[4] which follows the same principles, including entry structure, labeling of arguments etc.

Here is an example of a valency lexicon entry (for the base sense of *to give*, simplified):

```
give ACT(sb) PAT(dobj) ADDR(dobj2)
```

The verb lemma (`give`) is associated with its arguments, labeled by *functors*: `ACT` for actor (deep subject), `PAT` for Patient (deep object), and `ADDR` for addressee.[5]

In the valency lexicon entries, two more argument labels can be used: effect (`EFF`) and origin (`ORIG`). In addition, if a free modifier (e.g. adverbial, prepositional phrase, etc.) is so tightly associated to be deemed *obligatory* for the given verb sense, it is also explicitly put into the list of arguments. The P(CE)DT use about 35 free modifications (such as `LOC`, `DIR1`, `TWHEN`, `TTILL`, `CAUS`, `AIM`, ...), most of which can be marked as obligatory with certain verbs (verb senses).

At each valency slot, requirements on surface syntactic structure and inflectional properties of the arguments may be given. This is much more complex in inflective languages but it is used in English too, often as a 'code' assigned to a verb sense, e.g. in OALDCE (Crowther, 1998).

For details of surface-syntactic structural and morphological requirements related to Czech valency and subcategorization in Czech, see e.g. Urešová (2011a; 2011b).

For the annotation of (general) MWEs (Bejček and Straňák, 2010) in the P(CE)DT, the following principle have been chosen: each MWE is represented by a single node in the deep dependency tree. This accords with our principles that "deep" representation should abstract from (the peculiarities and idiosyncrasies of) surface syntax and represent "meaning."[6] The syntactic (and related morphological) representation of MWEs is annotated at a "lower", purely syntactic dependency layer (here, each word token is represented by its own node).

[1](Baldwin and Kim, 2010), Sect. 1.3.2.4

[2]Also available from LDC, Catalog No. LDC2012T08.

[3]`http://ufal.mff.cuni.cz/lindat/PDT-Vallex`

[4]`http://ufal.mff.cuni.cz/lindat/EngVallex`; since it was created for the WSJ/PTB annotation, the starting point was PropBank (Palmer et al., 2005) to which it is also linked.

[5]We say that a verb has (zero or more) *valency slots*; the verb `give` as presented here has three.

[6]Under this assumption, each node in such a dependency tree should ideally represent a single unit of meaning, and the "meaning" of the tree - typically representing a sentence - should be derived compositionally from the meanings of the individual nodes and their (labeled, dependency) relations (i.e. functors, as they are called in the PDT-style treebanks).

Subsequently, the two representations are linked.

However, here arises a problem with modifiable MWEs (such as *lose his/my/their/... head*): if the whole MWE is represented as a single node, the modifier relation to the MWE would be ambiguous if put simply as the dependent of the MWE (i.e., which part of the MWE does it modify?). Therefore, a rather technical, but unambiguous solution was adopted: the verb as the head of the verbal MWE is represented by a node, and the "rest" of the MWE gets its own appropriately marked node (technically dependent on the verb node). Such a relation is labeled with the `DPHR` functor ("Dependent part of a PHRase"). The modifier of the MWE can thus be unambiguously attached as either the dependent node of the verb (if it modifies the whole MWE, such as a temporal adverbial in *hit the books on Sunday*), or to the `DPHR` node (if it modifies only that part of the MWE, such as in *hit the history books*).[7] We believe that this solution which allows the flexibility of considering also modifiable verbal VNICs to be annotated formally in the same way as fully fixed VNICs is original in the PDT family of treebanks, since we have not seen it neither in the Penn Treebank nor in other treebanks, including dependency ones.

Since `DPHR` is technically a dependent node, it can then be formally included as a slot in the valency dictionary, adding the surface syntactic and/or morphological representation in the form of an encoded surface dependency representation, such as in the following example of an English VNIC:

```
make DPHR(mountain.Obj.sg[a],
         out[of,molehill.Adv.sg[a])
```

In Czech, the formal means are extended, e.g. for the required case (1 - nominative, 6- locative):[8]

```
běhat DPHR(mráz.S1,po[záda.P6])
```

[7]One can argue that in very complex MWEs, this simple split into two nodes might not be enough; in the treebanks we have explored no such multiple dependent modifiers exist.

[8]The repertoire of possible syntactic and morphological constraints, which can be used for the description of possible forms of the fixed part of the idiomatic expression, covers all aspects of Czech word formation: case, number, grammatical gender, possessive gender and number, degree of comparison, negation, short/long form of certain adjectives, analytical dependency function etc.

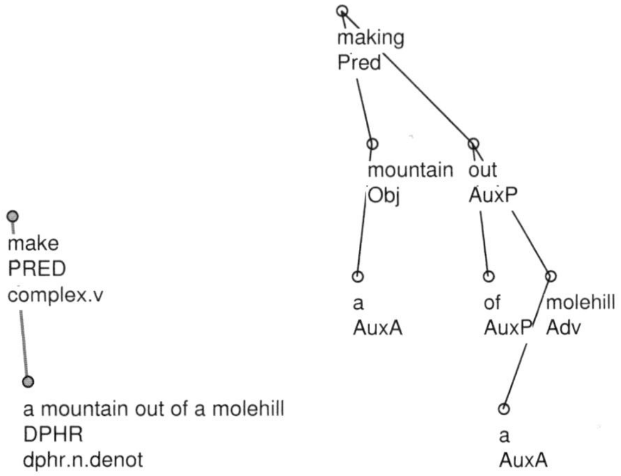

Figure 1: Verbal MWE: tectogrammatical (left) and syntactic (right) annotation of a VNIC

In Fig. 1, the phrase *making a mountain out of a mole* is syntactically annotated in the following way:

- *mountain* is annotated as the syntactic direct object of *making*,
- *out of a molehill* is annotated as a prepositional phrase (with the preposition as the head)

On the tectogrammatical layer of annotation, the verb is the head and the defining part of the MWE gets a separate node (marked by `DPHR`).

In the corpus-based analysis of verbal MWEs in the valency lexicons and the treebanks presented here, we concentrate mainly on VNICs (see Sect. 1) and briefly mention LVCs, since the boundary between them is often a bit grayish. In the P(CE)DT treebanks, LVCs are always represented as two nodes: the (light) verb node and the noun complement node. Formally, the representing structure is the same for both mentioned groups of MWEs, but it differs in the labels of the verb arguments: `CPHR` (Compound PHRase) for LVCs vs. `DPHR` for VNICs. Whereas lexical units marked as `DPHR`s are mostly limited to a fixed number of words and therefore are listed in the lexicon, lexical units marked as `CPHR`s are often not limited in their number and therefore it does not make sense to list them all in the lexicon.

A possible solution to the problem of automatic *identification* of (general) MWEs in texts using the annotation found in the PDT, which is related to the topic described in this paper but goes beyond its scope, can be found in (Bejcek et al., 2013).

3 Corpus Analysis

To compare annotation and use of VNICs in Czech and English, we have used the PCEDT. The PCEDT contains alignment information, thus it was easy to extract all cases where a VNIC was annotated (i.e. where the `DPHR` functor occurs).[9]

We found a total of 92890 occurrences of aligned (non-auxiliary) verbs. Czech VNICs were aligned with English counterparts not annotated as a VNIC in 570 cases, and there were 278 occurrences of English VNICs aligned with Czech non-VNICs, and only 88 occurrences of VNICs annotated on both sides were aligned.[10] These figures are surprisingly small (less than 1.5% of verbs are marked as VNICs), however, (a) it is only the VNIC type (e.g., phrasal verbs would account for far more), and (b) the annotator guidelines asked for "conservativeness" in creating new VNIC-type verb senses.[11]

Ideally (for NLP), VNICs would be translated as VNICs. However, as stated above, this occurred only in a 88 cases only (a few examples are shown below).

(1) (wsj0062) točit[*turn*] se[*oneself-acc.*] zády[*back-Noun-sg-instr.*]: thumb(ing) its nose

(2) (wsj0989) podřezávat[*saw down*] si[*oneself-dat.*] pod[*under*] sebou[*oneself-instr.*] větev[*branch-Noun-sg-acc.*]: bit(ing) the hand that feeds them

[9]The alignment is automatic, the Czech and English tectogrammatical annotation (including verb sense/frame assignment) is manual.

[10]The total number of Czech VNICs in the PCEDT (1300) is higher than the sum of extracted alignments (570+88=658). The difference is due to many of the Czech VNICs being aligned to a node which does not correspond to a verb, or which is not linked to an English node, or where the alignment is wrong.

[11]By "conservative" approach we mean that splitting of verb senses into new ones has been discouraged in the annotation guidelines.

Manual inspection of these alignments revealed (except for a few gray-area cases) no errors. We have thus concentrated on the asymmetric cases by manually exploring 200 such cases on each side. The results are summarized in Tab. 1.

Direction / Annotated as (by type)	VNIC in En, not Cz	VNIC in Cz, not En	Examples
Correctly annotated (as non-VNIC)			
LVC	26	4	lámat[*break*] rekordy: set records
non-MWE	138	124	přerušit [*interrupt*]: cut short
Annotation Error (should have been VNIC)			
LVC	7	17	držet[*hold*] krok[*step*]: keep abreast
non-MWE	28	52	zlomit (mu) srdce: break sb's heart
other error	1	3	

Table 1: Breakdown of VNICs linked to non-VNICs

3.1 English VNICs Linked to Non-VNIC Czech

The first column of counts in Tab. 1 refers to cases where the verb in the English original has been annotated as VNIC, but the Czech translation has been marked as a non-VNIC. We have counted cases, where we believe that the annotation is correct, even if it is not annotated as a VNIC (164 in total) and cases which should have been in fact annotated as a VNIC (35 cases). Within these two groups, we separately counted cases where the translation has not been annotated as a VNIC, but at least as a LVC, another MWE type (total of 33 such cases). The proportion of errors (approx. 18%) is higher than the 5.5% rate reported for semantic relation annotation (Štěpánek, 2006). Typically, the error would be corrected by adding a separate idiomatic verb sense into the valency lexicon and adjusting the annotation (verb sense and the `DPHR` label) accordingly.

3.2 Czech VNICs Linked to Non-VNIC English

The second column of counts in Tab. 1 shows the same breakdown as described in the previous section, but in the opposite direction: Czech VNICs which in the English original have been annotated differently. The first difference is in the number of erroneously annotated tokens, which is visibly higher (approx. twice as high) than in the opposite direction both for LVCs (17) and for constructions which have not been marked as MWEs at all (52). This suggests that the authors of the English valency lexicon and the annotators of the English deep structure have been even more "conservative" than their Czech colleagues by not creating many VNIC-typed verb senses.[12] Second, there are only 4 cases of VNICs translated into and correctly annotated as LVCs, compared to the English → Czech direction (26 cases).

4 Conclusions

We have described the treatment of (an enriched set of) verb-noun idiomatic combinations (and briefly other types of MWEs) in the PDT style treebanks and in the associated valency lexicons. We have explored the PCEDT to find interesting correspondences between the annotation and lexicon entries in the English and Czech annotation schemes.

We have found that VNICs, as one of the types of MWEs, are translated in different ways. A translation of a VNIC as a VNIC is rare, even if we take into account the annotation errors (88+7+17+28+52=192 cases of the 936 extracted). By far the most common case of translating a VNIC in both directions is the usage of a completely non-MWE phrase. There is also a substantial amount of errors in each direction, higher in cases where the Czech translation was annotated as a VNIC and the English original was not. While the low overall number of VNICs found in the parallel corpus can be explained by not considering standard phrasal verbs for this study and by the required conservatism in marking a phrase as a true VNIC, we can only speculate why only a small proportion of VNICs are translated as VNICs in(to) the other language: manual inspection of several cases suggested (but without a statistically significant conclusions) that this does not seem to be caused by the specific nature or genre of the Wall Street Journal texts, but rather by the fact that the two languages explored, Czech and English, went generally through different developments under different circumstances and contexts throughout the years they evolved separately.

While this paper describes only an initial analysis of multiword expressions (of the verb-noun idiomatic combination type) in parallel treebanks, we plan to apply the same classification and checks as described here to the whole corpus (perhaps automatically to a certain extent), to discover (presumably) even more discrepancies and also more correspondence types. These will again be classified and corrections in the data will be made. Eventually, we will be able to get a more reliable material for a thorough study of the use of MWEs in translation, with the aim of improving identification and analysis of MWEs (e.g., by enriching the approach taken by and described in (Bejcek et al., 2013)). We would also like to improve machine translation results by identifying relevant features of MWEs (including but not limited to VNICs) and using the associated information stored in the valency lexicons in order to learn translation correspondences involving MWEs.

Acknowledgments

The authors would like to thank the four reviewers, especially reviewer #4, for helpful comments which hopefully have lead to a clearer version of this paper. Also, we would like to thank to all the annotators and technical support staff who made our research possible by creating the treebanks and lexicons which we can now build upon.

References

Vilmos Ágel, Ludwig M. Eichinger, Hans-Werner Eroms, Peter Hellwig, Hans Jürgen Heringer, Henning Lobin, and Guta Rau. 2006. *Dependenz und Valenz*. Walter de Gruyter, Berlin & New York.

Timothy Baldwin and Su Nam Kim. 2010. Multiword expressions. In Nitin Indurkhya and Fred J. Damerau, editors, *Handbook of Natural Language Processing, Second Edition*. CRC Press, Taylor and Francis Group, Boca Raton, FL. ISBN 978-1420085921.

[12]None of the annotators of the English side of the parallel treebank was a fully native English speaker, which might also explain this "conservatism."

Eduard Bejček and Pavel Straňák. 2010. Annotation of multiword expressions in the prague dependency treebank. *Language Resources and Evaluation*, 44(1-2):7–21.

Eduard Bejcek, Pavel Pecina, and Pavel Stranak. 2013. Syntactic Identification of Occurrences of Multiword Expressions in Text using a Lexicon with Dependency Structures. In *Workshop on Multiword Expressions (NAACL 2013, this volume)*, New Jersey. Association for Computational Linguistics.

Alena Böhmová, Silvie Cinková, and Eva Hajičová. 2005. A Manual for Tectogrammatical Layer Annotation of the Prague Dependency Treebank (English translation). Technical report, ÚFAL MFF UK, Prague, Czech Republic.

Nicoletta Calzolari, Charles J. Fillmore, Ralph Grishman, Nancy Ide, Alessandro Lenci, Catherine Macleod, and Antonio Zampolli. 2002. Towards best practice for multiword expressions in computational lexicons. In *LREC*.

Jonathan Crowther. 1998. *Oxford Advanced Learner's Dictionary*. Cornelsen & Oxford, 5th edition.

A.E. Goldberg. 1995. *Constructions: A Construction Grammar Approach to Argument Structure*. University of Chicago Press.

Jan Hajič, Eduard Bejček, Jarmila Panevová, Jiří Mírovský, Johanka Spoustová, Jan Štěpánek, Pavel Straňák, Pavel Šidák, Pavlína Vimmrová, Eva Šťastná, Magda Ševčíková, Lenka Smejkalová, Petr Homola, Jan Popelka, Markéta Lopatková, Lucie Hrabalová, Natalia Klyueva, and Zdeněk Žabokrtský. 2012a. Prague Dependency Treebank 2.5. https://ufal-point.mff.cuni.cz/xmlui/handle/11858/00-097C-0000-0006-DB11-8.

Jan Hajič, Eva Hajičová, Jarmila Panevová, Petr Sgall, Ondřej Bojar, Silvie Cinková, Eva Fučíková, Marie Mikulová, Petr Pajas, Jan Popelka, Jiří Semecký, Jana Šindlerová, Jan Štěpánek, Josef Toman, Zdeňka Urešová, and Zdeněk Žabokrtský. 2012b. Announcing Prague Czech-English Dependency Treebank 2.0. In *Proceedings of the 8th International Conference on Language Resources and Evaluation (LREC 2012)*, pages 3153–3160, İstanbul, Turkey. ELRA, European Language Resources Association.

Václava Kettnerová. 2012. *Lexikálně-sémantické konverze ve valenčním slovníku*. Ph.D. thesis, Charles University, Prague, Czech Republic.

Markéta Lopatková. 2010. *Valency Lexicon of Czech Verbs: Towards Formal Description of Valency and Its Modeling in an Electronic Language Resource*. Prague.

Mitchell P. Marcus, Beatrice Santorini, and Mary Ann Marcinkiewicz. 1993. Building a Large Annotated Corpus of English: The Penn Treebank. *COMPUTATIONAL LINGUISTICS*, 19(2):313–330.

Martha Palmer, Daniel Gildea, and Paul Kingsbury. 2005. The Proposition Bank: An Annotated Corpus of Semantic Roles. *Computational Linguistics*, 31(1):71–106.

Jarmila Panevová. 1998. Ještě k teorii valence. *Slovo a slovesnost*, 59(1):1–14.

Jarmila Panevová. 1977. Verbal Frames Revisited. *The Prague Bulletin of Mathematical Linguistics*, (28):55–72.

Ivan A. Sag, Timothy Baldwin, Francis Bond, Ann Copestake, and Dan Flickinger. 2002. Multiword Expressions: A Pain in the Neck for NLP. In *Proc. of the 3rd International Conference on Intelligent Text Processing and Computational Linguistics (CICLing 2002)*, pages 1–15.

Petr Sgall, Eva Hajičová, and Jarmila Panevová. 1986. *The Meaning of the Sentence in Its Semantic and Pragmatic Aspects*. Dordrecht, Reidel, and Prague, Academia.

Petr Sgall. 1998. Teorie valence a její formální zpracování. *Slovo a slovesnost*, 59(1):15–29.

Jan Štěpánek. 2006. Post-annotation Checking of Prague Dependency Treebank 2.0 Data. In *Lecture Notes in Artificial Intelligence, Text, Speech and Dialogue. 9th International Conference, TSD 2006, Brno, Czech Republic, September 11–15, 2006*, volume 4188 of *Lecture Notes in Computer Science*, pages 277–284, Berlin / Heidelberg. Springer.

Lucien Tesnière. 1959. *Éléments de syntaxe structurale*. Editions Klincksieck, Paris.

Zdeňka Urešová. 2011a. *Valence sloves v Pražském závislostním korpusu*. Studies in Computational and Theoretical Linguistics. Ústav formální a aplikované lingvistiky, Prague.

Zdeňka Urešová. 2011b. *Valenční slovník Pražského závislostního korpusu (PDT-Vallex)*. Studies in Computational and Theoretical Linguistics. Ústav formální a aplikované lingvistiky, Prague.

Automatic Identification of Bengali Noun-Noun Compounds Using Random Forest

Vivekananda Gayen
Department of Computer Science and Technology
Central Calcutta Polytechnic
Kolkata-700014, India
vivek3gayen@gmail.com

Kamal Sarkar
Department of Computer Science and Engineering
Jadavpur University
Kolkata, India
jukamal2001@yahoo.com

Abstract

This paper presents a supervised machine learning approach that uses a machine learning algorithm called Random Forest for recognition of Bengali noun-noun compounds as multiword expression (MWE) from Bengali corpus. Our proposed approach to MWE recognition has two steps: (1) extraction of candidate multi-word expressions using Chunk information and various heuristic rules and (2) training the machine learning algorithm to recognize a candidate multi-word expression as Multi-word expression or not. A variety of association measures, syntactic and linguistic clues are used as features for identifying MWEs. The proposed system is tested on a Bengali corpus for identifying noun-noun compound MWEs from the corpus.

1 Introduction

Automatic identification of multiword expression (MWE) from a text document can be useful for many NLP (natural language processing) applications such as information retrieval, machine translation, word sense disambiguation. According to Frank Samadja (1993), MWEs are defined as "recurrent combinations of words that co-occur more often than expected by chance". Timothy Baldwin et al. (2010) defined multiword expressions (MWEs) as lexical items that: (a) can be decomposed into multiple lexemes; and (b) display lexical, syntactic, semantic, pragmatic and/or statistical idiomaticity. Most real world NLP applications tend to ignore MWE, or handle them simply by listing, but successful applications will need to identify and treat them appropriately.

As Jackendoff (1997) stated, the magnitude of this problem is far greater than has traditionally been realized within linguistics. He estimates that the number of MWEs in a native speakers's lexicon is of the same order of magnitude as the number of single words. In WordNet 1.7 (Fellbaum, 1999), for example, 41% of the entries are multiword.

MWEs can be broadly classified into lexicalized phrases and institutionalized phrases (Ivan A. sag et al., 2002). In terms of the semantics, compositionality is an important property of MWEs. Compositionality is the degree to which the features of the parts of a MWE combine to predict the features of the whole. According to the compositionality property, the MWEs can take a variety of forms: complete compositionality (also known as institutionalized phrases, e.g. many thanks, 'রাজ্য সরকার' (Rajya Sarkar, state government)), partial compositionality (e.g. light house, 'শপিং মল' (shopping mall), 'আম আদমি' (aam admi, common people)), idiosyncratically compositionality (e.g. spill the beans (to reveal)) and finally complete non-compositionality (e.g. hot dog, green card, 'উভয় সঙ্কট' (ubhoy sangkat, on the horns of a dilemma)).

Compound noun is a lexical unit. It is a class of MWE which is rapidly expanding due to the continuous addition of new terms for introducing new ideas. Compound nouns fall into both groups: lexicalized and institutionalized. A noun-noun compound in English characteristically occurs frequently with high lexical and semantic variability. A summary examination of the 90 million-word written component of the British National Corpus (BNC) uncover the fact that there are over 400,000 NN (Noun-Noun) compound types, with a combined token frequency of 1.3 million, that is, over 1% of words in the BNC are NN compounds (Timothy Baldwin et al., 2003). Since compound nouns are rather productive and new compound nouns are created from day to day, it is impossible to exhaustively store all compound nouns in a dictionary

It is also common practice in Bengali literature to use compound nouns as MWEs. Bengali new terms directly coined from English terms are also commonly used as MWEs in Bengali (e.g., 'ডেং থ্রি' (dengue three), 'ন্যানো সিম' (nano sim), 'ভিলেজ টুযরিজম' (village tourism), 'অ্যালার্ট মেসেজ' (alert message)).

The main focus of our work is to develop a machine learning approach based on a set of statistical, syntactic and linguistic features for identifying Bengali noun-noun compounds.

To date, not much comprehensive work has been done on Bengali multiword expression identification.

Different types of compound nouns in Bengali are discussed in section 2. Related works are presented in section 3. The proposed noun-noun MWE identification method has been detailed in section 4. The evaluation and results are presented in section 5 and conclusions and feature work are drawn in section 6.

2 Classification of Bengali Compound Nouns

In Bengali, MWEs are quite varied and many of these are of types that are not encountered in English. The primary types of compound nouns in Bengali are discussed below.

Named-Entities (NE): Names of people ('তীর্থ দাস' (Tirtha Das), 'নয়ন রায়' (Nayan Roy)). Name of the location ('হুগলি স্টেশন' (Hooghly Station), 'অশোক বিহার' (Ashok Bihar)). Names of the Organization ('আইডিয়াল কেব্ল অপারেটর্স অ্যাসোসিয়েশন' (Ideal cable operators association), 'রিবক ইন্ডিয়া' (Reebok India)). Here inflection can be added to the last word.

Idiomatic Compound Nouns: These are characteristically idiomatic and unproductive. For example, 'মা বাবা' (maa baba, father mother), 'কল কারখানা' (kaal karkhana, mills and workshops) are MWEs of this kind.

Idioms: These are the expressions whose meanings can not be recovered from their component words. For example, 'তাসের ঘর' (taser ghar, any construction that may tumble down easily at any time), 'পাখির চোখ' (pakhir chokh, target), 'সবুজ বিপ্লব' (sabuj biplab, green revolution) are the idioms in Bengali.

Numbers: These are productive in nature and little inflection like syntactic variation is also seen in number expression. For example, 'সোয়া তিন ঘন্টা' (soya teen ghanta, three hours and fifteen minutes), 'আড়াই গুণ' (arawi guun, two and a half times), 'সাড়ে তিনটে' (sharre teenta, three hours and thirty minutes), 'দেড় বছর' (der bachar, one and a half year) are MWEs of this kind.

Relational Noun Compounds: These are generally consists of two words, no word can be inserted in between. Some examples are: 'পিচতুতো ভাই' (pistuto bhai, cousin), 'মেজ মেয়ে' (majo meyya, second daughter).

Conventionalized Phrases (or Institutionalized phrases):

Institutionalized phrases are conventionalized phrases, such as ('বিবাহ বার্ষীকি' (bibaha barshiki, marriage anniversary, 'চাক্কা জ্যাম' (chakka jam, standstill), 'শেয়ার বাজার' (share bazar, share market)). They are semantically and syntactically compositional, but statistically idiosyncratic.

Simile terms: It is analogy term in Bengali and semi-productive ('হাতের পাঁচ' (hater panch, last resort), 'কথার কথা' (kather katha, a word for word's sake)).

Reduplicated terms: Reduplicated terms are non-productive and tagged as noun phrase. Namely Onomatopoeic expression ('খট খট' (khhat khhat, knock knock), 'হু হু' (hu hu, the noise made by a strong wind)), Complete reduplication ('বাড়ি বাড়ি' (bari bari, door to door), 'ব্লকে ব্লকে' (blocke blocke, block block)), Partial reduplication ('যন্তর মন্তর' (jantar mantar)), Semantic reduplication ('মাথা মুন্ডু' (matha mundu, head or tail)), Correlative reduplication ('মারামারি' (maramari, fighting)).

Administrative terms: These are institutionalized as administrative terms and are non-productive in nature. Here inflection can be added with the last word ('স্বরাষ্ট্র মন্ত্রক' (sarastra montrak, home ministry)), 'স্বাস্থ্য সচিব' (sastha sachib, health secretary)).

One of the component of MWE from English literature: Some examples of Bengali MWEs of this kind are 'মাদ্রাসা বোর্ড' (madrasha board), 'মেট্রো শহর' (metro sahar, metro city).

Both of the component of MWE from English literature: Some examples of Bengali MWEs of this kind are 'রোমিং চার্জ' (roaming charge), 'ক্রেডিট কার্ড' (credit card).

3 Related Work

The earliest works on Multiword expression extraction can be classified as: Association measure based methods, deep linguistic based methods, machine learning based methods and hybrid methods.

Many previous works have used statistical measures for multiword expression extraction. One of the important advantages of using statistical measures for extracting multiword expression is that these measures are language independent. Frank Smadja (1993) developed a system, Xtract that uses positional distribution and part-of-speech information of surrounding words of a word in a sentence to identify interesting word pairs. Classical statistical hypothesis test like Chi-square test, t-test, z-test, log-likelihood ratio (Ted Dunning, 1993) have also been employed to extract collocations. Gerlof Bouma (2009) has presented a method for collocation extraction that uses some information theory based association measures such as mutual information and pointwise mutual information.

Wen Zhang et al (2009) highlights the deficiencies of mutual information and suggested an enhanced mutual information based association measures to overcome the deficiencies. The major deficiencies of the classical mutual information, as they mention, are its poor capacity to measure association of words with unsymmetrical co-occurrence and adjustment of threshold value. Anoop et al (2008) also used various statistical measures such as point-wise mutual information (K. Church et al., 1990), log-likelihood, frequency of occurrence, closed form (e.g., blackboard) count, hyphenated count (e.g., black-board) for extraction of Hindi compound noun multiword extraction. Aswhini et al (2004) has used co-occurrence and significance function to extract MWE automatically in Bengali, focusing mainly on Noun-verb MWE. Sandipan et al (2006) has used association measures namely salience (Adam Kilgarrif et al., 2000), mutual information and log likelihood for finding N-V collocation. Tanmoy (2010) has used a linear combination of some of the association measures namely co-occurrence, Phi, significance function to obtain a linear ranking function for ranking Bengali noun-noun collocation candidates and MWEness is measured by the rank score assigned by the ranking function.

The statistical tool (e.g., log likelihood ratio) may miss many commonly used MWEs that occur in low frequencies. To overcome this problem, some linguistic clues are also useful for multiword expression extraction. Scott Songlin Paul et al (2005) focuses on a symbolic approach to multiword extraction that uses large-scale semantically classified multiword expression template database and semantic field information assigned to MWEs by the USAS semantic tagger (Paul Rayson et al.,2004). R. Mahesh et al (2011) has used a stepwise methodology that exploits linguistic knowledge such as replicating words (ruk ruk e.g. stop stop), pair of words (din-raat e.g. day night), samaas (N+N, A+N) and Sandhi (joining or fusion of words), Vaalaa morpheme (jaane vaalaa e.g. about to go) constructs for mining Hindi MWEs. A Rule-Based approach for identifying only reduplication from Bengali corpus has been presented in Tanmoy et al (2010). A semantic clustering based approach for indentifying bigram noun-noun MWEs from a medium-size Bengali corpus has been presented in Tanmoy et al (2011). The authors of this paper hypothesize that the more the similarity between two components in a bigram, the less the probability to be a MWE. The similarity between two components is measured based on the synonymous sets of the component words.

Pavel Pecina (2008) used linear logistic regression, linear discriminant analysis (LDA) and Neural Networks separately on feature vector consisting of 55 association measures for extracting MWEs. M.C. Diaz-Galiano et al. (2004) has applied Kohonen's linear vector quantization (LVQ) to integrate several statistical estimators in order to recognize MWEs. Sriram Venkatapathy et al. (2005) has presented an approach to measure relative compositionality of Hindi noun-verb MWEs using Maximum entropy model (MaxEnt). Kishorjit et al (2011) has presented a conditional random field (CRF) based method for extraction and transliteration of Manipuri MWEs.

Hybrid methods combine statistical, linguistic and/or machine learning methods. Maynard and Ananiadou (2000) combined both linguistics and statistical information in their system, TRUCK, for extracting multi-word terms. Dias (2003) has developed a hybrid system for MWE extraction, which integrates word statistics and linguistic information. Carlos Ramisch et al. (2010) presents a hybrid approach to multiword expression extraction that combines the strengths of different sources of information using a machine learning algorithm. Ivan A. Sag et al (2002) argued in favor of maintaining the right balance between symbolic and statistical approaches while developing a hybrid MWE extraction system.

4 Proposed Noun-Noun compound Identification Method

Our proposed noun-noun MWE identification method has several steps: preprocessing, candidate noun-noun MWE extraction and MWE identification by classifying the candidates MWEs into two categories: positive (MWE) and negative (non-MWE).

4.1 Preprocessing

At this step, unformatted documents are segmented into a collection of sentences automatically according to Dari (in English, full stop), Question mark (?) and Exclamation sign (!). Typographic or phonetic errors are not corrected automatically. Then the sentences are submitted to the chunker [1] one by one for processing. The chunked output is then processed to delete the information which is not required for MWE identification task. A Sample input sentence and the corresponding chunked sentence after processing are shown in figure 1.

Sample input sentence:

পরিবহণ একটি অত্যাবশ্যক শিল্প ।(paribhan ekti attyaboshak shilpo, Communication is a essential industry.)

Processed output from the chunker:

((NP পরিবহণ NN)) ((NP একটি QC অত্যাবশ্যক JJ শিল্প NN SYM))

Figure 1: A Sample input sentence and processed output from the chunker.

[1] http//ltrc.iiit.ac.in/analyzer/bengali

4.2 Candidate Noun-Noun MWE Extraction

The chunked sentences are processed to identify the noun-noun multi-word expression candidates. The multiword expression candidates are primarily extracted using the following rule:

Bigram consecutive noun-noun token sequence within same NP chunk is extracted from the chunked sentences if the Tag of the token is NN or NNP or XC (NN: Noun, NNP: Proper Noun, XC: compounds) (Akshar Bharati et al., 2006).

We observed that some potential noun-noun multi-word expressions are missed due to the chunker's error. For example, the chunked version of the sentence is ((NP কবেকার NN)) ((NP বিএসএ NN)) ((NP সাইকেল NN, SYM)). Here we find that the potential noun-noun multi-word expression candidate "বিএসএ সাইকেল" (BSA Cycle) cannot be detected using the first rule since "বিএসএ" (BSA) and সাইকেল (Cycle) belong to the different chunk.

To identify more number of potential noun-noun MWE candidates, we use some heuristic rules as follows:

Bigram noun-noun compounds which are hyphenated or occur within single quote or within first brackets or whose words are out of vocabulary (OOV) are also considered as the potential candidates for MWE.

4.3 Features

4.3.1 Statistical features: We use the association measures namely phi, point-wise mutual information (pmi), salience, log likelihood, poisson stirling, chi and t-score to calculate the scores of each noun-noun candidate MWE. These association measures use various types of frequency statistics associated with the bigram. Since Bengali is highly inflectional language, the candidate noun-noun compounds are stemmed while computing their frequencies.

The frequency statistics used in computing association measures are represented using a typical contingency table format (Satanjeev Banerjee et al., 2003). Table 1 shows a typical contingency table showing various types of frequencies associated with the noun-noun bigram <word, word2> (e.g., রাজ্য সরকার). The meanings of the entries in the contingency table are given below:

n_{11} = number of times the bigram occurs, joint frequency.

n_{12} = number of times word1 occurs in the first position of a bigram when word2 does not occur in the second position.

	সরকার (government)	~সরকার (~ government)	
রাজ্য (state)	n_{11}	n_{12}	n1p
~রাজ্য (~state)	n_{21}	n_{22}	n2p
	np1	np2	npp

Table 1: Contingency table

n_{21} = number of times word2 occurs in the second position of a bigram when word1 does not occur in the first position.

n_{22} = number of bigrams where word1 is not in the first position and word2 is not in the second position.

n1p = the number of bigrams where the first word is word, that is, n1p $=n_{11}+n_{12}$.

np1 = the number of bigrams where the second word is word2, that is np1$=n_{11}+n_{21}$.

n2p = the number of bigrams where the first word is not word1, that is n2p$=n_{21}+n_{22}$.

np2 = the number of bigrams where the second word is not word2, that is np2$=n_{12}+n_{22}$.

npp is the total number of bigram in the entire corpus.

Using the frequency statistics given in the contingency table, expected frequencies, m_{11}, m_{12}, m_{21} and m_{22} are calculated as follows:

$$m_{11} = (n1p*np1/npp)$$
$$m_{12} = (n1p*np2/npp)$$
$$m_{21} = (np1*n2p/npp)$$
$$m_{22} = (n2p*np2/npp)$$

where:

m_{11}: Expected number of times both words in the bigram occur together if they are independent.

m_{12}: Expected number of times word1 in the bigram will occur in the first position when word2 does not occur in the second position given that the words are independent.

m_{21}: Expected number of times word2 in the bigram will occur in the second position when word1 does not occur in the first position given that the words are independent.

m_{22}: Expected number of times word1 will not occur in the first position and word2 will not occur in the second position given that the words are independent.

The following association measures that use the above mentioned frequency statistics are used in our experiment.

Phi, Chi and T-score: The Phi, Chi and T-score are calculated using the following equations:

$$phi = ((n_{11}*n_{22})-(n_{12}*n_{21})) \Big/ \sqrt{(n1p*np1*np2*n2p)}$$

$$chi = 2*(((n_{11}-m_{11})/m_{11})^2 + ((n_{12}-m_{12})/m_{12})^2 + ((n_{21}-m_{21})/m_{21})^2 + ((n_{22}-m_{22})/m_{22})^2)$$

$$T-Score = (n_{11}-m_{11}) \Big/ \sqrt{n_{11}}$$

Log likelihood, Pmi, Salience and Poisson Stirling: Log likelihood is calculated as:

$$LL = 2*(n_{11}*\log(n_{11}*m_{11}) + n_{12}*\log(n_{12}*m_{12}) + n_{21}*\log(n_{21}*m_{21}) + n_{22}*\log(n_{22}*m_{22}))$$

Pointwise Mutual Information (pmi) is calculated as:

$$pmi = \log(n_{11}/m_{11})$$

The salience is defined as:

$$salience = (\log(n_{11}/m_{11})) * \log(n_{11})$$

The Poisson Stirling measure is calculated using the formula:

$$Poisson - Stirling = n_{11} * ((\log(n_{11}/m_{11}) - 1)$$

Co-occurrence: Co-occurrence is calculated using the following formula (Agarwal et al., 2004):

$$co(w1, w2) = \sum_{s \in S(w1,w2)} e^{-d(s,w1,w2)}$$

Where co(w1,w2)=co-occurrence between the words (after stemming).

S(w1,w2)= set of all sentences where both w1 and w2 occurs.

d(s,w1,w2)= distance between w1 and w2 in a sentence in terms of words.

Significance Function: The significance function (Aswhini Agarwal et al., 2004) is defined as:

$$sig_{w1}(w2) = \sigma[k1(1 - co(w1, w2).\frac{f_{w1}(w2)}{f(w1)})].\sigma[k2.\frac{f_{w1}(w2)}{\lambda} - 1]$$

$$sig(w1, w2) = sig_{w1}(w2).\exp[\frac{f_{w1}(w2)}{\max(f_{w1}(w2))} - 1]$$

Where:

$sig_{w1}^{(w2)}$ = significance of w2 with respect to w1.

$f_{w1}^{(w2)}$ = number of w1 with which w2 has occurred.

Sig(w1,w2)= general significance of w1 and w2, lies between 0 and 1.

σ(x)= sigmoid function =exp(-x)/(1+exp(-x))]

k1 and k2 define the stiffness of the sigmoid curve (for simplicity they are set to 5.0)

λ is defined as the average number of noun-noun co-occurrences.

4.3.2 Syntactic and linguistic features: Other than the statistical features discussed in the above section, we also use some syntactic and linguistic features which are listed in the table 2.

Feature name	feature description	Feature value
AvgWordLength	average length of the components of a candidate MWE	Average length of the words in a candidate MWE
Whether-Hyphenated	Whether a candidate MWE is hyphenated	Binary
Whether-Within-Quote	Whether a candidate MWE is within single quote	Binary
Whether-Within-Bracket	Whether a candidate MWE is within first brackets	Binary
OOV	Whether candidate MWE is out of vocabulary	Binary
First-Word-Inflection	Whether the first word is inflected	Binary
Second-Word-Inflection	Whether second word is inflected	Binary
TagOf-FirstWord	Lexical category of the first word of a candidate.	XC (compound), NN (noun), NNP (proper noun)
TagOfSecondWord	Lexical category of the second word of a candidate	XC (compound), NN (noun), NNP (proper noun)

Table2. Syntactic and linguistic features

4.4 Noun-noun MWE identification using random forest

Random forest (Leo Breiman, 2000) is an ensemble classifier that combines the predictions of many decision trees using majority voting to output the class for an input vector. Each decision tree participated in ensembling chooses a subset of features randomly to find the best split at each node of the decision tree. The method combines the idea of "bagging" (Leo Breiman, 1996) and the random selection of features. We use this algorithm for our multiword identification task for several reasons: (1) For many data sets, it produces a highly accurate classifier (Rich Caruana et al, 2008), (2) It runs efficiently on large databases and performs well consistently across all dimensions and (3) It generates an internal unbiased estimate of the generalization error as the forest building progresses.

The outline of the algorithm is given in the figure 2.

Training Random Forests for noun-noun MWE identification requires candidate noun-noun MWEs to be represented as the feature vectors. For this purpose, we write a computer program for automatically extracting values for the features characterizing the noun-noun MWE candidates in the documents. For each noun-noun candidate MWE in a document in our corpus, we extract the values of the features of the candidate using the measures discussed in subsection 4.3. If the noun-noun candidate MWE is found in the list of manually identified noun-noun MWEs, we label the MWE as a "Positive" example and if it is not found we label it as a "negative" example. Thus the feature vector for each candidate looks like {<a_1 a_2 a_3 ….. a_n>, <label>} which becomes a training instance (example) for the random forest, where a_1, a_2 . . .a_n, indicate feature values for a candidate. A training set consisting of a set of instances of the above form is built up by running a computer program on the documents in our corpus.

For our experiment, we use Weka (www.cs.waikato.ac.nz/ml/weka) machine learning tools. The *random forest* is included under the panel Classifier/ trees of WEKA workbench.. For our work, the random forest classifier of the WEKA suite has been run with the default values of its parameters. One of the important parameters is number of trees in the forest. We set this parameter to its default value of 10.

Random forest learning algorithm

Training phrase:
For each of N decision trees to be built
- Select a new bootstrap sample from training set
- Grow an un-pruned decision tree on this bootstrap.
- While growing a decision tree, at each internal node, randomly select m_{try} predictors (features) and determine the best split using only these predictors.
- Do not perform pruning. Save the decision tree.

Testing phase:
For an input vector, output the class that is the mode of the classes produced by the all individually trained decision trees.

Figure 2. Random forest learning algorithm

5 Evaluation and results

For evaluating the performance of our system the traditional precision, recall and F-measure are computed by comparing machine assigned labels to the human assigned labels for the noun-noun candidate MWEs extracted from our corpus of 274 Bengali documents.

5.1 Experimental dataset

Our corpus is created by collecting the news articles from the online version of well known Bengali newspaper ANANDABAZAR PATRIKA during the period spanning from 20.09.2012 to 19.10.2012. The news articles published online under the section Rajya and Desh on the topics bandh-dharmoghat, crime, disaster, jongi, mishap, political and miscellaneous are included in the corpus. It consists of total 274 documents and all those documents contain 18769 lines of Unicode texts and 233430 tokens. We have manually identified all the noun-noun compound MWEs in the collection and labeled the training data by assigning positive labels to the noun-noun compounds and negative labels to the expressions which are not noun-noun compounds. It consists of 4641 noun-noun compound MWEs. Total 8210 noun-noun compound MWE candidates are automatically extracted employing chunker and using heuristic rules as described in subsection 4.2.

5.2 Results

To estimate overall accuracy of our proposed noun-noun MWE identification system, 10-fold cross validation is done. The dataset is randomly reordered and then split into *n* parts of equal size. For each of 10 iterations, one part is used for testing and the other *n*-1 parts are used for training the classifier. The test results are collected and averaged over all folds. This gives the cross-validation estimate of the accuracy of the proposed system. J48 which is basically a decision tree included in WEKA is used as a single decision tree for comparing our system. The table 2 shows the estimated accuracy of our system. The comparison of the performance of the proposed random forest based system to that of a single decision tree is also shown in table 2. Our proposed random forest based system gives average F-measure of 0.852 which is higher than F-measure obtained by a single decision tree for bigram noun-noun compound recognition task.

Systems	Precision	Recall	F-measure
Random Forest	0.852	0.852	0.852
Single Decision Tree	0.831	0.83	0.831

Table 2: Comparisons of the performances of the proposed *random forest* based system and a single decision tree based system for bigram noun-noun compound recognition task.

6 Conclusion and Future Work

This paper presents a machine learning based approach for identifying noun-noun compound MWEs from a Bengali corpus. We have used a number of association measures, syntactic and linguistic information as features which are combined by a random forest learning algorithm for recognizing noun-noun compounds.

As a future work, we have planned to improve the noun-noun candidate MWE extraction step of the proposed system and/or introduce new features such as lexical features and semantic features for improving the system performance.

References

Adam Kilgarrif and Joseph Rosenzweig. 2000. Framework and Results for English Senseval. *Computer and the Humanities*, 34(1): pp 15-48.

Akshar Bharati, Dipti Misra Sharma, Lakshmi Bai, Rajeev Sangal. 2006. AnnCorra : Annotating Corpora Guidelines For POS And Chunk Annotation For Indian Languages.

Anoop Kunchukuttan and Om P. Damani. 2008. A System for Compound Noun Multiword Expression Extraction for Hindi. *In proceeding of 6th International Conference on National Language Processing (ICON).* pp. 20-29.

Aswhini Agarwal, Biswajit Ray, Monojit Choudhury, Sudeshna Sarkar and Anupam Basu. 2004. Automatic Extraction of Multiword Expressions in Bengali: An Approach for Miserly Resource Scenario. *In Proceedings of International Conference on Natural Language Processing (ICON),* pp. 165-174

Carlos Ramisch, Helena de Medeiros Caseli, Aline Villavicencio, André Machado, Maria José Finatto: *A Hybrid Approach for Multiword Expression Identification.* PROPOR 2010: 65-74

Fellbaum, Christine, ed.: 1998, WordNet: An Electronic Lexical Database, *Cambridge,MA: MIT Press*.

Frank Smadja 1993. "Retrieving Collocation from Text: Xtract." *Computational Linguistics*. 19.1(1993):143-177.

Gerlof Bouma. 2009. "Normalized (pointwise) mutual information in collocation extraction." *Proceedings of GSCL* (2009): 31-40.

Ivan A. Sag, Timothy Baldwin, Francis Bond, Ann Copestake and Dan Flickinger.2002. Multi-worh expression: A Pain in the neck for NLP. *CICLing*, 2002.

Jackendoff, Ray: 1997, The Architecture of the Language Faculty, *Cambridge, MA: MIT Press*.

Kishorjit Nongmeikapam, Ningombam Herojit Singh, Bishworjit Salam and Sivaji Bandyopadhyay. 2011. Transliteration of CRF Based Multiword Expression (MWE) in Manipuri: From Bengali Script Manipuri to Meitei Mayek (Script) Manipuri. *International Journal of Computer Science and Information Technology*, vol.2(4) . pp. 1441-1447

K. Church and P. Hanks. 1990. Word association norms, mutual information, and lexicography. *Computational Linguistics*. 16(1). 1990.

Leo Breiman . 1996. "Bagging predictors". *Machine Learning* 24 (2): 123–140.

Leo Breiman . 2001. "Random Forests". *Machine Learning* 45 (1): 5–32.

M.C. Diaz-Galiano, M.T. Martin-Valdivia, F. Martinez-Santiago, L.A. Urea-Lopez. 2004. Multiword Expressions Recognition with the LVQ Algorithm. *Workshop on methodologies and evaluation of Multiword Units in Real-word Applications associated with the 4th International Conference on Languages Resources and Evaluation*, Lisbon, Portugal. pp.12-17

Paul Rayson, Dawn Archer, Scott Piao and Tony McEnery. 2004. The UCREL semantic analysis system. *In Proceedings of the LREC-04 Workshop, beyond Named Entity Recognition Semantic Labelling for NLP Tasks*, Lisbon, Portugal, pp.7-12.

Pavel Pecina. 2008. Reference data for czech collocation extraction. *In Proc. Of the LREC Workshop Towards a Shared Task for MWEs (MWE 2008)*. pp. 11-14, Marrakech, Morocco, Jun.

Rich Caruana, Nikos Karampatziakis and Ainur Yessenalina (2008). "An empirical evaluation of supervised learning in high dimensions". *Proceedings of the 25th International Conference on Machine Learning (ICML).*

R. Mahesh and K. Sinha. 2011. Stepwise Mining of Multi-Word Expressions in Hindi. *Proceedings of the Workshop on Multiword Expressions: from Parsing and Generation to the Real World (MWE 2011)* pp. 110-115

Sandipan Dandapat, Pabitra Mitra and Sudeshna Sarkar. 2006. Statistical Investigation of Bengali Noun-Verb (N-V) Collocations as Multi-word expressions. *In the Proceedings of MSPIL*, Mumbai, pp 230-233.

Santanjeev Banerjee and Ted Pedersen. 2003. "The Design, Implementation and Use of the Ngram Staistics Package." *Proceedings of the Fourth International Conference on Intelligent Text Processing and Computational Linguistics.* Pp. 370-381

Scott Songlin Piao, Paul Rayson, Dawn Archer, Tony McEnery. 2005. Comparing and combining a semantic tagger and a statistical tool for MWE extraction. *Computer Speech and Language (ELSEVIER) 19 (2005)* pp. 378-397

Sriram Venkatapathy, Preeti Agrawal and Aravind K. Joshi. Relative Compositionality of Noun+Verb Multi-word Expressions in Hindi. *In Proceedings of ICON-2005*, Kanpur.

Takaaki Tanaka, Timothy Baldwin. 2003. "Noun-Noun Compound Machine Translation: a Feasibility Study on Shallow Processing." *Proceeings of the ACL 2003 workshop on Multiword expressions.* pp. 17-24

Tanmoy Chakraborty. 2010. Identification of Noun-Noun(N-N) Collocations as Multi-Word Expressions in Bengali Corpus. *8th International Conference on Natural Language Processing (ICON 2010).*

Tanmoy Chakraborty and Sivaji Bandyopadhyay. 2010. Identification of Reduplication in Bengali Corpus and their Semantic Analysis: A Rule-Based Approach. *Proceedings of Workshop on Multiword Expressions: from Theory to Applications* (MWE 2010) pp. 72-75

Tanmoy Chakraborty, Dipankar Das and Sivaji Bandyopadhyay. 2011. Semantic Clustering: an Attempt to Identify Multiword Expressions in Bengali. Proceedings of Workshop on Multiword Expressions: from Parsing and Generation to the Real World(MWE 2011*). Association for Computational Linguistics*. Portland, Oregon, USA, 23 June 2011.

Ted Dunning. 1993. Accurate Method for the Statistic of Surprise and Coincidence. *In Computational Linguistics*, pp. 61-74

Timothy Baldwin and Su Nam Kim (2010), in Nitin Indurkhya and Fred J. Damerau (eds .) Handbook of Natural Language Processing, *Second Edition, CRC Press,* Boca Raton, USA, pp. 267-292.

Automatic Detection of Stable Grammatical Features in N-Grams

Mikhail Kopotev[1] **Lidia Pivovarova**[1,2] **Natalia Kochetkova**[3] **Roman Yangarber**[1]
[1] University of Helsinki, Finland
[2] St.Petersburg State University, Russia
[3] Moscow Institute of Electronics and Mathematics, NRU HSE, Russia

Abstract

This paper presents an algorithm that allows the user to issue a query pattern, collects multi-word expressions (MWEs) that match the pattern, and then ranks them in a uniform fashion. This is achieved by quantifying the strength of all possible relations between the tokens and their features in the MWEs. The algorithm collects the frequency of morphological categories of the given pattern on a unified scale in order to choose the stable categories and their values. For every part of speech, and for all of its categories, we calculate a normalized Kullback-Leibler divergence between the category's distribution in the pattern and its distribution in the corpus overall. Categories with the largest divergence are considered to be the most significant. The particular values of the categories are sorted according to a frequency ratio. As a result, we obtain morphosyntactic profiles of a given pattern, which includes the most stable category of the pattern, and their values.

1 Introduction

In n-grams, the relations among words and among their grammatical categories cover a wide spectrum, ranging from idioms to syntactic units, such as a verb phrase. In most cases, the words are linked together by both grammatical and lexical relations. It is difficult to decide, which relation is stronger in each particular case. For example, in the idiomatic phrase *meet the eye*, the relationship is lexical rather than grammatical. A phrasal verb *meet up* is similar to single-word verbs and has its own meaning. It can be interpreted as one lexeme, spelled as two words.

On the other hand, phrases like *meet the requirements*, *meet the specifications*, *meet the demands* are traditionally called "collocations." However, the question arises about the role played by the noun following the verb: is it a lexically free direct object, or a part of stable lexical unit, or to some extend both? These words are bound by both grammatical and lexical relations, and we assume that the majority of word combinations in any language have such a dual nature.

Lastly, the relationship between the words in the English phrase *meet her* differs from those above in that it may be described as purely grammatical—the verb *meet* receives a direct object.

Distinguishing *collocations*, i.e. "co-occurrences of words" from *colligations*, i.e. "co-occurrence of word forms with grammatical phenomena" (Gries and Divjak, 2009) is not always a simple task; there is no clear boundary between various types of word combinations inasmuch as they can be simultaneously a collocation and a colligation—this type of MWE is called *collostructions* in (Stefanowitsch and Gries, 2003). It was proposed that language as such is a "constructicon" (Goldberg, 2006), which means that fusion is its core nature. For this reason, devising formal methods to measure the strength of morphological or lexical relations between words becomes a challenge.

Our approach aims to treat multi-word expressions (MWEs) of various nature—idioms, multi-word lexemes, collocations and colligations—*on an equal basis*, and to compare the strength of various possible relations between the tokens in a MWE quantitatively. We search for "the underlying cause" for the frequent co-occurrence of certain words: whether it is due to their morphological categories, or lexical compatibility, or a combination of both. In this paper, however, we focus on colligations, ignoring collocations and collostructions.

For languages with rich morphology the situation is more complicated, because each word may have several morphological categories that are not independent and interact with each other. This paper focuses on Russian, which not only has free word order and rich morphology,[1] but is also a language that is well-investigated. A good number of corpora and reference grammars are available to be used for evaluation. The data we use in this work is the n-gram corpus, extracted from a deeply annotated and carefully disambiguated (partly manually) sub-corpus of the Russian National Corpus (RNC). The size of disambiguated corpus used in this paper is 5 944 188 words of running text.

2 Related Work

Much effort has been invested in automatic extraction of MWEs from text. A great variety of method are used, depending on the data, the particular tasks and the types of MWEs to be extracted. Pecina (2005) surveys 87 statistical measures and methods, and even that is not a complete list. The most frequently used metrics, *inter alia*, are Mutual Information (MI), (Church and Hanks, 1990), t-score (Church et al., 1991), and log-likelihood (Dunning, 1993). The common disadvantage of these is their dependency on the number of words included in the MWE. Although there is a large number of papers that use MI for bigram extraction, only a few use the MI measure for three or more collocates, e.g., (Tadić and Šojat, 2003; Wermter and Hahn, 2006; Kilgarriff et al., 2012),

Frantzi et al. (2000) introduced the c-value and nc-value measures to extract terms of different lengths. Daudaravicius (2010) has developed a promising method that recognizes collocations in text. Rather than extracting MWEs, this method cuts the text into a sequence of MWEs of length from 1 to 7 words; the algorithm may produce different chunking for the same segment of text within different corpora. Nevertheless, extraction of variable-length MWE is a challenging task; the majority of papers in the field still use measures that take the number of collocates as a core parameter.

Entropy and other probabilistic measures have been used for MWE extraction since the earliest work. For example, the main idea in (Shimohata et al., 1997; Resnik, 1997), is that the MWE's idiosyncrasy, (Sag et al., 2002), is reflected in the distributions of the collocates. Ramisch et al. (2008) introduced the Entropy of Permutation and Insertion:

$$EPI = -\sum_{a=0}^{m} p(ngram_a) \log[p(ngram_a)] \quad (1)$$

where $ngram_0$ is the original MWE, and $ngram_a$ are its syntactically acceptable permutations. Kullback-Leibler divergence was proposed by Resnik (1997) to measure selective preference for the word sense disambiguation (WSD) task. Fazly and Stevenson (2007) applied a set of statistical measures to classify *verb+noun* MWEs and used Kullback-Leibler divergence, among other methods, to measure the syntactic cohesion of a word combination. Van de Cruys and Moirón (2007) used normalized Kullback-Leibler divergence to find idiomatic expression with verbs in Dutch.

Russian MWE-studies have emerged over the last decade. Khokhlova and Zakharov (2009) applied MI, t-score and log-likelihood to extract verb collocations; Yagunova and Pivovarova (2010) studied the difference between Russian lemma/token collocations and also between various genres; Dobrov and Loukachevitch (2011) implemented term extraction algorithms. However, there is a lack of study of both colligations and collostructions in Russian. The only work known to us is by Sharoff (2004), who applied the MI-score to extract prepositional phrases; however, the only category he used was the POS.

As far as we aware, the algorithm we present in this paper has not been applied to Russian or to other languages.

3 Method

The input for our system is any n-gram of length 2–4, where one position is a gap—the algorithm aims

[1]The Multitext-East specification, which aims to create an unified cross-language annotation scheme, defines 156 morpho-syntactic tags for Russian as compared to 80 tags for English (http://nl.ijs.si/ME/V4/msd/html).

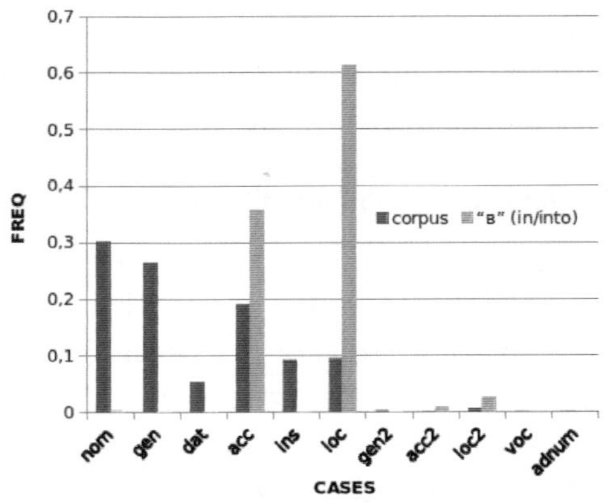

Figure 1: Distributions of noun cases in the corpus and in a sample—following the preposition "в" (*in*)

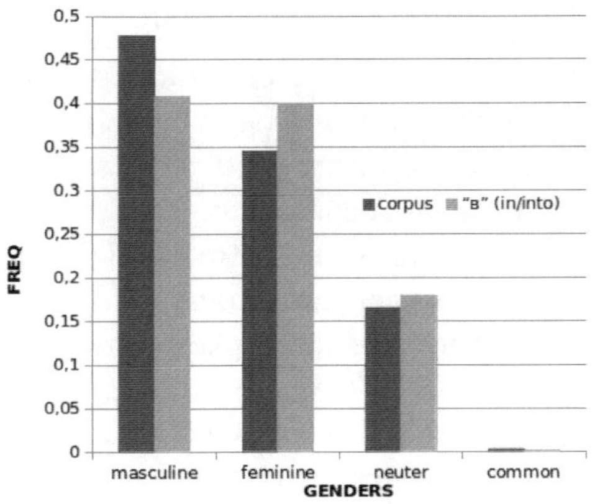

Figure 2: Distributions of nominal gender in the corpus and in a sample—following the preposition "в" (*in*)

to find the most stable morphological categories of words that can fill this gap. Moreover, the user can specify the particular properties of words that can fill the gap—for example, specify that the output should include only plural nouns. Thus, the combination of the surrounding words and morphological constrains form an initial query *pattern* for the algorithm.

Our model tries to capture the difference between distributions of linguistic features in the general corpus as compared to distributions within the given pattern. For example, Figure 1 shows the distribution of cases in the corpus overall vs. their distribution in words following the preposition "в" (*in/into*). Figure 2 shows the corresponding distributions of gender. Gender is distributed similarly in the corpus and in the sample restricted by the pattern; by contrast, the distribution of cases is clearly different. This is due to the fact that the preposition governs the case of the noun, but has no effect on gender. To measure this difference between the distributions we use the Kullback-Leibler divergence:

$$Div(C) = \sum_{i=1}^{N} P_i^{pattern} \times \log(\frac{P_i^{pattern}}{P_i^{corpus}}) \quad (2)$$

where C is the morphological category in a pattern—e.g., case or gender,—having the values $1..N$, $P_i^{pattern}$ is the relative frequency of value i restricted by the pattern, and P_i^{corpus} is the relative frequency of the same value in the general corpus. Since the number of possible values for a category is variable—e.g., eleven for case, four for gender, and hundreds of thousands for lemmas—the divergence needs to be normalized. The normalization could be done in various ways, e.g., against the entropy or some maximal divergence in the data; in our experiments, the best results were obtained using a variant proposed in (Bigi, 2003), where the divergence between the corpus distribution and the uniform distribution is used as the normalizing factor:

$$NormDiv(C) = \frac{Div(C)}{E(C) + \log(n)} \quad (3)$$

where $E(C)$ is the entropy of category C and n is the number of possible values of C; the term $\log(n)$ is the entropy of the uniform distribution over n outcomes (which is the maximal entropy). The category with the highest value of normalized divergence is seen as maximally preferred by the pattern.

However, divergence is unable to determine the exact *values* of the category, and some of these values are clearly unreliable even if they seem to appear in the pattern. For example, Figure 1 shows that preposition "в" (*in*) in the data is sometimes followed by the nominative case, which is grammatically impossible. This is due to a certain amount of noise, which is unavoidable in a large corpus due to mark-up errors or inherent morphological ambiguity. In Russian, the nominative and accusative cases often syncretize (assume identical forms), which can cause inaccuracies in annotation. On the other hand, some values of a category can be extremely rare; thus, they will be rare within patterns as well. For instance, the so-called "second accusative" case (labeled "acc2" in Figure 1) is rare in modern Russian, which is why its appearance in combination with preposition "в" (*in*) is significant, even though its frequency is not much higher than the frequency of the (erroneous) nominative case in the same pattern.

To find the significant values of a particular category we use the ratio between the frequencies of the value in a sample and in the corpus:

$$frequency\_ratio = \frac{P_i^{pattern}}{P_i^{corpus}} \quad (4)$$

If $frequentcy\_ratio > 1$, then the category's value is assumed to be *selected* by the pattern.

Finally, we note that the distribution of POS varies considerably within every pattern as compared to its distribution in the corpus. For example, prepositions can be followed only by noun groups and can never be followed by verbs or conjunctions. This means the Kullback-Leibler divergence for any POS, naturally assumes the highest value in *any* pattern; for this reason, we exclude the POS category from consideration in our calculation, aiming to find more subtle and interesting regularities in the data.

To summarize, the algorithm works as follows: for a given *query pattern*

1. search all words that appear in the query pattern and group them according to their POS tags.
2. for every POS, calculate the normalized Kullback-Leibler divergence for all of its categories; categories that show the maximum divergence are considered to be the most significant for the given pattern;
3. for every relevant category, sort its values according to the frequency ratio; if frequency ratio is less than 1, the value considered to be irrelevant for this pattern.

4 Experiments

In this paper, we conduct an in-depth evaluation focusing on a limited number of linguistic phenomena, namely: bigrams beginning with single-token prepositions, which impose strong morpho-syntactic constraints in terms of case government. We investigate 25 prepositions, such as "без" (*without*), "в" (*in/to*), etc. We evaluate the corpus of bigrams systematically against these queries, although we expect that the model we propose here produces relevant results for a much wider range of constructions—to be confirmed in further work.

4.1 Prepositions and Morphological Category

A syntactic property of prepositions in Russian is that they govern nominal phrases, i.e., that we expect the largest normalized divergence in queries such as $\{$ Preposition + X $\}$, where the POS of X is *noun*, to occur exactly with the category of case. Figure 3 shows the normalized divergence for four lexical and morphological categories. Among them, Case has the maximal divergence for all prepositions, which matches our expectation with 100% accuracy.

According to the figure, the morphological category of Animacy[2] is also interesting, in that it has a high value for some prepositions, like "из-под" (*from under*), "под" (*under*), "над" (*above*). A good example is the preposition "из-под" (*from under*). Its semantic properties cause inanimate nouns to appear much more frequently than animate ones. Consequently, we observe a higher divergence, due to inanimate nouns like "из-под земли" (*from under ground*), "из-под снега" (*from under the snow*), etc. Another good example of hidden semantic properties is a pair of prepositions "под" (*under*) and "над" (*above*). One can expect that their syntactic behaviour is more or less similar, but the histogram shows that Animacy (surprisingly) has a much higher divergence for "под" (*under*) to be ignored. Indeed, a deeper corpus-based analysis reveals a stable, frequently used construction, which gives many points to animate nouns, e.g., "замаскированный под невесту" (*disguised as a bride*). It is notable that this particular effect is not mentioned in any grammar book, (to the best of our knowledge).

To conclude, the Case category is the clear winner in terms of having the greatest normalized divergence, and the output fully matches the expectation on all 25 common prepositions that we tested. Other results are also clearly interesting due to their links to semantic properties, that is, to collocations. The next task is, therefore to discriminate

[2]Animacy is a morphological category of Russian nouns based on whether the referent of the noun is considered sentient or living. Most nouns denoting humans and animals are animate, while the majority of other nouns are inanimate.

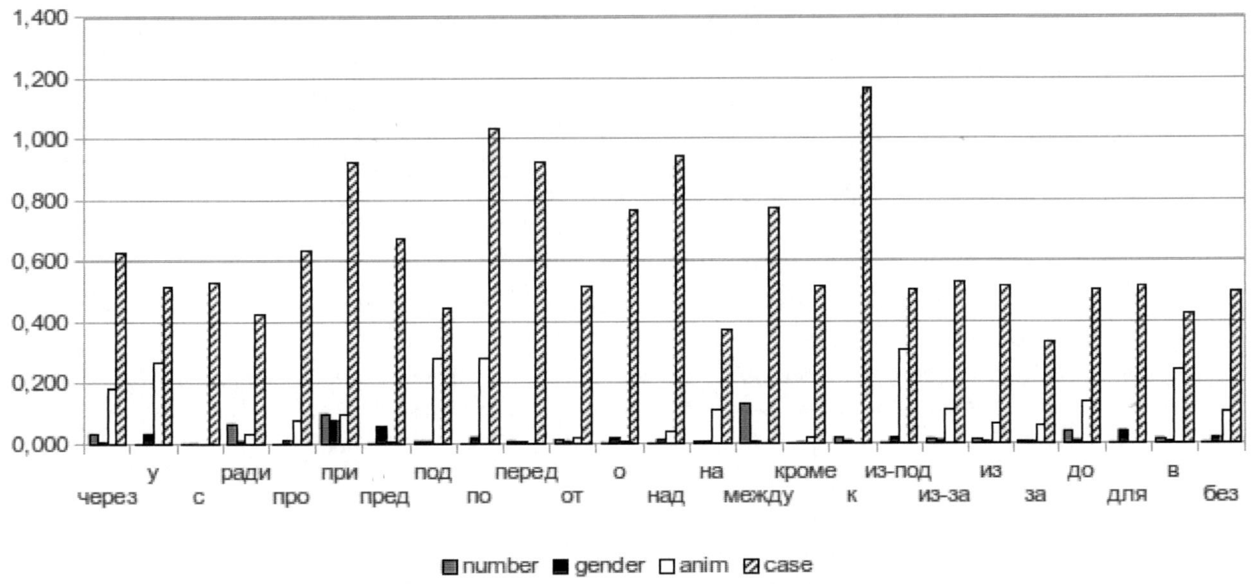

Figure 3: Normalized divergence of noun categories (grammemes) for pattern *preposition+X*.

between the runners-up, like Animacy for "под" (*under*), which seem to be interesting to some extent, and clear losers like Gender, in the example above. To do that we need to find an appropriate threshold—preferably automatically—between relevant and non-relevant results. The algorithm ranks the categories according to their divergence; the category that has the top rank is certainly meaningful. The question is how to determine which among the rest are significant as well; this is left for future work.

4.2 Specific Values of the Category with Maximum Divergence

The next question we explore is which particular *values* of the maximally divergent category—here, Case—are selected by a given preposition. As we mentioned above, we use the frequency ratio for this task. We collected a list of cases[3] that appear after the given preposition, according to the algorithm with $frequency\_ratio > 1$; which cases are possible according to grammatical descriptions,[4] which cases were produced by the algorithm, and the number of correct cases in the system's response. We expect that by using the frequency ratio we can reduce the noise; for example, of the eight cases that match the pattern { "с" (*with*) + Noun } only four are relevant.

The algorithm predicts the correct relevant set for 21 of 25 prepositions, giving a total precision of 95%, recall of 89%, and F-measure of 92%. The prepositions highlighted in bold in Table 1 are those that were incorrectly processed for various reasons; the error analysis is presented below.

14: "о" (*about*) The algorithm unexpectedly flags the *voc* (vocative) as a possible case after this preposition. This is incorrect; checking the data we discovered that this mistake was due to erroneous annotation: the interjection "о" (*oh*), as in "О боже!" (*Oh God!*), is incorrectly annotated as the preposition "о" (*about*). The error occurs twice in the data. However, as the vocative is extremely rare in the data (its frequency in the corpus is less than 0,0004), two erroneous tags are sufficient to give it a high rank. Similar annotation errors for more frequent cases are eliminated by the algorithm. For example, as we mentioned in the previous section, the nominative

[3]The current annotation scheme of our data has eleven case tags, namely: nom, voc, gen, gen2, dat, acc, acc2, ins, loc, loc2, adnum.

[4]Note, that not all possible prep+case combinations are represented in the corpus; for example, the combination { "ради" (*for the sake of*) + gen2 } does not appear in our data, and only eight times in the RNC overall. For evaluation we take into consideration only those prep+case combinations that appear at least once in our dataset.

	Preposition	Meaning	Expected cases	Response
1	без	*without*	gen/gen2	gen/gen2
2	в	*in/into*	acc/acc2/loc/loc2	acc/acc2/loc/loc2
3	для	*for*	gen/gen2	gen/gen2
4	до	*until*	gen/gen2	gen/gen2
5	за	*behind*	acc/ins	acc/ins
6	из	*from*	gen/gen2	gen/gen2
7	из-за	*from behind*	gen/gen2	gen/gen2
8	из-под	*from under*	gen/gen2	gen/gen2
9	к	*to*	dat	dat
10	кроме	*beyond*	gen	gen
11	между	*between*	ins	ins
12	на	*on*	acc/loc/loc2	acc/loc/loc2
13	над	*above*	ins	ins
14	о	*about*	**acc/loc**	**loc/voc**
15	от	*from*	gen/gen2	gen/gen2
16	перед	*in front of*	ins	ins
17	пред	*in front of*	ins	ins
18	по	*by/up to*	**dat/loc/acc**	**dat**
19	под	*under*	acc/ins	acc/ins
20	при	*at/by*	loc	loc
21	про	*about*	acc	acc
22	ради	*for*	gen	gen
23	с	*with*	**gen/gen2/acc/ins**	**gen2/ins**
24	у	*near*	gen	gen
25	через	*through*	**acc**	**acc/adnum**

Expected	45	**Precision**	0.95
Response	42	**Recall**	0.89
Correct	40	**F-measure**	0.92

Table 1: Noun cases expected and returned by the algorithm for Russian prepositions.

case after preposition "в" (*in*) appears 88 times in our data; however this case is not returned by the algorithm, since it is below the frequency ratio threshold.

25: "через" (*through/past*) The adnumerative (adnum) is a rare case in our data, so even a single occurrence in a sample is considered important by the algorithm. A single bigram is found in the data, where the token "часа" (*hours*)—correctly annotated with the *adnum* tag—predictably depends on the Numeral, i.e., "два" (*two*), rather than on preposition "через" (*through/past*), see Figure 4. The numeral appears in *post-position*—a highly marked word order that is admissible in this colloquial construction in Russian: "через часа два" (*lit.: after hours two = idiom: after about two hours*), where

Figure 4: Distributions of cases in the corpus and in a sample. (Arrows indicate syntactic dependency.)

the preposition governs the Case of the numeral, and the numeral governs a noun that *precedes* it.

Because our algorithm at the moment processes linear sequences, these kinds of syntactic inversion phenomena in Russian will pose a challenge. In general this problem can be solved by using tree-banks for MWE extraction, (Seretan, 2008; Martens and Vandeghinste, 2010). However, an appropriate treebank is not always available for a given language; in fact, we do not have access to any Russian tree-bank suitable for this task.

23: "с" (*with*) This is a genuine error. The algorithm misses two of four correct cases, Genitive and Accusative, because both are widely used across the corpus, which reduces their frequency ratio in the sub-sample. Our further work will focus on finding flexible frequency ratio thresholds, which is now set to one. Two of the correct cases (Instrumental and Gen2) are well over the threshold, while Genitive, with 0.6924, and Accusative, with 0.0440, fall short.

18: "по" (*by/along*) For this preposition the algorithm predicts 1 case out of 3. This situation is slightly different from the previous ones, since the accusative and locative cases are much more rare with preposition "по" (*by/along*) than the dative: 245 instances out of 15387 for accusative, and 222 for locative in our data. We hypothesize that this means that such "Prep+case" combinations are constrained lexically to a greater extent than grammatically. To check this hypothesis we calculate the frequency ratio for all lemmas that appear with the respective patterns { "по" (*by/along*) + acc } and { "по" (*by/along*) + loc }. As a result, 15 distinct lemmas were extracted by { "по" (*by*) + acc }; 13 out of them have $frequency\_ratio > 1$. The majority of the lemmas belong to the semantic class "part of the body" and are used in a very specific Russian construction, which indicates "an approximate level", e.g. "по локоть" (*up to (one's) elbow*), cf. English *"up to one's neck in work"*. This construction has limited productivity, and we are satisfied that the Accusative is omitted in the output for grammatical categories, since the algorithm outputs all tokens that appear in the { "по" (*by/along*) + acc } as relevant lemmas.

The case of { "по" (*by*) + loc } is more complex: 44 of 76 combinations return a frequency greater than 1. Analysis of annotation errors reveals a compact collection of bureaucratic cliches, like "по прибытии" (*upon arrival*), "по истечении" (*upon completion*), etc., which all share the semantics of "*immediately following X*", and are pragmatically related. These are expressions belonging to the same bureaucratic jargon and sharing the same morphological pattern, however, they are below the threshold. Again, we are faced with need to tune the threshold to capture this kind of potentially interesting lexical combinations. In general, semantic and pragmatic factors influence the ability of words to combine, and the algorithm shows it in some way, though these aspects of the problem are beyond the scope of our experiments in the current stage.

5 Discussion and Future Work

5.1 Development of the algorithm

We have presented a part an overall system under development. In the preceding sections, we investigate an area where collocations and colligations meet. To summarize, the algorithm, based on the corpus of n-grams, treats both morpho-syntactic and lexical co-occurrences as a unified continuum, which has no clear borders. The evaluation of the morphological output raises some new questions for further development:

- At present, the low precision for both low- and high-frequency tags depends on the threshold, which needs to be studied further.

- The values of divergences are currently not normalized among the different query patterns. This may be a difficult question, and we plan to investigate this further. The algorithm provides a way to compare the strength of very diverse collocations, which have nothing in common, in terms of their degree of idiomatization.

- We observe that the longer the n-gram, the more we expect it to be a collocation; stable bigrams appear more frequently to be colligations, while stable 4-grams are more often collocations. The problem is that those collocations with a highly frequent first collocate, e.g., "в" (*in*), cannot be found using our algorithm as it stands now.

- Token/lexeme stability is the next task we will concentrate on. Wermter and Hahn (2006) and Kilgarriff et al. (2012) proposed that sorting tokens/lexemes according to plain frequency works well if there is no grammatical knowledge at hand. We do have such knowledge. To improve the accuracy of lexeme/token extraction we rely on the idea of grammatical profiles, introduced by Gries and Divjak (2009). We plan to develop this approach with the further assumption that the distribution of tokens/lexemes within a pattern is based on relevant grammatical properties, which are obtained in an earlier step of our algorithm. For instance, for "не до X" (*not up to X*) we have found that the grammatical profile for X is N.gen/gen2, and the token $frequency\_ratio$ is greater than 1 as well. Building the list of tokens that are the most stable for this pattern, we compare their distributions within the pattern to all N.gen/gen2 tokens in the corpus. This yields the following tokens as the most relevant: "не до смеха" (*lit.: not up to laughter.gen = idiom: no laughing matter*);"не до жиру" (*lit. not up to fat.gen2 = idiom: no time/place for complacency*), which reveals an interesting set of idioms.

5.2 Extensions and Applications

The model has no restriction on the length of data to be used, and is applicable to various languages. Finnish (which is morphologically rich) and English (morphologically poor) will be examined next. As for Russian, so far the algorithm has been systematically evaluated against bigrams, although we have 3-, 4- and 5-grams at our disposal for future work.

A reliable method that is able to determine patterns of frequently co-occurring lexical and grammatical features within a corpus can have far-reaching practical implications. One particular application that we are exploring is the fine-tuning of semantic patterns that are commonly used in information extraction (IE), (Grishman, 2003). Our work on IE focuses on different domains and different languages, (Yangarber et al., 2007; Atkinson et al., 2011). Analysis of MWEs that occur in extraction patterns would provide valuable insights into how the patterns depend on the particular style or *genre* of the corpus, (Huttunen et al., 2002). Subtle, genre-specific differences in expression can indicate whether a given piece of text is signaling the presence an event of interest.

5.3 Creating Teaching-Support Tools

Instructors teaching a foreign language are regularly asked how words co-occur: What cases and word forms appear after a given preposition? Which ones should I learn by rote and which ones follow rules? The persistence of such questions indicates that this is an important challenge to be addressed—we should aim to build a system that can automatically generate an integrated answer. A tool that produces answers to these questions would be of great help for teachers as well as students. The presented algorithm can support an easy-to-use Web-based application, or an application for a mobile device. We plan to develop a service, which is able to process queries described in the paper. This service would be an additional interface to a corpus, aimed at finding not only the linear context of words but also their collocational and constructional preferences. We believe that such an interface would be useful for both research and language-learning needs.

Acknowledgments

We are very grateful to the Russian National Corpus developers, especially E. Rakhilina and O. Lyashevskaya, for providing us with the data.

References

Martin Atkinson, Jakub Piskorski, Erik van der Goot, and Roman Yangarber. 2011. Multilingual real-time event extraction for border security intelligence gathering. In U. Kock Wiil, editor, *Counterterrorism and Open Source Intelligence*, pages 355–390. Springer Lecture Notes in Social Networks, Vol. 2, 1st edition.

Brigitte Bigi. 2003. Using Kullback-Leibler distance for text categorization. In Fabrizio Sebastiani, editor, *Advances in Information Retrieval*, volume 2633 of *Lecture Notes in Computer Science*, pages 305–319. Springer Berlin, Heidelberg.

Kenneth Ward Church and Patrick Hanks. 1990. Word association norms, mutual information, and lexicography. *Computational linguistics*, 16(1):22–29.

Kenneth Church, William Gale, Patrick Hanks, and Donald Kindle. 1991. Using statistics in lexical analysis. *Lexical acquisition: exploiting on-line resources to build a lexicon.*

Vidas Daudaravicius. 2010. Automatic identification of lexical units. *Computational Linguistics and Intelligent text processing CICling-2009.*

Boris Dobrov and Natalia Loukachevitch. 2011. Multiple evidence for term extraction in broad domains. In *Proceedings of the 8th Recent Advances in Natural Language Processing Conference (RANLP 2011). Hissar, Bulgaria*, pages 710–715.

Ted Dunning. 1993. Accurate methods for the statistics of surprise and coincidence. *Computational linguistics*, 19(1):61–74.

Afsaneh Fazly and Suzanne Stevenson. 2007. Distinguishing subtypes of multiword expressions using linguistically-motivated statistical measures. In *Proceedings of the Workshop on A Broader Perspective on Multiword Expressions*, pages 9–16. Association for Computational Linguistics.

Katerina Frantzi, Sophia Ananiadou, and Hideki Mima. 2000. Automatic recognition of multi-word terms: the c-value/nc-value method. *International Journal on Digital Libraries*, 3(2):115–130.

Adele Goldberg. 2006. *Constructions at work: The nature of generalization in language*. Oxford University Press, USA.

Stefan Th. Gries and Dagmar Divjak. 2009. Behavioral profiles: a corpus-based approach to cognitive semantic analysis. *New directions in cognitive linguistics*, pages 57–75.

Ralph Grishman. 2003. Information extraction. In *The Handbook of Computational Linguistics and Natural Language Processing*, pages 515–530. Wiley-Blackwell.

Silja Huttunen, Roman Yangarber, and Ralph Grishman. 2002. Diversity of scenarios in information extraction. In *Proceedings of the Third International Conference on Language Resources and Evaluation (LREC 2002)*, Las Palmas de Gran Canaria, Spain, May.

Maria Khokhlova and Viktor Zakharov. 2009. Statistical collocability of Russian verbs. *After Half a Century of Slavonic Natural Language Processing*, pages 125–132.

Adam Kilgarriff, Pavel Rychlỳ, Vojtech Kovár, and Vıt Baisa. 2012. Finding multiwords of more than two words. In *Proceedings of EURALEX2012*.

Scott Martens and Vincent Vandeghinste. 2010. An efficient, generic approach to extracting multi-word expressions from dependency trees. In *CoLing Workshop: Multiword Expressions: From Theory to Applications (MWE 2010)*.

Pavel Pecina. 2005. An extensive empirical study of collocation extraction methods. In *Proceedings of the ACL Student Research Workshop*, pages 13–18. Association for Computational Linguistics.

Carlos Ramisch, Paulo Schreiner, Marco Idiart, and Aline Villavicencio. 2008. An evaluation of methods for the extraction of multiword expressions. In *Proceedings of the LREC Workshop-Towards a Shared Task for Multiword Expressions (MWE 2008)*, pages 50–53.

Philip Resnik. 1997. Selectional preference and sense disambiguation. In *Proceedings of the ACL SIGLEX Workshop on Tagging Text with Lexical Semantics: Why, What, and How*, pages 52–57. Washington, DC.

Ivan Sag, Timothy Baldwin, Francis Bond, Ann Copestake, and Dan Flickinger. 2002. Multiword expressions: A pain in the neck for NLP. *Computational Linguistics and Intelligent Text Processing*, pages 189–206.

Violeta Seretan. 2008. *Collocation extraction based on syntactic parsing*. Ph.D. thesis, University of Geneva.

Serge Sharoff. 2004. What is at stake: a case study of Russian expressions starting with a preposition. In *Proceedings of the Workshop on Multiword Expressions: Integrating Processing*, pages 17–23. Association for Computational Linguistics.

Sayori Shimohata, Toshiyuki Sugio, and Junji Nagata. 1997. Retrieving collocations by co-occurrences and word order constraints. In *Proceedings of the eighth conference on European chapter of the Association for Computational Linguistics*, pages 476–481. Association for Computational Linguistics.

Anatol Stefanowitsch and Stefan Th Gries. 2003. Collostructions: Investigating the interaction of words and constructions. *International journal of corpus linguistics*, 8(2):209–243.

Marko Tadić and Krešimir Šojat. 2003. Finding multiword term candidates in Croatian. In *Proceedings of IESL2003 Workshop*, pages 102–107.

Tim Van de Cruys and Begona Villada Moirón. 2007. Lexico-semantic multiword expression extraction. In *Proceedings of the 17th Meeting of Computational Linguistics in the Netherlands (CLIN)*, pages 175–190.

Joachim Wermter and Udo Hahn. 2006. You can't beat frequency (unless you use linguistic knowledge) – a qualitative evaluation of association measures for collocation and term extraction. In *Proceedings of the 21st International Conference on Computational Linguistics and 44th Annual Meeting of the Association for Computational Linguistics*, pages 785–792.

Elena Yagunova and Lidia Pivovarova. 2010. The nature of collocations in the Russian language. The experience of automatic extraction and classification of the material of news texts. *Automatic Documentation and Mathematical Linguistics*, 44(3):164–175.

Roman Yangarber, Clive Best, Peter von Etter, Flavio Fuart, David Horby, and Ralf Steinberger. 2007. Combining information about epidemic threats from multiple sources. In *Proceedings of the MMIES Workshop, International Conference on Recent Advances in Natural Language Processing (RANLP 2007)*, Borovets, Bulgaria, September.

Exploring MWEs for Knowledge Acquisition from Corporate Technical Documents

Bell Manrique Losada
Universidad de Medellín
Cra. 87 30-65 Belén
Medellín, AQ, Colombia
bmanrique@udem.edu.co

Carlos M. Zapata Jaramillo
Universidad Nacional de Colombia
Cra. 80 65-223 Robledo
Medellín, AQ, Colombia
cmzapata@unal.edu.co

Diego A. Burgos
Wake Forest University
Greene Hall, P.O. Box 7566
Winston Salem, NC 27109, USA
burgosda@wfu.edu

Abstract

High frequency can convert a word sequence into a multiword expression (MWE), *i.e.*, a collocation. In this paper, we use collocations as well as syntactically-flexible, lexicalized phrases to analyze 'job specification documents' (a kind of corporate technical document) for subsequent acquisition of automated knowledge elicitation. We propose the definition of structural and functional patterns of specific corporate documents by analyzing the contexts and sections in which the expression occurs. Such patterns and its automated processing are the basis for identifying organizational domain knowledge and business information which is used later for the first instances of requirement elicitation processes in software engineering.

1 Introduction

In software engineering, business knowledge and the needs of a system's users are analyzed and specified by a process called requirement elicitation (RE). Traditionally, RE has been carried out by human analysts through techniques such as interviews, observations, questionnaires, etc. The information obtained by the analyst is then converted to a controlled language used further stages of software implementation. These techniques, however, necessarily increase costs and imply a certain degree of subjectivity. Sometimes, as an alternative approach for RE, human analysts elicit requirement from documents instead of from clients or users. The present work, proposes the use multiword expressions (MWEs) such as collocations and syntactically-flexible, lexicalized phrases to detect relevant patterns in 'job specification documents' (a kind of corporate technical document). The approach contributes to the task of generating controlled language used in subsequent automated knowledge representation.

MWEs are lexical items which can be decomposed into multiple lexemes with lexical, syntactic, semantic, pragmatic, and/or statistical idiomaticity (Baldwin *et al.*, 2010). According to Bauer (1983), MWEs can be broadly classified into lexicalized phrases and institutionalized phrases. Institutionalized phrases, or collocations, basically require a high frequency of co-occurrence of their components. Lexicalized phrases (LP), on the other hand, may present other kind of idiomaticity, but not only statistical. Along with collocations, out of the set of lexicalized phrase types, we find syntactically-flexible, lexicalized phrases and semi-fixed phrases of special interest for the present work.

Based on an experimental corpus, we identify when and how a MWE is used in order to identify patterns, infer organizational relationships, and generate corporate information and/or conceptual models for further requirement elicitation.

We propose context analysis—in which MWEs occur—would contribute by adding essential information to the pattern definition. Such patterns are conceived from the structural and functional components inherent to corporate documents. This means that we classify MWEs according to the section in the document where they prevail. We expect the automated processing of such patterns helps in the identification and understanding of domain knowledge and business information from an organization.

The remainder of this paper is organized as follows: in Section 2 we describe the conceptual framework and background. Section 3 presents examples and analysis of the MWEs used for this study. Last, Section 4 draws conclusions and outlines future work.

2 Conceptual Framework and Background

Two main lines converge on this study, namely requirements elicitation belonging to software engineering and linguistic description and parsing related to natural language processing.

Requirements elicitation (RE) is the initial process from requirement engineering in the software development process lifecycle. RE involves seeking, uncovering, capturing, and elaborating requirements, based on activities of the business analysis initially performed. This process comprises functional, behavioral, and quality properties of the software to be developed (Castro-Herrera *et al.*, 2008). In order to accomplish RE, an analyst should increasingly and iteratively develop several actions involving natural language analysis and modeling (Li *et al.*, 2003).

On the other hand, a user of a language has available a large number of pre-constructed phrases conforming single choices, even though they might appear to be analyzable into segments (Sinclair, 1991). Such phrases are known as lexical phrases (LPs) and may have a pragmatic function. According to Pérez (1999), the importance of LPs lies in their usage and domain, which constitute an integral part of the communicative competence. In the same line of thought, López-Mezquita (2007) categorizes LPs into polywords, institutionalized expressions, phrasal constraints, and sentence builders.

For this study, we use the classification of MWEs proposed by Baldwin *et al.* (2010). This and other classifications have been used in natural language processing techniques for text-mining and information extraction. They also have been applied to the analysis of many kinds of documents, *e.g.*, technical documents, patents, and software requirement documents.

Cascini *et al.* (2004) present a functional analysis of patents and their implementation in the PAT-Analyzer tool. They use techniques based on the extraction of the interactions between the entities described in the document and expressed as subject-action-object triples, by using a suitable syntactic parser.

Rösner *et al.* (1997) use techniques to automatically generate multilingual documents from knowledge bases. The resulting documents can be represented in an interchangeable, reusable way. The authors describe several techniques for knowledge acquisition from documents by using particular knowledge structures from particular contexts. Breaux *et al.* (2006) describe the extraction of rights and obligations from regulation texts restated into restricted natural language statements. In this approach, the authors identify normative phrases that define what stakeholders are permitted or required to do, and then extract rights and obligations by using normative phrases.

For knowledge acquisition, several authors have applied NLP techniques for handling MWEs. Jackendoff (1997) and Aussenac-Gilles *et al.* (2000) extract knowledge from existing documents and demonstrate its usage on the ontological engineering research domain.

Some other contributions are related to the extraction of multiword expressions from corpora, empirical work on lexical semantics in comparative fields, word sense disambiguation, and ontology learning (Bannard, 2005). In the intersection of NLP and requirement elicitation, Lee and Bryant (2002) use contextual techniques to overcome the ambiguity and express domain knowledge in the DARPA agent markup language (DAML). The resulting expression from the linguistic processing is a formal representation of the informal natural language requirements.

For processing technical and organizational documentation, Dinesh *et al.* (2007) propose the description of organizational procedures and the validation of their conformance to regulations, based on logical analysis. Lévy *et al.* (2010) present an environment that enables semantic annotations of document textual units (e.g., words, phrases, paragraphs, etc.) with ontological information (concepts, instances, roles, etc.). This approach provides an ontology-driven interpretation of the document contents.

Some work has been also developed to perform corpus-based analysis from several technical documents, as follows: for the use of frequency and concordance data from a corpus, Flowerdew (1993) work on English biology lectures; Lam (2007) propose the processing of English tourism documents looking for pedagogical implications of its usage; and Henry and Roseberry (2001) observe English application letters.

In other lines of thought, we found language models accounting for documents oriented to audit linguistic expertise and analyze communicative and health texts (Fernández & García, 2009).

3 Exploration of MWEs in Corporate Documents

3.1 Corpus and Analysis Tools

We collected and analyzed a set of documents from the corporate domain in different subject fields such as medicine, forestry, and laboratory. The corpus used as the basis for this preliminary study consists of 25 English-written documents with independence of its variety.

The documents selected are a small sample belonging to the 'Job Specification Document' (JSD) category and were collected following representativeness and ecological criteria, *i.e.*, looking for the collection of documents produced, created, or promoted in the corporate or business environment. All the documents were taken from different corporations and sum 31627 tokens and 3839 types.

The initial exploration of this experimental corpus was supported by AntConc 3.3.5w® (Anthony, 2009) and TermoStatWeb™ (Drouin, 2003). AntConc was used to manually and systematically find frequent expressions and select their contexts, and TermoStatWeb™ was used to list most frequent verbs, nouns, and adjectives which could become part of MWEs.

3.2 Identification of Relevant MWEs

Relevant MWEs are identified in the experimental corpus according to the flow chart shown in Figure 1. From each technical document belonging to the corpus, we carried out the task of LP extraction (institutionalized expressions or lexicalized expressions) and classification (analysis by categories).

We classify the extracted expressions based on the document section where they prevail (see Table 1). Each section corresponds to a structural component of the JSD which also reflects the communicative intention of the writer.

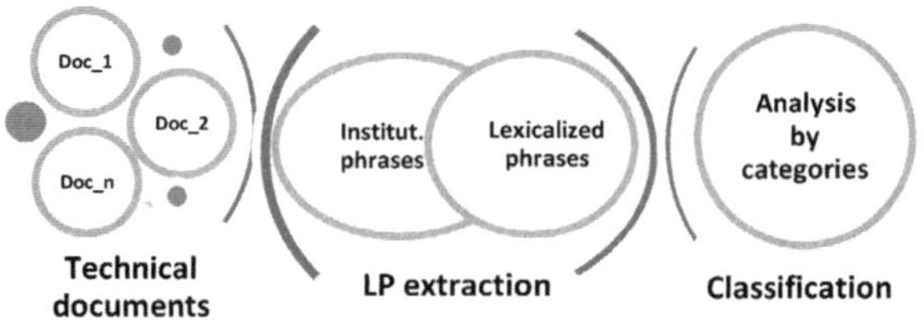

Figure 1. Flow chart for identifying MWEs

No.	*Description section*
i	Job purpose / objective
ii	Main responsibilites / functions
iii	Knowledge and skills
iv	Requirements

Table 1. Sections of JSD

Table 2 shows the relevant MWEs identified, as follows: i) the selected expressions with the corresponding MWE category (C) according to the classification proposed by Baldwin *et al.* (2010); ii) the frequency (F) of occurrence for each expression; and, iii) the section number (S) where the expression prevails in the JSD (from the Table 1).

C	*MWEs*			*F*	*S*
1. Statistically-idiomatic phrases	*be*	*Able*	*to*	13	iii
	be	*required*	*to*	13	ii
	are	*required*	*to*	7	iv
	be	*responsible*	*for*	5	ii
	-	*knowledge*	*of*	49	iii
	-	*experience*	*in*	15	iv
	-	*ability*	*to*	61	iii
	related	*duties*	*as*	11	Ii
	the	*duties*	*of*	6	ii
	skills	*and*	*abilities*	11	iii
	level	*experience*	-	12	iv
	job	*code*	-	4	i
	job	*description*	-	9	i
	job	*specification*	-	7	i
	office	*equipment*	-	5	ii,iii
	working	*relationships*	*with*	12	ii,iii
	at	*all*	*times*	10	ii
	as	*well*	*as*	11	ii
2. Syntactically-flexible phrases	*be*	*[adquired]*	*on*	5	iv
	to	*[support]*	*the*	29	ii
	the	*[priority] and [schedule]*	*of*	24	ii,iii
	the	*[work] of*	*[others]*	12	iii,iv
	by	*[giv]ing*	*[time]*	11	iii,iv
	in	*[contacts] with the*	*[public]*	13	ii
3. Semi-fixed phrases	-	*work*	*in*	7	ii,iii
	-	*work*	*of*	6	ii
	-	*work*	*with*	5	iii
	-	*may*	*be*	30	ii
	-	*may*	*have*	5	iv
	-	*follow*	*up*	4	i,ii
	-	*carry*	*out*	9	i,

Table 2. Extracted MWEs

We use brackets for indicating semi-fixed phrases or variable uses of the expression (they can take values with the same conjugation). In this way, we identify and prioritize the most frequents MWEs and patterns in each category, as follows:

1. <u>*ability to, knowledge of, experience in, be able to, be required to*</u>
2. <u>*to-V-the, the-N-and-N-of, in-N-with-the-N*</u>
3. <u>*may be, carry out, work in, work of*</u>

Likewise, we also found useful identifying the most frequent lexical items that could become part of MWEs and alternate with the expressions and patterns presented above. For that purpose, TermoStatWeb was used to generate a map with the most frequent verbs, nouns, and adjectives. Some examples are shown in Figure 2.

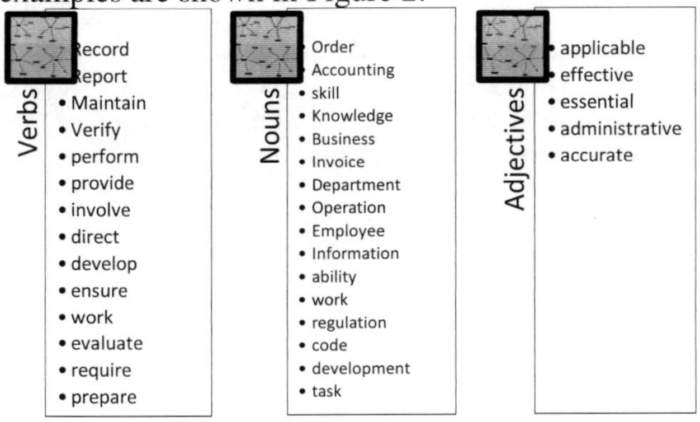

Figure 2. Some frequent verbs, nouns, and adjectives.

The high frequency of these items in the corpus suggests that they could probably be part of MWEs conveying corporate information. Also, when placed in the slots of the patterns observed in Table 2, they increase their chance to become relevant MWEs useful to detect specific corporate knowledge.

The following paragraph is an example of how this can happen. The source text belongs to a JSD from our corpus and shows how two frequent items (*evaluate* and *work*) co-occur in a collocation. Then, identified corporate information is expected to be generated by other means into specific organizational information in a controlled language:

<u>Source paragraph</u>

...A City Manager <u>*plans, organizes, evaluates,*</u> *and* <u>*controls*</u> *the* ***work*** *of all* City departments <u>*to ensure*</u> *that* **operations** *and* ***services*** <u>*comply*</u> *with the* ***policies...***

<u>Generated organizational information</u>:

[City_manager <u>*plans*</u> ***work***. City_manager <u>*organizes*</u> ***work***. City_manager <u>*evaluates*</u> ***work*** City_manager <u>*controls*</u> ***work***] [City_department *has* ***work***] [City_manager <u>*ensures*</u> ***operations***] [City_department *has* ***operations***] [City_department *has* ***services***] [***operations*** <u>*comply*</u> ***policies***]

In terms of organizational knowledge, an analyst can find information from JSDs about roles, responsibilities, actions, and constraints, as an approach for understanding an organizational domain. Such entities are expressed in a JSD as subject, actions, and object triples, as suggested by some instances in Table 2. This information can be represented either into models or controlled language discourses, among other specifications.

4 Conclusions

This study aims at characterizing JSDs by revealing key MWEs used in an English corpus. We proposed a set of MWEs of a JSD, as a corporate technical document, which can be processed as input for further knowledge engineering processes. The appropriateness of JSDs in requirements elicitation was verified with this study.

The analysis shows frequencies and patterns of relevant MWEs as well as their contexts and inflectional forms extracted via a concordance tool. The performed analysis is a preliminary study for knowledge acquisition and understanding of organizational domains. Such knowledge is expected to be readily available to future applications in specific domains in order to validate the findings and then to automate the process.

As future work, we expect to increase the number of documents in the corpus and refine the study of lexical and textual features. Statistical association measures can be also considered as a way to reinforce MWEs and term identification and extraction in the frame of knowledge acquisition from corporate documents. Likewise, given the importance of the syntactic structure given by the triple subject-verb-object, dependency parsing seems to be a promising approach for the identification of roles and responsibilities in JSDs.

Acknowledgments

This work is funded by the Vicerrectoría de Investigación from both the Universidad de Medellín and the Universidad Nacional de Colombia, under the project: *"Método de transformación de lenguaje natural a lenguaje controlado para la obtención de requisitos, a partir de documentación técnica"*.

References

Anthony, L. 2009. *Issues in the design and development of software tools for corpus studies: The case for collaboration*. Contemporary corpus linguistics, London: P. Baker Ed.: 87-104.

Aussenac-Gilles, N. Biébow, B. and Szulman, S. 2000. *Revisiting Ontology Design: A Method Based on Corpus Analysis. Knowledge Engineering and Knowledge Management*. Methods, Models, and Tools, 1937:27–66.

Baldwin, Timothy and Su Nam Kim (2010) Multiword Expressions, in Nitin Indurkhya and Fred J. Damerau (eds.) Handbook of Natural Language Processing, Second Ed., CRC Press, USA, pp. 267-292.

Bannard, C. 2005. Learning about the meaning of verb–particle constructions from corpora. *Computer Speech & Language*, 19(4): 467-478.

Bauer, L. 1983. *English Word-Formation*. London: Cambridge University Press, 311.

Breaux, T.D., Vail, M.W. and Antón, A.I. 2006. Towards Regulatory Compliance: Extracting Rights and Obligations to Align Requirements with Regulations. North Carolina State University TR-2006-6.

Cascini, G. Fantechi, A. and Spinicci, E. 2004. Natural Language Processing of Patents and Technical Documentation. *Lecture Notes in Computer Science*, 3163:508-520.

Castro-Herrera, C., Duan, C., Cleland-Huang, J. and Mobasher, B. Using data mining and recommender systems to facilitate large-scale, open, and inclusive requirements elicitation processes. *Proceedings of 16th IEEE Inter. Requirements Eng. Conference*, pp.165–168, 2008.

Dinesh, N. Joshi, A. Lee, I. and Sokolski, O. 2007. *Logic-based regulatory conformance checking*. In 14th Monterey Workshop, ScholarlyCommons Penn.

Drouin, P. 2003. *TermoStat Web 3.0*. Désormais utilisable qu'après enregistremen. Available in: http://olst.ling.umontreal.ca/~drouinp/termostat_web/

Fernández, L. and García, F.J. 2009. Texto y empresa. *Applied Linguistics Now: Understanding Language and Mind*, pp.655-665. Universidad de Almería, España.

Flowerdew, J. 1993. Concordancing as a Tool in Course Design. *System*, 21(2): 231-244.

Henry, A. and Roseberry, R.L. 2001. *Using a Small Corpus to Obtain Data for Teaching a Genre*. In Ghadessy/Henry/Roseberry: 93-133.

Jackendoff, R. 1997. *The architecture of the language faculty*. MIT Press, Cambridge, MA, USA.

Lam, P. Y. 2007. A *Corpus-driven Léxico-grammatical Analysis of English Tourism Industry Texts and the Study of its Pedagogic Implications in ESP*. In Hidalgo/Quereda/Santana: 71-90.

Lee, B. and Bryant, B. R. 2002. *Contextual Natural Language Processing and DAML for Understanding Software Requirements Specifications*. In 19th International Conference on Computational Linguistics, Taipei, Taiwan.

Levy, F. Guisse, A. Nazarenko, A. Omrane, N. and Szulman, S. 2010. An Environment for the Joint Management of Written Policies and Business Rules. 22nd IEEE International Conference on Tools with Artificial Intelligence. *IEEE Computer Society*, 2:142-149.

Li, K., Dewar, R.G. and Pooley, R.J. Requirements capture in natural language problem statements. Heriot-Watt University, 2003. Available in http://www.macs.hw.ac.uk:8080/techreps/docs/files/HW-MACS-TR-0023.pdf

López-Mezquita, M.T. 2007. La evaluación de la competencia léxica: tests de vocabulario. Su fiabilidad y validez. *Centro de Investigación y Documentación Educativa*, 177(1): 488.

López Rodríguez, C. I., Faber, P., León- Araúz, P., Prieto, J. A. and Tercedor, M. 2010. La Terminología basada en marcos y su aplicación a las ciencias medioambientales: los proyectos MarcoCosta y Ecosistema. *Arena Romanistica*, 7 (10): 52-74.

Peleg, M. Gutnik, L.A. Snow, V. and Patel, V.L. 2005. Interpreting procedures from descriptive guidelines. *Journal of Biomedical Informatics*, 39(1):184–195.

Perez, C. 1999. *La enseñanza del vocabulario desde una perspectiva lingufstica y pedagogica*. In S. Salaberri (Ed.), Lingutstica Aplicada a las Lenguas Extranjeras, Almería: Univ. de Almería: 262-307.

Rösner, D., Grote, B., Hartmann, K. and Höfling. B. 1997. From Natural Language Documents to Sharable Product Knowledge: A Knowledge Engineering Approach. Journal of Universal Computer Science. 3(8): 955-987.

Sinclair, J. 1991. Corpus, concordance, collocation. Oxford: Oxford University Press.

Soler, C. and Gil, I. 2010. Posibilidades y límites de los tesauros frente a otros sistemas de organización del conocimiento: folksonomías, taxonomías y ontologías. *Revista Interamericana de Bibliotecología*, 33(2): 361-377.

MWE in Portuguese: Proposal for a Typology for Annotation in Running Text

Sandra Antunes and **Amália Mendes**
Centro de Linguística da Universidade de Lisboa
Av. Prof. Gama Pinto, 2
1649-003 Lisboa, Portugal
{sandra.antunes, amalia.mendes}@clul.ul.pt

Abstract

Based on a lexicon of Portuguese MWE, this presentation focuses on an ongoing work that aims at the creation of a typology that describes these expressions taking into account their semantic, syntactic and pragmatic properties. We also plan to annotate each MWE-entry in the mentioned lexicon according to the information obtained from that typology. Our objective is to create a valuable resource, which will allow for the automatic identification MWE in running text and for a deeper understanding of these expressions in their context.

1 Introduction

As it is widely known, the lexicon does not consist mainly of simple lexical items but appears to be populated with numerous chunks, more or less predictable, though not fixed (Firth, 1955). In fact, the development of computer technologies and corpus-based approaches has enabled the identification of complex patterns of word associations, proving that the speakers use a large number of preconstructed phrases that constitute single choices (Sinclair, 1991:110). Several studies have also shown that great part of a speaker's lexicon is composed by these word associations (Jackendoff, 1997; Fellbaum, 1998). These multiword expressions (MWE)[1] appear in every kind of spoken and written discourse and, despite the fact that they don't pose any problems from the speaker's point of view (we easily recognize that they function as a single unit that may have a specific meaning), natural language processing (NLP) applications, on the other hand, find notorious difficulties when dealing with them (Sag et al., 2000).

Bearing in mind the extreme importance of the study of this linguistic phenomenon for the improvement of NLP systems, this paper will address an ongoing analysis that aims to create a typology for MWE in Portuguese (based on a MWE lexicon previously extracted from a 50 million word written corpus) that will be used to enrich that lexicon with extensive information regarding these expressions. This annotated lexicon will be a resource that will allow for the annotation of these expressions in running text (Hendrickx et al., 2010a).

This presentation will briefly discuss compilation of the lexicon and the methodology adopted for MWE selection and organization (section 2), the typology based on syntactic, semantic and statistic criteria (section 3), the annotation proposal of the lexicon (section 4) and applications of the work (section 5).

2 MWE: Corpus and Lexicon

The work we are going to present used the lexicon of word combinations[2] that was created within the scope of the project COMBINA-PT – Word Combinations in Portuguese Language[3]. The corpus used for their extraction was 50 million word writ-

[1] The term multiword expression will be used to refer to any sequence of words that act as a single unit, embracing all different types of word combinations (collocations, compound nouns, light verbs, institutionalized phrases, idioms, etc.).

[2] The lexicon is available at Meta-Share repository: http://www.meta-net.eu/meta-share.

[3] https://www.clul.ul.pt/en/research-teams/187-combina-pt-word-combinations-in-portuguese-language

ten corpus extracted from the Reference Corpus of Contemporary Portuguese[4], and has the constitution presented in Table 1 (Mendes et al., 2006):

CORPUS CONSTITUTION	
Newspapers	**30.000.000**
Books	**10.917.889**
Magazines	**7.500.000**
Miscellaneous	**1.851.828**
Leaflets	**104.889**
Supreme court verdicts	**313.962**
Parliament sessions	**277.586**
TOTAL	**50.966.154**

Table 1. Constitution of the corpus

The MWE in the lexicon are organized in order to identify a main lemma (from which the MWE was selected) and a group lemma, which corresponds to the canonical form of the MWE and covers all the variants that occurred in the corpus. Concordances lines for each MWE are also available in KIWIC format. Table 2 illustrates some MWE that were identified when analyzing the lemma *fogo* 'fire'.

Main Lemma
fogo 'fire'
Group Lemma
arma de fogo 'firearm'
Concordances
uma arma de fogo relativamente leve 'a relatively light firearm' *800 mil portugueses possuem armas de fogo* '800 thousand Portuguese have firearms'
Group Lemma
baptismo de fogo 'baptism of fire'
Concordances
teve o seu baptismo de fogo no assalto 'he had his baptism of fire in a robbery'
Group Lemma
fogo cruzado 'crossfire'
Concordances
civis apanhados no fogo cruzado entre o exército 'civilians were caught in a crossfire between the army'
Group Lemma
fogo de artifício 'firework'
Concordances
espectáculos de fogo de artifício 'firework shows' *à 1 hora haverá fogos de artifício* 'there will be fireworks at 1:00 a.m.'

Table 2. Example of MWE for the lemma *fogo* 'fire'

[4] CRPC is a monitor corpus of 311 million words, constituted by sampling from several types of written and spoken text and comprising all the national and regional varieties of Portuguese (https://www.clul.ul.pt/en/research-teams/183-reference-corpus-of-contemporary-portuguese-crpc).

In all, the lexicon comprises 1.180 main lemmas, 14.153 group lemmas and 48.154 word combinations.

Mendes et al. (2006) describe the criteria used for MWE selection: following the results of previous studies (Evert and Krenn, 2001; Pereira and Mendes, 2002), the authors first selected groups with MI[5] values between 8 and 10, and, throughout manual validation, applied several criteria upon which usually relies the definition of a MWE:
a) lexical and syntactic fixedness that can be observed through the possibility of replacing elements, inserting modifiers, changing the syntagmatic structure or gender/number features;
b) total or partial loss of compositional meaning, which means that the meaning of the expressions can not be predicted by the meaning of the parts;
c) frequency of occurrence, which means that the expressions may be semantically compositional but occur with high frequency, revealing sets of favoured co-occurring forms, which could tell that they may be in their way to a possible fixedness.

3 Data Analysis: Towards a Typology

In contrast to languages for which there is a wide range of studies regarding MWE both from a linguistic and a computational point of view, for Portuguese little work has been done so far. Great part of the existing studies had paid more attention to idiomatic expressions and compound nouns in general, relegating the analysis of other types of expressions to the morphossyntactic properties of its elements (Macário Lopes, 1992; Chacoto, 1994; Baptista, 1994; Vilela, 2002; Ranchhod, 2003)[6].

Considering the existence of different types of MWE with different degrees of syntactic and semantic cohesion, our analysis tries to categorize these expressions taking into account their lexical, syntactic, semantic and pragmatic properties. Thus, from a semantic standpoint, three major classes were considered: (i) expressions with compositional meaning (*pão de centeio* 'rye bread'); (ii) expressions with partial idiomatic meaning, i.e., at least one of the elements keeps its literal meaning

[5] Statistical association measure (Church and Hanks, 1990).

[6] Some research has been carried out regarding the identification and annotation of Complex Predicates, usually called in the literature Light Verb Constructions or Support Verb Constructions (Hendrickx et al., 2010b; Duran et al., 2011; Zeller and Padó, 2012).

(*vontade de ferro* 'iron will'); (iii) expressions with total idiomatic meaning (*pés de galinha* 'crow's feet').

Note, however, that one may find notorious difficulties regarding the evaluation of the meaning of certain expressions that seems to be linked to two major factors: (i) the polysemous nature of the words (it is necessary to establish a boundary between compositional and figurative meanings. If we consider the literal meaning to be the first prototypical meaning of a word, this restrictive definition will trigger us to consider a large number of MWE as idiomatic); (ii) the awareness of the semantic motivation that had led to the idiomatic meanings, which depends on cultural and social factors.

This semantic criterion implies that the same type of MWE may occur in different classes. It is the case with compound nouns. Although we tried to accentuate the different degrees of lexicalization of this type of expressions, we are acutely aware that drawing this dividing line neither is easy nor allows for accurate definitions and divisions.

Within each of these three semantic categories, the expressions are also analyzed according to their grammatical category and lexical and syntactic fixedness. Regarding the latest aspect, the expressions may be: (i) fixed (no variation); (ii) semi-fixed (nominal/verbal inflection)[7]; (iii) with variation: lexical (permutation, replacement of elements, insertion of modifiers) and/or syntactic (constructions with passives, relatives, pronouns, extraction, adjectival vs. prepositional modifiers).

Our typology relies, then, on several categories, some of which we will briefly present.

Expressions with Compositional Meaning

➢ Favoured co-occurring forms – expressions that occurred with high frequency in the corpus, revealing a tendency to co-occur in certain contexts (*pão seco* 'dry bread', *desvendar o mistério* 'unravel the mystery'). Expressions with full lexical and syntactic variation[8].

➢ Compound nouns – expressions that represent a single concept (*noite de núpcias* 'wedding night', *cama de casal* 'double bed', *cavalo alazão*[9] 'chestnut horse', *Idade do Ferro* 'Iron Age'). Usually, these expressions are semi-fixed. However, we also observed that some combinations may occur in a small distributional paradigm (*cama de solteiro* 'single bed') that allows for predicative constructions (*a cama é de solteiro* lit. 'the bed is single'). Entities are fixed.

➢ Institutionalized expressions – expressions observed with higher frequency than any alternative lexicalization of the same concept (*lufada de ar fresco* 'breath of fresh air', *condenar ao fracasso* 'doomed to failure', *abrir um precedente* 'set a precedent'). Apart from inflection, since there are alternative expressions, we also observed lexical variation, such as substitution (*rajada de ar fresco* 'rush of fresh air'), insertion of modifiers (*condenar este projecto ao fracasso* lit. 'to doom this project to failure') and change in the syntagmatic structure (*o precedente foi aberto* 'a precedent has been set', *abertura de um precedente* lit. 'the opening of a precedent').

➢ Ligh verb constructions – expressions where the noun is used in a normal sense and the verb meaning appears to be bleached (*dar um passeio* 'take a walk'). Expressions with lexical and syntactic variation (substitution, insertion of modifiers, change in the syntagmatic structure).

➢ proverbs (*no poupar é que está o ganho* 'profit is in saving'). Despite our conception of proverbs as frozen expressions, the fact is that speakers' lexical creativity may result in the production of expressions such as *no anunciar/atacar/descontar/esperar/comparar é que está o ganho* 'profit is in announcing/attacking/discounting/waiting/comparing'.

Expressions with Partial Idiomatic Meaning

➢ Expressions with an additional meaning that can not be derived from the meaning of its parts[10], (*cinturão negro* 'black belt' + martial arts expert, *abrir a boca* 'open the mouth' + to speak/to yawn, *deitar as mãos à cabeça* lit. 'throw the hands in the head' (throw one's hands up) + despair). Nominal expressions are semi-fixed while verbal expressions may undergo inflection and lexical variation, such as substitution (*levar/lançar as mãos à cabeça* lit. 'put/lay the hands in the head') and insertion of modifiers (*deitou logo as mãos à cabeça* lit. 'put immediately his hands in his head').

[7] Since Portuguese is a highly inflectional language, practically all the verbs and nouns that occur in MWE inflect.

[8] More examples of variation will be included in Section 4.

[9] "Lexikalische Solidaritäten" (Coseriu, 1967).

[10] Quasi-phrasemes or quasi-idioms (Mel'cuk, 1998).

➢ Compound nouns: (i) the meaning does not occur in any other combination (*sorriso amarelo* lit. 'yellow smile' → yellow = wry); (ii) the meaning may occur in different combinations (*café fresco* 'fresh coffe', *pão fresco* 'fresh bread' → fresh = recent); (iii) periphrastic nouns[11] (*continente negro* 'black continent' = Africa); (iv) entities (*dama de ferro* 'iron lady'). Apart from inflection, some expressions are subject to lexical and syntactic variation, namely insertion of modifiers (*sorriso muito amarelo* lit. 'smile very yellow'), alternation between simple elements and elements with suffixes (*sorrisinho amarelo* lit. 'little yellow smile') and alternation between adjectival and prepositional modifiers (*silêncio mortal* 'deadly silence', *silêncio de morte* 'silence of death'). Entities are fixed.

Expressions with Total Idiomatic Meaning

➢ Expressions transposed to another semantic field by metaphoric process (*balde de água fria* 'cold shower', *faca de dois gumes* 'double-edge knife', *esticar o pernil* 'kick the bucket', *deitar água na fervura* 'pour oil on troubled waters', *a sangue frio* 'in cold blood'). Adverbial expressions are fixed. Some of the nominal and verbal structures may undergo lexical and syntactic variation, such as substitution (*arma/espada/pau de dois gumes* 'double-edge weapon/sword/stick'), insertion of modifiers (*deitar mais água na fervura* 'pour more oil on troubled waters'), permutation (*estar de mãos e pés atados* 'bound hand and foot', *estar de pés e mãos atados* 'bound foot and hand' (helpless)) and occurrence both in negative and affirmative sentences (*ter olhos na cara* lit. 'have eyes in the face' (put things in perspective), *não ter olhos na cara* lit. 'do not have eyes in the face').

➢ Compound nouns (*flor de estufa* 'greenhouse plant' (delicate person); *mão de ferro* 'iron fist'). Apart from inflection, we observed alternation between simple elements and elements with suffixes.

➢ Proverbs (*grão a grão enche a galinha o papo* lit. 'grain by grain the hen fills its belly' (little strokes fell great oaks)). As in compositional proverbs, we also observed lexical variation (*grão a grão enche muita gente o papo* lit. 'grain by grain lots of people fill their bellies').

[11] Cf. Sanromán, 2000.

In what idiomatic expressions are concerned, it is important to note the fact that the transposition of an expression to another semantic field is a synchronic process that usually implies that at some point in time (including the present day) the expressions may simultaneously present compositional and idiomatic meanings (*porto de abrigo* 'harbor'; 'safe haven'). Curiously, from a statistical point of view, our study showed that the idiomatic meaning is the one that usually presents high frequency of occurrence. This information, together with the interpretation of the context, may help the automatic systems to decide whether they face a compositional or idiomatic expression.

In a sweeping look at the data, we observed that MWE show particular properties according to their syntactic pattern. Thus, at the sentence level (proverbs and aphorisms), MWE usually do not accept syntactic changes (the possible change seems to be lexical, when speakers substitute one or more elements), while verb phrases admit much more morphossyntactic variation. Noun phrases, on the other hand, raise specific issues. Compositional groups can behave as idiomatic ones and it is not always easy to distinguish them. The modifiers of the noun can express different semantic relations (part of, made of, used for) that may interact with the meaning (literal or idiomatic) of the noun.

4 Annotation of the Lexicon

The information presented on our typology will allow us to enrich the lexicon mentioned in Section 2. Our purpose is to have each MWE entry in the lexicon labeled regarding: (i) canonical form of the expression; (ii) definition of idiomatic expressions through synonyms or literal paraphrases; (iii) grammatical category of both the expression and its elements; (iv) idiomatic property and additional meanings; (v) possible variation; (vi) function of MWE parts (e.g., obligatory, optional, free).

As we have seen before, MWE have different types of variation for which we have to account for. We will briefly discuss our proposal for handling the annotation of some cases of lexical and syntactic variation in the lexicon.

Lexical Variation

➢ Insertion of modifiers – lexical elements (usually with an emphatic function) that do not belong to the canonical form are not part of the MWE and are not labeled (*sorriso muito amarelo* lit. 'smile very yellow').

- Lexical substitution – This variation is restricted to limited set of alternatives. This set is recorded in the MWE lexicon as *'obligatory parts of the MWE and member of a set list'* (*comer/vender/comprar/impingir/levar gato por lebre* lit. 'eat/sell/buy/impose/take a cat instead of a hare' (buy a pig in a poke)).
- Free lexical elements – These elements are marked in the lexicon with, e. g., a pronoun (*ALGUÉM* 'someone', *ALGUM* 'something') or a particular phrase (NP, PP) (*estar nas mãos de ALGUÉM* 'to be in the hands of someone').

There are also cases where parts of the MWE may freely vary, while other parts remain fixed (*a educação é a mãe de todas as civilizações* 'education is the mother of all civilizations', *a liberdade é a mãe de todas as virtudes* 'liberty is the mother of all virtues'). These cases are treated likewise (*ALGO é a mãe de todas as NOUN-PL* 'something is the mother of all NOUN-PL')

Also, since creative use of language can lead to MWEs that only partly match the canonical MWE (cf. proverbs), we label these parts as *'different from canonical form'*.

Syntactic Variation

- Pronouns/Possessives – These elements will be marked up as part of the MWE, but will have an additional label to signal that they are optional (*estar nas mãos dele/estar nas suas mãos* 'to be in the hands of him'/'to be in his hands').
- From active to passive voice – Auxiliary verbs are not labeled as part of the MWE (*passar ALGO a pente fino/ALGO foi passado a pente fino* lit. 'pass something with a fine toothcomb'/'something was passed with a fine toothcomb' (to scrutinize)).

According to Hendrickx et al. (2010a), this annotated lexicon could be the basis for the annotation of idiomatic MWE in running text[12]. Each MWE encountered in the corpus would be annotated with a link to the corresponding entry in the lexicon. Linking each MWE to its canonical form would allow for an easier detection of all occurrences of one particular MWE and check its variation in the corpus. The annotation process would combine automatic retrieval with manual validation in order to better account for variable expressions. Without doubt, the corpus would contain many MWE that were not yet listed in the lexicon. Therefore, each sentence would need to be checked manually for new MWE and the newly discovered expression would be manually added to the lexicon.

[12] The authors' approach is to annotate CINTIL corpus, a 1M word corpus of both spoken and written data from different sources that has been previously annotated with linguistic information such as part-of-speech, lemma, inflection, proper names, etc. (http://cintil.ul.pt/pt/).

5 Conclusion

This paper has shown the ongoing research that aims to describe, as detailed as possible, the syntactic and semantic properties of different types of Portuguese MWE. During our analysis, we encountered two major problems: (i) the evaluation of the meaning of certain expressions (compositional or idiomatic); (ii) the attempt to account for all possible lexical and syntactic variation. The information obtained from the typology will be used to annotate a MWE lexicon. Having a resource with such information (that includes additional meanings, possible variation that accounts for obligatory and optional elements, etc.) will be of extreme value for the development and evaluation of automatic MWE identification systems.

References

Baptista Jorge. 1994. *Estabelecimento e Formalização de Classes de Nomes Compostos*. MA Thesis, Faculdade de Letras da Universidade de Lisboa, Lisbon.

Chacoto Luísa. 1994. *Estudo e Formalização das Propriedades Léxico-Sintácticas das Expressões Fixas Proverbiais*. MA Thesis, Faculdade de Letras da Universidade de Lisboa, Lisboa.

Church Kenneth and Patrick Hanks. 1990. Word Association Norms, Mutual Information and Lexicography. *Proceedings of the 27th Annual Meeting of the Association for Computational Linguistics*. Vancouver, Canada, pp. 76-83.

Coseriu Eugenio. 1967. Lexikalische Solidaritäten. *Poetica 1*. pp. 293-303.

Duran Magali Sanches, Carlos Ramish, Sandra Maria Aluísio and Aline Villavicencio. 2011. Identifying and Analyzing Brazilian Portuguese Complex Predicates. *Proceedings of the Workshop on Multiword Expressions*. Association for Computational Linguistics. Portland, Oregon, USA, pp. 74-82.

Evert Stephan and Brigitte Krenn. 2001. Methods for the Qualitative Evaluation of Lexical Association Measures. *Proceedings of the 39th Annual Meeting of the Association for Computational Linguistics.* Toulouse, France, pp. 188-195.

Fellbaum Christiane. 1998. *An WordNet Electronic Lexical Database.* The MIT Press, Cambridge, MA.

Firth R. John. 1955. Modes of meaning. *Papers in Linguistics 1934-1951.* London, Oxford University Press, pp. 190-215.

Hendricks Iris, Amália Mendes and Sandra Antunes. 2010a. Proposal for Multi-word Expression Annotation in Running Text. *Proceedings of the fourth Linguistic Annotation Workshop.* Association for Computational Linguistics. Uppsala, Sweden, pp. 152-156.

Hendricks Iris, Amália Mendes, Sílvia Pereira, Anabela Gonçalves and Inês Duarte. 2010b. Complex Predicates annotation in a corpus of Portuguese. *Proceedings of the fourth Linguistic Annotation Workshop.* Association for Computational Linguistics. Uppsala, Sweden, pp 100-108.

Jackendoff Ray. 1997. *The Architecture of the Language Faculty.* The MIT Press, Cambridge, MA.

Macário Lopes Ana Cristina. 1992. *Texto Proverbial Português: elementos para uma análise semântica e pragmática.* PhD Dissertation, Universidade de Coimbra, Coimbra.

Mel'čuk Igor. 1998. Collocations and Lexical Functions. Cowie, A. P. (ed.), *Phraseology. Theory, Analysis, and Applications.* Oxford University Press, Oxford, pp. 23-53.

Mendes Amália, Sandra Antunes, Maria Fernanda Bacelar do Nascimento, João M. Casteleiro, Luísa Pereira and Tiago Sá. 2006. COMBINA-PT: A Large Corpus-extracted and Hand-checked Lexical Database of Portuguese Multiword Expressions. *Proceedings of the Fifth International Conference on Language Resources and Evaluation.* Genoa, Italy, pp. 1900-1905.

Pereira Luísa and Amália Mendes. 2002. An Electronic Dictionary of Collocations for European Portuguese: Methodology, Results and Applications. Braasch, A. and C. Povlsen (eds.), *Proceedings of the 10th International Congress of the European Association for Lexicography.* Copenhagen, Denmark, vol. II, pp. 841-849.

Ranchhod Elisabete. 2003. O Lugar das Expressões 'Fixas' na Gramática do Português. Castro, I. and I. Duarte (eds.), *Razões e Emoção. Miscelânea de Estudos oferecida a Maria Helena Mira Mateus.* Imprensa Nacional Casa da Moeda, Lisboa, pp. 239-254.

Sag Ivan, Timothy Baldwin, Francis Bond, Ann Copestake and Dan Flickinger. 2002. Multiword Expressions: A Pain in the Neck for NLP. Gelbukh A. (ed.), *Proceedings of the Third International Conference on Intelligent Text Processing and Computational Linguistics.* Mexico City, Mexico, pp. 1-15.

Sanromán A. Iriarte. 2000. *A Unidade Lexicográfica. Palavras, Colocações, Frasemas, Pragmatemas.* PhD Dissertation, Universidade do Minho, Braga.

Sinclair John. 1991. *Corpus, Concordance and Collocation.* Oxford University Press, Oxford.

Vilela Mário. 2002. *Metáforas do Nosso Tempo.* Almedina, Coimbra.

Zeller Britta and Sebastian Padó. 2012. Corpus-Based Acquisition of Support Verb Constructions for Portuguese. *Proceedings of the 10th International Conference on Computational Processing of the Portuguese Language.* Coimbra, Portugal, pp. 73-84.

Identifying Pronominal Verbs: Towards Automatic Disambiguation of the Clitic *se* in Portuguese

Magali Sanches Duran♡**, Carolina Evaristo Scarton**♡**,**
Sandra Maria Aluísio♡**, Carlos Ramisch**♠

♡ University of São Paulo (Brazil)
♠ Joseph Fourier University (France)
magali.duran@uol.com.br, carol.scarton@gmail.com
sandra@icmc.usp.br, carlosramisch@gmail.com

Abstract

A challenging topic in Portuguese language processing is the multifunctional and ambiguous use of the clitic pronoun *se*, which impacts NLP tasks such as syntactic parsing, semantic role labeling and machine translation. Aiming to give a step forward towards the automatic disambiguation of *se*, our study focuses on the identification of pronominal verbs, which correspond to one of the six uses of *se* as a clitic pronoun, when *se* is considered a CONSTITUTIVE PARTICLE of the verb lemma to which it is bound, as a multiword unit. Our strategy to identify such verbs is to analyze the results of a corpus search and to rule out all the other possible uses of *se*. This process evidenced the features needed in a computational lexicon to automatically perform the disambiguation task. The availability of the resulting lexicon of pronominal verbs on the web enables their inclusion in broader lexical resources, such as the Portuguese versions of Wordnet, Propbank and VerbNet. Moreover, it will allow the revision of parsers and dictionaries already in use.

1 Introduction

In Portuguese, the word *se* is multifunctional. POS taggers have succeeded in distinguishing between *se* as a conjunction (meaning *if* or *whether*) and *se* as a pronoun (see Martins et al. (1999) for more details on the complexity of such task). As a clitic[1] pronoun, however, *se* has six uses:

1. marker of SUBJECT INDETERMINATION:
   Já se falou muito nesse assunto.
   **Has-SE already spoken a lot about this matter.*
   One has already spoken a lot about this matter.
2. marker of pronominal PASSIVE voice (synthetic passive voice):
   Sugeriram-se muitas alternativas.
   **Have-SE suggested many alternatives.*
   Many alternatives have been suggested.
3. REFLEXIVE pronoun (-self pronouns):
   Você deveria se olhar no espelho.
   **You should look-SE on the mirror.*
   You should look at yourself on the mirror.
4. RECIPROCAL pronoun (each other):
   Eles se cumprimentaram com um aperto de mão.
   **They greeted-SE with a handshake.*
   They greeted each other with a handshake.
5. marker of causative-INCHOATIVE alternation[2]:
   Esse esporte popularizou-se no Brasil.
   **This sport popularED-SE in Brazil.*
   This sport became popular in Brazil.
6. CONSTITUTIVE PARTICLE of the verb lexical item (pronominal verb):
   Eles se queixaram de dor no joelho.
   **They complained-SE about knee pain.*
   They complained about knee pain.

[1] A clitic is a bound form, phonologically unstressed, attached to a word from an open class (noun, verb, adjective, adverbial). It belongs to closed classes, that is, classes that have grammatical rather than lexical meaning (pronouns, auxiliary verbs, determiners, conjunctions, prepositions, numerals).

[2] Causative-inchoative alternation: a same verb can be used two different ways, one transitive, in which the subject position is occupied by the argument which causes the action or process described by the verb (causative use), and one intransitive, in which the subject position is occupied by the argument affected by the action or process (inchoative use).

Clitic *se* uses	Syntactic function	Semantic function
SUBJECT INDETERMINATION	NO	YES[3]
PASSIVE	YES	YES[3]
REFLEXIVE	YES	YES
RECIPROCAL	YES	YES
INCHOATIVE	YES	NO
CONSTITUTIVE PARTICLE	NO	NO

Table 1: Uses of the clitic *se* from the point of view of syntax and semantics.

The identification of these uses is very important for Portuguese language processing, notably for syntactic parsing, semantic role labeling (SRL) and machine translation. Table 1 shows which of these six uses support syntactic and/or semantic functions.

Since superficial syntactic features seem not sufficient to disambiguate the uses of the pronoun *se*, we propose the use of a computational lexicon to contribute to this task. To give a step forward to solve this problem, we decided to survey the verbs undergoing *se* as an integral part of their lexical form (item 6), called herein *pronominal verbs*, but also known as *inherent reflexive verbs* (Rosário Ribeiro, 2011). Grammars usually mention this kind of verbs and give two classical examples: *queixar-se* (*to complain*) and *arrepender-se* (*to repent*). For the best of our knowledge, a comprehensive list of these multiword verbs is not available in electronic format for NLP uses, and not even in a paper-based format, such as a printed dictionary.

An example of the relevance of pronominal verbs is that, in spite of not being argumental, that is, not being eligible for a semantic role label, the use of *se* as a CONSTITUTIVE PARTICLE should integrate the verb that evokes the argumental structure, as may be seen in Figure 1.

The identification of pronominal verbs is not a trivial task because a pronominal verb has a negative definition: if *se* does not match the restrictions imposed by the other five uses, so it is a CONSTITUTIVE PARTICLE of the verb, that is, it composes a multiword. Therefore, the identification of pronominal verbs requires linguistic knowledge to distinguish *se* as a CONSTITUTIVE PARTICLE from the other uses of the the pronoun *se* (SUBJECT INDETERMINATION, PASSIVE, REFLEXIVE, RECIPROCAL and INCHOATIVE.)

[3]In these cases, the clitic may support the semantic role label of the suppressed external argument (agent).

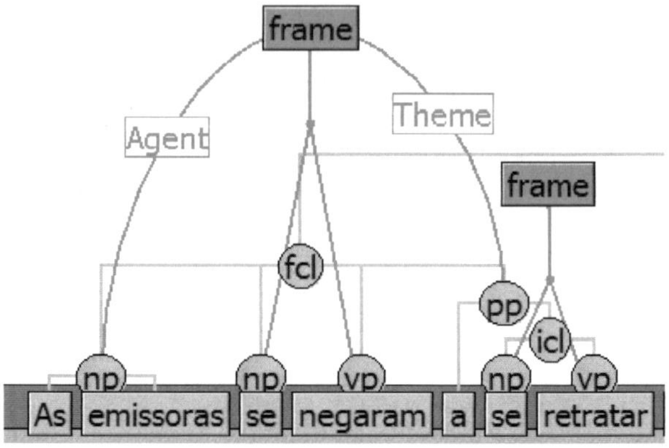

Figure 1: Sentence *The broadcasters refused to apologize* includes pronominal verbs *negar-se* (*refuse*) and *retratar-se* (*apologize*) that evoke frames in SRL.

There are several theoretical linguistic studies about the clitic pronoun *se* in Portuguese. Some of these studies present an overview of the *se* pronoun uses, but none of them prioritized the identification of pronominal verbs. The study we report in this paper is intended to fill this gap.

2 Related Work

From a linguistic perspective, the clitic pronoun *se* has been the subject of studies focusing on: SUBJECT INDETERMINATION and PASSIVE uses (Morais Nunes, 1990; Cyrino, 2007; Pereira-Santos, 2010); REFLEXIVE use (Godoy, 2012), and INCHOATIVE use (Fonseca, 2010; Nunes-Ribeiro, 2010; Rosário Ribeiro, 2011). Despite none of these works concerning specifically pronominal verbs, they provided us an important theoretical basis for the analysis undertaken herein.

The problem of the multifunctional use of clitic pronouns is not restricted to Portuguese. Romance languages, Hebrew, Russian, Bulgarian and others also have similar constructions. There are crosslinguistic studies regarding this matter reported in Siloni (2001) and Slavcheva (2006), showing that there are partial coincidence of verbs taking clitic pronouns to produce alternations and reflexive voice.

From an NLP perspective, the problem of the ambiguity of the clitic pronoun *se* was studied by Martins et al. (1999) to solve a problem of categorization, that is, to decide which part-of-speech tag should be assigned to *se*. However, we have not found studies regarding pronominal verbs aiming at Portuguese automatic language processing.

Even though in Portuguese all the uses of the clitic pronoun *se* share the same realization at the surface form level, the use as a CONSTITUTIVE PARTICLE of pronominal verbs is the only one in which the verb and the clitic form a multiword lexical unit on its own. In the other uses, the clitic keeps a separate syntactic and/or semantic function, as presented in Table 1.

The particle *se* is an integral part of pronominal verbs in the same way as the particles of English phrasal verbs. As future work, we would like to investigate possible semantic contributions of the *se* particle to the meaning of pronominal verbs, as done by Cook and Stevenson (2006), for example, who try to automatically classify the uses of the particle *up* in verb-particle constructions. Like in the present paper, they estimate a set of linguistic features which are in turn used to train a Support Vector Machine (SVM) classifier citecook:2006:mwe.

3 Methodology

For the automatic identification of multiword verb+*se* occurrences, we performed corpus searches on the PLN-BR-FULL corpus (Muniz et al., 2007), which consists of news texts extracted from a major Brazilian newspaper, *Folha de São Paulo*, from 1994 to 2005, with 29,014,089 tokens. The corpus was first preprocessed for sentence splitting, case homogenization, lemmatization, morphological analysis and POS tagging using the PALAVRAS parser (Bick, 2000). Then, we executed the corpus searches using the `mwetoolkit` (Ramisch et al., 2010). The tool allowed us to define two multilevel word patterns, for proclitic and enclitic cases, based on surface forms, morphology and POS. The patterns covered all the verbs in third person singular (POS=`V*`, morphology=`3S`) followed/preceded by the clitic pronoun *se* (surface form=*se*, POS=`PERS`). The patterns returned a set of *se* occurrences, that is, for each verb, a set of sentences in the corpus in which this verb is followed/preceded by the clitic *se*.

In our analysis, we looked at all the verbs taking an enclitic *se*, that is, where the clitic *se* is attached after the verb. We could as well have included the occurrences of verbs with a proclitic *se* (clitic attached before the verb). However, we suspected that this would increase the number of occurrences (sentences) to analyze without a proportional increase in verb lemmas. Indeed, our search for proclitic *se* occurrences returned 40% more verb lemmas and 264% more sentences than for the enclitic *se* (59,874 sentences), thus confirming our hypothesis. Moreover, as we could see at a first glance, proclitic *se* results included *se* conjunctions erroneously tagged as pronouns (when the parser fails the categorial disambiguation). This error does not occur when the pronoun is enclitic because Portuguese orthographic rules require a hyphen between the verb and the clitic when *se* is enclitic, but never when it is proclitic.

We decided to look at sentences as opposed to looking only at candidate verb lemmas, because we did not trust that our intuition as native speakers would be sufficient to identify all the uses of the clitic *se* for a given verb, specially as some verbs allow more than one of the six uses we listed herein.

For performing the annotation, we used a table with the verb lemmas in the lines and a column for each one of the six uses of *se* as a clitic pronoun. Working with two screens (one for the table and the other for the sentences), we read the sentences and, once a new use was verified, we ticked the appropriate column. This annotation setup accelerated the analyses, as we only stopped the reading when we identified a new use. The annotation was performed manually by a linguist, expert in semantics of Portuguese verbs, and also an author of this paper.

After having summarized the results obtained from corpus analysis, we realized that some cliticized verb uses that we know as native speakers did not appear in the corpus (mainly reflexive and reciprocal uses). In these cases, we added a comment on our table which indicates the need to look for the use in another corpus aiming to confirm it.

For example, the most frequent cliticized verb, *tratar-se* has no occurrence with the meaning of *to take medical treatment*. We checked this meaning in another corpus and found one example: *O senador se tratou com tecido embrionário...* (**The senator treated himself with embryonic tissue...*), proving that our intuition may help us to improve the results with specific corpus searches. A comparative multi-corpus extension of the present study is planned as future work.

The strategy we adopted to analyze the sentences in order to identify pronominal verbs was to make a series of questions to rule out the other possible *se* uses.

Question 1 Does the *se* particle function as a marker of PASSIVE voice or SUBJECT INDETERMINATION?

In order to answer this question, it is important to know that both uses involve the suppression of the external argument of the verb. The difference is that, in the pronominal PASSIVE voice, the remaining NP (noun phrase) is shifted to the subject position (and the verb must then be inflected according to such subject), whereas in SUBJECT INDETERMINATION, the remaining argument, always a PP (prepositional phrase), remains as an indirect object. For example:

- Pronominal PASSIVE voice:
  Fizeram-se várias tentativas.
  **Made-SE several trials.*
  Several trials were made.
- SUBJECT INDETERMINATION:
  Reclamou-se de falta de hygiene.
  **Complained-SE about the lack of hygiene.*
  One has complained about the lack of hygiene.

Question 2 Is it possible to substitute *se* for *a si mesmo* (*-self*)?

If so, it is a case of REFLEXIVE use. A clue for this is that it is always possible to substitute *se* for another personal pronoun, creating a non-reflexive use keeping the same subject. For example:

- *Ele perguntou-**se** se aquilo era certo.*
  *He asked **himself** whether that was correct.*
- *Ele perguntou-**me** se aquilo era certo.*
  *He asked **me** whether that was correct.*

Question 3 Is it possible to substitute *se* for *um ao outro* (*each other*)?

If so, it is a case of RECIPROCAL use. A clue for this interpretation is that, in this case, the verb is always in plural form as the subject refers to more than one person. RECIPROCAL uses were not included in the corpus searches, as we only looked for cliticized verbs in third person singular. However, aiming to gather data for future work, we have ticked the table every time we annotated sentences of a verb that admits reciprocal use. The reciprocal use of such verbs have been later verified in other corpora.

- *Eles se beijaram.*
  They kissed each other.

Question 4 Has the verb, without *se*, a transitive use? If so, are the senses related to causative-inchoative alternation? In other words, is the meaning of the transitive use *to cause X become Y*?

If so, it is a case of INCHOATIVE use, for example:

- *A porta abriu-se.*
  The door opened.

Compare with the basic transitive use:

- *Ele abriu a porta.*
  He opened the door.

It is important to mention that verbs which allow causative-inchoative alternation in Portuguese may not have an equivalent in English that allows this alternation, and vice-versa. For example, the inchoative use of the verb *tornar* corresponds to the verb *to become* and the causative use corresponds to the verb *to make*:

- *Esse fato tornou-se conhecido em todo o mundo.*
  This fact became known all around the world.

- *A imprensa tornou o fato conhecido em todo o mundo.*
  The press made the fact known all around the world.

If the verb being analyzed failed the four tests, the clitic *se* has neither semantic nor syntactic function and is considered a CONSTITUTIVE PARTICLE of the verb, for example:

- *Ele vangloriou-se de seus talentos.*
  He boasted of his talents.

Therefore, we made the identification of pronominal verbs based on the negation of the other possibilities.

4 Discussion

The corpus search resulted in 22,618 sentences of cliticized verbs, corresponding to 1,333 verb lemmas. Some verbs allow only one of the uses of the clitic *se* (unambiguous cliticized verbs), whereas others allow more than one use (ambiguous cliticized verbs), as shown in Table 2. Therefore, a lexicon can only disambiguate part of the cliticized verbs (others need additional features to be disambiguated).

The analysis of the verbs' distribution reveals that 10% of them (133) account for 73% of the sentences. Moreover, among the remaining 90% verb lemmas, there are 477 *hapax legomena*, that is, verbs that occur only once. Such distribution indicates that computational models which focus on very frequently cliticized verbs might significantly improve NLP applications.

Contrary to our expectations, very frequently cliticized verbs did not necessarily present high polysemy. For example, the most frequent verb of our corpus is *tratar*, with 2,130 occurrences. Although *tratar-se* has more than one possible use, only one appeared in the corpus, as a marker of SUBJECT INDETERMINATION, for example:

- *Trata-se de uma nova tendência.*
  It is the case of a new tendency.

Despite being very frequent, when we search for translations of *tratar-se de* in bilingual (parallel) Portuguese-English corpora and dictionaries available on the web,[4,5,6] we observed that there are several solutions to convey this idea in English (determining a subject, as English does not allow subject omission). Six examples extracted from the Compara corpus illustrate this fact:

[4] http://www.linguateca.pt/COMPARA/

[5] http://www.linguee.com.br/portugues-ingles

[6] http://pt.bab.la/dicionario/portugues-ingles

***se* uses**	**Unamb.**	**Amb.**	**Total**
SUBJECT INDETERMINATION	17	6	23
PASSIVE	467	630	1097
REFLEXIVE	25	333	358
INCHOATIVE	190	64	254
RECIPROCAL	0	33	33
CONSTITUTIVE PARTICLE	83	104	187
Total	782	1170	1952

Table 2: Proportion of unambiguous (Unamb.) and ambiguous (Amb.) verbs that allow each *se* use.

- **Trata-se de** *recriar o próprio passado.*
  It's a question of *re-creating your own past.*
- *Mas o assunto era curioso,* **trata-se do** *casamento, e a viúva interessa-me.*
  But the subject was a curious one; **it was about** *her marriage, and the widow interests me.*
- *Não há mais dúvidas,* **trata-se** *realmente* **de** *um louco.*
  There's no longer any doubt; **we're** *truly* **dealing with** *a maniac.*
- **Trata-se** *realmente* **de** *uma emergência, Sr. Hoffman.*
  This really **is a matter of** *some urgency, Mr Hoffman.*
- **Trata-se de** *um regime repousante e civilizado.*
  It is *a restful, civilized régime.*
- **Trata-se de** *um simples caso de confusão de identidades, dizem vocês.*
  (??) Simple case of mistaken identity.

In what concerns specifically pronominal verbs, our analysis of the data showed they are of three kinds:

1. Verbs that are used exclusively in pronominal form, as *abster-se* (*to abstain*). This does not mean that the pronominal form is unambiguous, as we found some pronominal verbs that present more than one sense, as for example the verb *referir-se*, which means *to refer* or *to concern*, depending on the subject's animacy status [+ human] or [− human], respectively;

2. Verbs that have a non-pronominal and a pronominal form, but both forms are not related, e.g.: *realizar* (*to make* or *to carry on*, which allows the passive alternation *realizar-se*); and the pronominal form *realizar-se* (*to feel fulfilled*);
3. Verbs that have pronominal form, but accept clitic drop in some varieties of Portuguese without change of meaning, as *esquecer-se* and *esquecer* (both mean *to forget*)

We did not study the clitic drop (3), but we uncovered several pronominal verbs of the second kind above (2). The ambiguity among the uses of *se* increases with such cases. The verb *desculpar* (*to forgive*), for example, allows the REFLEXIVE use *desculpar-se* (*to forgive oneself*), but also constitutes a pronominal verb: *desculpar-se* (*to apologize*). The verb *encontrar* (*to find*) allows the REFLEXIVE use (*to find oneself*, from a psychological point of view) and the PASSIVE use (*to be found*). The same verb also constitutes a pronominal verb which means *to meet* (1) or functions as a copula verb, as *to be* (2):

1. *Ele encontrou-se com o irmão.*
   He met his brother.
2. *Ele encontra-se doente.*
   He is ill.

In most sentences of cliticized verbs' occurrences, it is easy to observe that, as a rule of thumb:[7]

- SUBJECT INDETERMINATION uses of *se* do not present an NP before the verb, present a PP after the verb and the verb is always inflected in the third person singular;
- PASSIVE uses of *se* present an NP after the verb and no NP before the verb;
- INCHOATIVE uses of *se* present an NP before the verb and almost always neither a PP nor a NP after the verb;
- CONSTITUTIVE PARTICLE uses of *se* present an NP before the verb and a PP after the verb;
- RECIPROCAL uses of *se* only occur with verbs taking a plural inflection.

Problems arise when a sentence follows none of these *rules*. For example, subjects in PASSIVE use of *se* usually come on the right of the verb. Thus, when the subject appears before the verb, it looks, at a first glance, to be an active sentence. For example:

- *O IDH baseia-se em dados sobre renda, escolaridade e expectativa de vida.*
  **The HDI bases-SE on income, education and life expectancy data.*
  The HDI is based on income, education and life expectancy data.

These cases usually occur with stative passives (see Rosário Ribeiro (2011, p. 196)) or with ditransitive action verbs[8] when a [− animate] NP takes the place usually occupied by a [+ animate] NP. Semantic features, again, help to disambiguate and to reveal a non-canonical passive.

The opposite also occurs, that is, the subject, usually placed on the left of the verb in active voice, appears on the right, giving to the sentence a false passive appearance:

- *Desesperaram-se todos os passageiros.*
  **Fell-SE into despair all the passengers.*
  All the passengers fell into despair.

Sometimes the meaning distinctions of a verb are very subtle, making the matter more complex. In the following sections, we comment two examples of difficult disambiguation.

4.1 Distinguishing Pronominal PASSIVE Voice from Pronominal Verbs

The verb *seguir* (*to follow*) conveys the idea of *obeying* when it has a [+ human] subject in the active voice (an agent). The passive voice may be constructed using *se*, like in (2). Additionally, this verb has a pronominal active use, *seguir-se*, which means *to occur after*, as shown in (3):

1. Active voice:
   - *[Eles]$_{Agent}$ seguem [uma série de convenções]$_{Theme\ -\ thing\ followed}$.*
     They follow a series of conventions.

[7] Syntactic clues do not help to identify REFLEXIVE verbs. The distinction depends on the semantic level, as the reflexive use requires a [+ animate] subject to play simultaneously the roles of agent and patient.

[8] Ditransitive verbs take two internal arguments: an NP as direct object and a PP as indirect object.

2. PASSIVE voice:

    - *Segue-se [uma série de convenções]$_{Theme\ -\ thing\ followed}$.*
      A series of conventions are followed.

3. Pronominal verb – active voice:

    - *[A queda]$_{Theme\ -\ thing\ occurring\ after}$ seguiu-se [à divulgação dos dados de desemprego em o país]$_{Theme\ -\ thing\ occurring\ before}$.*
      The drop followed the announcement of unemployment figures in the country.

The preposition *a* introducing one of the arguments in (3) distinguishes the two meanings, as the PASSIVE voice presents an NP and not a PP immediately after or before the verb.

4.2 Distinguishing REFLEXIVE, INCHOATIVE and PASSIVE Uses

The verb *transformar*, when cliticized, may be interpreted as a PASSIVE (*to be transformed*), as a REFLEXIVE (*to transform oneself*) or as an INCHOATIVE use (*to become transformed*). The PASSIVE voice is identified by the subject position, after the verb (1). The difference between the REFLEXIVE (2) and INCHOATIVE (3) uses, on its turn, is a semantic feature: only a [+ human] subject may act to become something (REFLEXIVE use):

1. PASSIVE:
    Transformou-se o encontro em uma grande festa.
    The meeting was transformed into a big party.

2. REFLEXIVE:

    - *A mulher jovem transformou-se em uma pessoa sofisticada.*
      The young woman transformed herself into a sophisticated person.

3. INCHOATIVE:

    - *O encontro transformou-se em uma grande festa.*
      The meeting transformed into a big party.

5 Conclusions and Future Work

The lexicon gathered through this research will partially enable disambiguating the uses of the clitic pronoun *se*, as there are several verbs that allow only one of the *se* clitic uses. For the other verbs, whose polysemy entails more than one possible use of *se*, it is necessary to add further information on each verb sense.

The analysis we reported here evidenced the need for enriching Portuguese computational lexicons, encompassing (a) the semantic role labels assigned by each verb sense, (b) the selectional restrictions a verb imposes to its arguments, and (c) the alternations a verb (dis)allows. The semantic predicate decomposition used by Levin (1993) has proved to be worthy to formalize the use of *se* in reflexive constructions (Godoy, 2012) and we think it should be adopted to describe other uses of the pronoun *se*. Another alternative is to construct a detailed computational verb lexicon along the lines suggested by Gardent et al. (2005), based on Maurice Gross' lexicon-grammar.

The data generated by this study can also be used to automatically learn classifiers for ambiguous uses of the clitic *se*. On the one hand, the annotation of uses can be semi-automatically projected on the sentences extracted from the corpus. On the other hand, the findings of this work in terms of syntactic and semantic characteristics can be used to propose features for the classifier, trying to reproduce those that can be automatically obtained (e.g., subcategorization frame) and to simulate those that cannot be easily automated (e.g., whether the subject is animate). For these future experiments, we intend to compare different learning models, based on SVM and on sequence models like conditional random fields (Vincze, 2012).

As languages are different in what concerns allowed alternations, the use of clitic *se* in Portuguese becomes even more complex when approached from a bilingual point of view. Depending on how different the languages compared are, the classification of *se* adopted here may be of little use. For example, several verbs classified as reflexive in Portuguese, like *vestir-se* (*to dress*), *barbear-se* (*to shave*) and *demitir-se* (*to resign*) are not translated into a reflexive form in English (**to dress oneself*, **to shave oneself* and **to dismiss oneself*). Similarly, typical inchoative verb uses in Portuguese need to be translated into a periphrasis in English, like *surpreender-se* (*to be surprised at*), *orgulhar-se* (*to be proud of*) and *irritar-se* (*to get angry*). Such evidences lead us to conclude that it would be useful to count on a bilingual description not only of pronominal, but also of the other *se* uses.

The results of this work are available at `www.nilc.icmc.usp.br/portlex`.

Acknowledgments

This study was funded by FAPESP (process 2011/22337-1) and by the CAMELEON project (CAPES-COFECUB 707-11).

References

Eckhard Bick. 2000. *The parsing system Palavras*. Aarhus University Press. 411 p.

Paul Cook and Suzanne Stevenson. 2006. Classifying particle semantics in English verb-particle constructions. In *Proceedings of MWE 2006*, pages 45–53, Sydney, Australia.

Sonia Maria Lazzarino Cyrino. 2007. Construções com SE e promoção de argumento no português brasileiro: Uma investigação diacrônica. *Revista da ABRALIN*, 6:85–116.

Paula Fonseca. 2010. *Os verbos pseudo-reflexos em Português Europeu*. Master's thesis, Universidade do Porto.

Claire Gardent, Bruno Guillaume, Guy Perrier, and Ingrid Falk. 2005. Maurice gross' grammar lexicon and natural language processing. In *Proceedings of the 2nd Language and Technology Conference*, Poznań, Poland.

Luisa Andrade Gomes Godoy. 2012. *A reflexivização no PB e a decomposição semântica de predicados*. Ph.D. thesis, Universidade Federal de Minas Gerais.

Beth Levin. 1993. *English Verb Classes and Alternations: a preliminary investigation*. The University of Chicago Press, Chicago, USA.

Ronaldo Teixeira Martins, Gisele Montilha, Lucia Helena Machado Rino, and Maria da Graça Volpe Nunes. 1999. Dos modelos de resolução da ambiguidade categorial: o problema do SE. In *Proceedings of IV Encontro para o Processamento Computacional da Língua Portuguesa Escrita e Falada (PROPOR 1999)*, pages 115–128, Évora, Portugal, September.

Jairo Morais Nunes. 1990. *O famigerado SE: uma análise sincrônica e diacrônica das construções com SE apassivador e indeterminador*. Master's thesis, Universidade Estadual de Campinas.

Marcelo Muniz, Fernando V. Paulovich, Rosane Minghim, Kleber Infante, Fernando Muniz, Renata Vieira, and Sandra Aluísio. 2007. Taming the tiger topic: an XCES compliant corpus portal to generate subcorpus based on automatic text topic identification. In *Proceedings of The Corpus Linguistics Conference (CL 2007)*, Birmingham, UK.

Pablo Nunes-Ribeiro. 2010. *A alternância causativa no Português do Brasil: a distribuição do clítico SE*. Master's thesis, Universidade Federal do Rio Grande do Sul.

José Ricardo Pereira-Santos. 2010. *Alternância passiva com verbos transitivos indiretos do português do Brasil*. Master's thesis, Universidade de Brasília.

Carlos Ramisch, Aline Villavicencio, and Christian Boitet. 2010. Multiword expressions in the wild? the mwetoolkit comes in handy. In *Proceedings of the 23rd COLING (COLING 2010) - Demonstrations*, pages 57–60, Beijing, China.

Sílvia Isabel do Rosário Ribeiro. 2011. *Estruturas com "se" Anafórico, Impessoal e Decausativo em Português*. Ph.D. thesis, Faculdade de Letras da Universidade de Coimbra.

Tal Siloni. 2001. Reciprocal verbs. In *Online Proceedings of IATL 17*, Jerusalem, Israel.

Milena Slavcheva. 2006. Semantic descriptors: The case of reflexive verbs. In *Proceedings of LREC 2006*, pages 1009–1014, Genoa, Italy.

Veronika Vincze. 2012. Light verb constructions in the szegedparalellFX English–Hungarian parallel corpus. In *Proceedings of LREC 2012*, Istanbul, Turkey.

A Repository of Variation Patterns for Multiword Expressions

Malvina Nissim
FICLIT, University of Bologna
malvina.nissim@unibo.it

Andrea Zaninello
Zanichelli Editore, Humanities Department
andrea.zaninello@gmail.com

1 Introduction and Background

One of the crucial issues in the analysis and processing of MWEs is their internal variability. Indeed, the feature that mostly characterises MWEs is their fixedness at some level of linguistic analysis, be it morphology, syntax, or semantics. The morphological aspect is not trivial in languages which exhibit a rich morphology, such as Romance languages.

The issue is relevant in at least three aspects of MWE representation and processing: lexicons, identification, and extraction (Calzolari et al., 2002). At the lexicon level, MWEs are usual stored as one form only, the so-called *quotation form* (or *citation form*). However, *some* variations of the quotation form might also be valid instances of MWEs (Bond et al., 2005) — some but not all, as some of them might actually be plain compositional phrases.

This becomes relevant for automatic identification and extraction. If a lexicon stores the quotation form only, identification on a corpus done via matching lexicon strings as such would miss valid variations of a given MWE. Identification could be done exploiting lemmas rather than quotation forms, but an unrestricted match would also possibly return compositional phrases. Extraction is usually done applying association measures over instances of given POS patterns (Evert and Krenn, 2005), and because lemmas are matched, no restrictions on internal variation is enforced as such. Knowing *which* variations should be allowed for the quotation form of a given MWE would help in increasing recall while keeping precision high. However, specifying such variations for *each* MWE would be too costly and wouldn't help in extraction, as no specifications could be done a priori on yet unknown MWEs. Optimally, one would need to find more general variation patterns that could be applied to *classes* of MWEs. Indeed, the main idea behind this work is that MWEs can be handled through more general patterns. This is also claimed, for instance, by Masini (2007) whose analysis on Italian MWEs takes a constructionist perspective (Goldberg, 2003), by Weller and Heid (2010), who treat verbal expressions in German, and also by Grégoire (2010), who bases his work on the Equivalence Class Method (ECM, (Odijk, 2004)) assuming that MWEs may be clustered according to their *syntactic* pattern and treated homogeneously. We suggest that variation patterns can be found and defined over POS sequences. Working on Italian, in this paper we report the results of ongoing research and show how such patterns can be derived, we then propose a way to encode them in a repository, which can be combined with existing lexicons of MWEs. For the moment, we restrict our study to contiguous MWEs although we are aware that non-contiguous expressions are common and should be treated, too (see also (Pianta and Bentivogli, 2004)). Thus, only morphological variation is considered at this stage, while phenomena such as insertion and word order variation are left for future work.

2 Obtaining Variation Patterns

Variation patterns refer to POS sequences and rely on frequencies. The main resources needed for obtaining them are a MWE lexicon and a reference corpus (pos-tagged and lemmatised).We use a MWE lexicon derived from an existing online dictionary for Italian (Zaninello and Nissim, 2010), and the corpus "La Repubblica" (Baroni et al., 2004) for obtaining frequencies.

A *variation pattern* encodes the way a given instance of a MWE morphologically differs from its original quotation form in each of its parts. All tokens that correspond to the quotation form are marked as fix whereas all tokens that do not are marked as $flex$. Consider Example (1):

(1) a. quotation form: "casa di cura" (nursing home)
  b. instance: "case di cura" (nursing homes)
  c. variation pattern: $flex\_fix\_fix$

The pattern for the instance in (1b) is $flex\_fix\_fix$ because the first token, "case" (houses) is a plural whereas the quotation form features a singular ("casa", house), thus is assigned a $flex$ label, whereas the other two tokens are found exactly as they appear in the quotation form, and are therefore labelled as fix.

At this point, it is quite important to note that a binary feature applied to each token makes *flexibility* underspecified in at least two ways. First, the value $flex$ does not account by itself for the degree of variation: a token is $flex$ if it can be found in one variation as well as many. We have addressed this issue elsewhere via a dedicated measure (Nissim and Zaninello, 2011), but we do not pick it up here again. In any case, the degree of variation could indeed be included as additional information. Second, we only specify which part of the MWEs varies but do not make assumptions on the type of variation encountered (for example, it doesn't distinguish at the level of gender or number).

We believe this is a fair tradeoff which captures generalisations at a level which is intermediate between a word-by-word analysis and considering the entire MWE as a single unit. Additionally, it does not require finer-grained annotation than POS-tagging and lemmatisation, and allows for the discovery of possibly unknown and unpredicted variations. Morphological analysis, when needed, is of course still possible *a posteriori* on the instances found, but it is useful that at this stage flexibility is left underspecified.

As said, validating variation patterns per MWE would be impractical and uninformative with respect to the extraction of previously unseen MWEs. Thus, we define variation patterns over part-of-speech sequences. More specifically, we operate as follows:

1. search all MWEs contained in a given lexicon on a large corpus, matching all possible variations (lemma-based, or unconstrained, search);

2. obtain variation patterns for all MWEs by comparing each instance to its quotation form;

3. group all MWEs with the same POS sequence;

4. for each POS sequence collect all variation patterns of all pertinent MWEs.

In previous work (Nissim and Zaninello, 2013), we have observed that frequency is a good indicator of valid patterns: the most frequent variation patterns correlate with variations annotated as correct by manual judges. Patterns for two nominal POS were evaluated, and they were found to be successful. In this paper we pick three further POS sequences per expression type for a total of nine POS patterns, and evaluate the precision of a pattern selection measure.

The availability of variation patterns per POS sequences (and expression type) can be of use both in identification as well as in extraction. In identification, patterns can be used as a selection strategy for all of the matched instances. One could just use frequency directly from the corpus where the identification is done, but this might not always be possible due to corpus size. This is why using an external repository of patterns evaluated against a large reference corpus for a given language might be useful.

In extraction tasks, patterns can be used as filters, either as a post-processing phase after matching lemmas for given POS sequences, or directly extracting only allowed configurations which could be specified for instance in extraction tools such as `mwetoolkit` (Ramisch et al., 2010). In previous work we have shown that patterns can be derived comparing found instances against their lemmatised form, making this a realistic setting even in extraction where quotation forms are not known (Nissim and Zaninello, 2013).

3 Ranking

For ranking variation patterns we take into account the following figures:

- the total number of different variation patterns per POS sequence
- the total number of instances (hits on the corpus) with a given variation pattern

For example, the POS sequence ADJ_PRE_NOUN characterising some adjectival expressions is featured by 9 different original multiword expressions that were found in the corpus. The variations with respect to the quotation form (indicated as fix_fix_fix and found for seven different types) in which instances have been found are four: $flex\_fix\_fix$ (13 times), $flex\_fix\_flex$ (7 times), fix_fix_flex (3 times), and fix_flex_flex (one time), for a total of 31 variations. Each instance yielding a given pattern was found at least once in the corpus, but possibly more times. We take into account this value as well, thus counting the number of single *instances* of a given pattern. So, while "degni di nota" ("worth$_{pl}$ mentioning", quotation form: "degno di nota", "worth$_{sg}$ mentioning") would serve as *one* variation of type $flex\_fix\_fix$, counting instances would account for the fact that this expression was found in the corpus 38 times. For the ADJ_PRE_NOUN sequence, instances of pattern fix_fix_fix were found 130 times, instances of $flex\_fix\_fix$ 219, $flex\_fix\_flex$ 326, fix_fix_flex 90, and fix_flex_flex just once, for a total of 766 instances.

Such figures are the basis for pattern ranking and are used in the repository to contribute to the description of variation patterns (Figure 1). We use the share of a given variation pattern (vp) over the total number of variations (*pattern share*). In the example above, the share of $flex\_fix\_fix$ (occurring 13 times) would be 13/31 (41.9%), as 31 is the total of encountered variations for the ADJ_PRE_NOUN POS sequence. We also use the *instance share*, which for the same variation pattern would be 219/766 (12.0%) and combine it with the pattern share to obtain an overall share ($share_{vp}$):

$$share_{vp} = \left(\frac{\#variations_{vp}}{\#variations_{pos}} + \frac{\#instances_{vp}}{\#instances_{pos}}\right)/2$$

As a global ranking score (GRS_{vp}), the resulting average share is combined with the *spread*, namely the ratio of instances over variations (219/13 for $flex\_fix\_fix$), a pattern-internal measure indicating the average instances per variation pattern.

$$spread_{vp} = \frac{\#instances_{vp}}{\#variations_{vp}}$$

$$GRS_{vp} = share_{vp} * spread_{vp}$$

Only patterns with $GRS > 1$ are kept, with the aim of maximising precision. Evaluation is done against some POS sequences for which extracted instances have been manually annotated. Precision, recall, and f-score are reported in Table 1. Results for an unconstrained search (no pattern selection) are also included for comparison. The number of variation patterns that we keep on the basis of the ranking score includes the fix_fix_fix pattern.

From the table, we can see that in most cases precision is increased over an unconstrained match. However, while for verbal expressions the boost in precision preserves recall high, thus yielding f-scores that are always higher than for an unconstrained search, the same isn't true for adjectives and adverbs. In two cases, both featuring the same POS sequence (PRE_NOUN_ADJ) though for different expression types, recall is heavily sacrificed. In three cases, the GRS doesn't let discard any patterns, thus being of no use in boosting precision. These are cases where only two variation patterns were observed, indicating that possibly other ranking measures could be explored for better results under such conditions. In previous work we have seen that selecting variation patterns works well for nominal expressions (Nissim and Zaninello, 2013).

Overall, even though in some cases our method does not yield different results than an unconstrained search, whenever it does, precision is always higher. It is therefore worth applying whenever boosting precision is desirable.

4 Repository and Encoding

We create an XML-based repository of POS patterns with their respective variation patterns. Variation patterns per POS sequence are reported according to the ranking produced by the GRS. However, we

Table 1: Evaluation of pattern selection for some POS sequences according to the Global Ranking Score.

			GRS			unconstrained		
expr type	POS sequence	# vp kept	prec	rec	f-score	prec	rec	f-score
verbal	VER:infi_ARTPRE_NOUN	2/4	1.000	0.998	0.999	0.979	1.000	0.989
	VER:infi:cli_ART_NOUN	2/7	0.965	0.981	0.973	0.943	1.000	0.971
	VER:infi_ADV	2/4	0.997	0.978	0.987	0.951	1.000	0.975
adjectival	ADJ_PRE_NOUN	2/2	0.379	1.000	0.550	0.379	1.000	0.550
	PRE_NOUN_ADJ	1/4	1.000	0.590	0.742	0.848	1.000	0.918
	PRE_VER:fin	4/5	1.000	0.968	0.984	1.000	1.000	1.000
adverbial	PRE_ADV	2/2	0.671	1.000	0.803	0.671	1.000	0.803
	PRE_NOUN_ADJ	1/4	1.000	0.746	0.854	0.899	1.000	0.947
	PRE_ADJ	2/2	0.362	1.000	0.532	0.362	1.000	0.532

include all observed patterns equipped with the frequency information we used, so that other ranking measures or different thresholds could be applied.

The repository is intended as connected to two sources, namely a lexicon to obtain quotation forms of MWEs to be searched, and the corpus where expressions were searched, which provides the figures.

POS patterns are listed as elements for each `expression` element, whose attribute `type` specifies the grammatical type—for example "verbal". The same POS pattern can feature under different expression types, and could have different constraints on variation according to the grammatical category of the MWE (in extraction this issue would require dedicated handling, as the grammatical category is not necessarily known in advance). For the element `pattern`, which specifies the POS sequence, the attribute `mwes` indicates how many different original mews were found for that sequence, and the attributes `variations` and `instances` the number of variations and instances (Section 3). Actual patterns are listed as data of a `vp` (variation pattern) element, according to decreasing GRS, with values obtained from the reference corpus (specified via a `corpus` element). Attributes for the `vp` element are `vshare` (variation share), `ishare` (instance share), `spread`, and `grs` (see again Section 3). In Figure 1 we provide a snapshot of what the repository looks like.

The POS sequence of a MWE in the original lexicon can be matched to the same value in the repository, and so can the expression type, which should also be specified in the lexicon, so that the relative variation patterns can be inherited by the MWE.

References

M. Baroni, S. Bernardini, F. Comastri, L. Piccioni, A. Volpi, G. Aston, and M. Mazzoleni. 2004. Introducing the La Repubblica Corpus: A Large, Annotated, TEI(XML)-Compliant Corpus of Newspaper Italian. In *Proceedings of LREC 2004*, pages 1771–1774.

F. Bond, A. Korhonen, D. McCarthy, and A. Villavicencio. 2005. Multiword Expressions: Having a crack at a hard nut. *Computer Speech and Language*, 19:365–367.

N. Calzolari, C. J. Fillmore, R. Grishman, N. Ide, A. Lenci, C. MacLeod, and A. Zampolli. 2002. Towards best practice for multiword expressions in computational lexicons. In *Proceedings of LREC 2002*, pages 1934–1940.

Stefan Evert and Brigitte Krenn. 2005. Using small random samples for the manual evaluation of statistical association measures. *Computer Speech & Language*, 19(4):450–466. Special issue on Multiword Expressions.

Adele Goldberg. 2003. Constructions: a new theoretical approach to language. *Trends in Cognitive Sciences*, 7(5):219–224.

Nicole Grégoire. 2010. DuELME: a Dutch electronic lexicon of multiword expressions. *Language Resources and Evaluation*, 44(1-2):23–39.

Francesca Masini. 2007. *Parole sintagmatiche in italiano*. Ph.D. thesis, University of Roma Tre, Rome, Italy.

Malvina Nissim and Andrea Zaninello. 2011. A quantitative study on the morphology of Italian multiword expressions. *Lingue e Linguaggio*, X:283–300.

Malvina Nissim and Andrea Zaninello. 2013. Modelling the internal variability of multiword expressions through a pattern-based method. *ACM Transactions on Speech and Language Processing*, Special issue on Multiword Expressions.

```
<corpus name="larepubblica">
 <expression type="verbal">
  <patterns>
   <pattern pos="VER:infi_ARTPRE_NOUN" mwes="55" variations="671" instances="9046">
    <vp vshare="0.896" ishare"0.740" spread="42.1" grs="9.109">flex_fix_fix</vp>
    <vp vshare="0.082" ishare"0.256" spread="11.1" grs="7.127">fix_fix_fix</vp>
    <vp vshare="0.016" ishare"0.003" spread="2.6" grs="0.026">flex_flex_fix</vp>
    <vp vshare="0.006" ishare"0.000" spread="1.2" grs="0.004">flex_flex_flex</vp>
   </pattern>
   <pattern pos="VER:infi:cli_ART_NOUN" mwes="41" variations="600" instances="3703">
    <vp vshare="0.065" ishare"0.267" spread="25.3" grs="4.203">fix_fix_fix</vp>
    <vp vshare="0.893" ishare"0.723" spread="5" grs="4.040">flex_fix_fix</vp>
    <vp vshare="0.030" ishare"0.008" spread="1.6" grs="0.029">flex_flex_flex</vp>
    <vp vshare="0.005" ishare"0.000" spread="1" grs="0.003">flex_flex_fix</vp>
    <vp vshare="0.003" ishare"0.000" spread="1" grs="0.002">fix_flex_flex</vp>
    <vp vshare="0.002" ishare"0.000" spread="2" grs="0.002">fix_flex_fix</vp>
    <vp vshare="0.002" ishare"0.000" spread="1" grs="0.000">flex_fix_flex</vp>
   </pattern>
   <pattern ...>
    ...
   </pattern>
  </patterns>
 </expression>
 <expression type="adverbial">
  <patterns>
   <pattern pos="PRE_NOUN_ADJ" mwes="53" variations="79" instances="12202">
    <vp vshare="0.671" ishare"0.989" spread="227.7" grs="189.0">fix_fix_fix</vp>
    <vp vshare="0.076" ishare"0.007" spread="14" grs="0.580">fix_flex_flex</vp>
    <vp vshare="0.190" ishare"0.004" spread="2.9" grs="0.284">fix_fix_flex</vp>
    <vp vshare="0.063" ishare"0.000" spread="1" grs="0.032">fix_fix_fix</vp>
   </pattern>
   ...
  </patterns>
 </expression>
 <expression type="adjectival">
  <patterns>
   ...
  </patterns>
 </expression>
</corpus>
```

Figure 1: Snapshot of the XML repository of variation patterns over POS patterns, listed by expression types. See text for element and attribute explanation..

J. Odijk. 2004. A proposed standard for the lexical representation of idioms. In *Proceedings of EURALEX 2004*, pages 153–164.

Emanuele Pianta and Luisa Bentivogli. 2004. Annotating discontinuous structures in xml: the multiword case. In *Proceedings of LREC Workshop on XML-based Richly Annotated Corpora*, pages 30–37, Lisbon, Portugal.

Carlos Ramisch, Aline Villavicencio, and Christian Boitet. 2010. mwetoolkit: a framework for multiword expression identification. In Nicoletta Calzolari, Khalid Choukri, Bente Maegaard, Joseph Mariani, Jan Odijk, Stelios Piperidis, Mike Rosner, and Daniel Tapias, editors, *Proceedings of the International Conference on Language Resources and Evaluation, LREC 2010, 17-23 May 2010, Valletta, Malta*. European Language Resources Association.

Marion Weller and Ulrich Heid. 2010. Extraction of German Multiword Expressions from Parsed Corpora Using Context Features. In *Proceedings of the seventh conference on International Language Resources and Evaluation (LREC 2010)*, pages 3195–3201. European Language Resources Association.

Andrea Zaninello and Malvina Nissim. 2010. Creation of Lexical Resources for a Characterisation of Multiword Expressions in Italian. In *Proceedings of LREC 2010*, pages 655–661, Valletta, Malta, may. European Language Resources Association (ELRA).

Syntactic Identification of Occurrences of Multiword Expressions in Text using a Lexicon with Dependency Structures

Eduard Bejček, Pavel Straňák, Pavel Pecina
Charles University in Prague, Faculty of Mathematics and Physics,
Institute of Formal and Applied Linguistics
Malostranské náměstí 25, 118 00 Praha 1, Czechia
{bejcek,stranak,pecina}@ufal.mff.cuni.cz

Abstract

We deal with syntactic identification of occurrences of multiword expression (MWE) from an existing dictionary in a text corpus. The MWEs we identify can be of arbitrary length and can be interrupted in the surface sentence. We analyse and compare three approaches based on linguistic analysis at a varying level, ranging from surface word order to deep syntax. The evaluation is conducted using two corpora: the Prague Dependency Treebank and Czech National Corpus. We use the dictionary of multiword expressions SemLex, that was compiled by annotating the Prague Dependency Treebank and includes deep syntactic dependency trees of all MWEs.

1 Introduction

Multiword expressions (MWEs) exist on the interface of syntax, semantics, and lexicon, yet they are almost completely absent from major syntactic theories and semantic formalisms. They also have interesting morphological properties and for all these reasons, they are important, but challenging for Natural Language Processing (NLP). Recent advances show that taking MWEs into account can improve NLP tasks such as dependency parsing (Nivre and Nilsson, 2004; Eryiğit et al., 2011), constituency parsing (Arun and Keller, 2005), text generation (Hogan et al., 2007), or machine translation (Carpuat and Diab, 2010).

The Prague Dependency Treebank (PDT) of Czech and the associated lexicon of MWEs SemLex[1] offer a unique opportunity for experimentation with MWEs. In this paper, we focus on identification of their syntactic structures in the treebank using various levels of linguistic analysis and matching algorithms.[2] We compare approaches operating on manually and automatically annotated data with various depth of annotation from two sources: the Prague Dependency Treebank and Czech National Corpus (CNC).

The remainder of the paper is organised as follows. Section 2 describes the state of the art of in acquisition and identification of MWEs. Section 3 explains what we consider a MWE. In Section 4 we describe the data used for our experiments. Section 5 gives the details of our experiments, and in Section 6 we analyse and discuss the results. Conclusions from the analysis are drawn in Section 7.

2 Processing of Multiword Expressions and Related Work

Automatic processing of multiword expressions includes two distinct (but interlinked) tasks. Most of the effort has been put into **acquisition** of MWEs appearing in a particular text corpus into a lexicon of MWEs (types) not necessarily linked with their occurrences (instances) in the text. The best-performing methods are usually based on lexical association measures that exploit statistical evidence of word occurrences and co-occurrences acquired from a corpus to determine degree of lexical association between words (Pecina, 2005). Expressions that consist of words with high association are then

[1] http://ufal.mff.cuni.cz/lexemann/mwe/semlex.zip

[2] We do not aim at disambiguating the occurrences as figurative or literal. We have not observed enough literal uses to substantiate working on this step. There are bigger improvements to be gained from better identification of syntactic occurrences.

denoted as MWEs. Most of the current approaches are limited to bigrams despite the fact that higher-order MWEs are quite common.

The task of **identification** of MWE occurrences expects a list of MWEs as the input and identifies their occurrences (instances) in a corpus. This may seem to be a trivial problem. However, the complex nature of this phenomenon gives rise to problems on all linguistic levels of analysis: morphology, syntax, and semantics.

In *morphologically* complex languages, a single MWE can appear in a number of morphological variants, which differ in forms of their individual components; and at the same time, a sequence of words whose base forms match with base forms of components of a given MWE do not necessarily represent an instance of this MWE (*Pracoval dnem i nocí / He's been working day and night* vs. *Ti dva byli jako den a noc / Those two were as day and night*).

MWEs differ in the level of *syntactic* fixedness. On the one hand, certain MWEs can be modified by inserting words in between their components or by changing word order. Such expressions can only be identified by matching their syntactic structures, but only if a reliable syntactic information is available in both the lexion and text (*Po převratu padaly hlavy / After the coup, heads were rolling* vs. *Hlavy zkorumpovaných náměstků budou padat jedna za druhou / One head of a corrupt deputy will be rolling after the other*). On the other hand, some MWEs can appear only as fixed expressions with no modifications allowed. In that case, the syntactic matching approach can miss-indicate their instances because of an inserted word or altered word order (*Vyšší společnost / High society* vs. **Vyšší bohatší společnost / High rich society*).

From the *semantic* point of view, MWEs are often characterized by more or less non-compositional (figurative) meaning. Their components, however, can also occur with the same syntax but compositional (literal) semantics, and therefore not acting as MWEs (*Jedinou branku dal až v poslední minutě zápasu / He scored his only goal in the last minute of the match.* vs. *Rozhodčí dal branku zpět na své místo / The referee put a goal back to its place*).

Automatic discrimination between figurative and literal meaning is a challenging task similar to word sense disambiguation which has been studied extensively: Katz and Giesbrecht (2006), Cook et al. (2007), Hashimoto and Kawahara (2008), Li and Sporleder (2009), and Fothergill and Baldwin (2011). Seretan (2010) includes MWE identification (based on a lexicon) in a syntactic parser and reports an improvement of parsing quality. As a by-product, the parser identified occurrences of MWEs from a lexicon. Similarly, Green et al. (2013) embed identification of some MWEs in a Tree Substitution Grammar and achieve improvement both in parsing quality and MWE identification effectiveness. None of these works, however, attempt to identify all MWEs, regardless their length or complexity, which is the main goal of this paper.

3 Definition of Multiword Expressions

We can use the rough definition of MWEs put forward by Sag et al. (2002): *"idiosyncratic interpretations that cross word boundaries (or spaces)"*. We can also start from their – or Bauer's (1983) – basic classification of MWEs as *lexicalised* or *institutionalised phrases*, where lexicalised phrases include some syntactic, semantic or lexical (i.e. word form) element, that is idiosyncratic. Institutionalised phrases are syntactically and semantically compositional, but still require a particular lexical choice, e.g. disallowing synonyms (mobile phone, but not *movable phone).

We need to make just one small adjustment to the above: "phrase" above must be understood as a subtree, i.e. it can have holes in the surface sentence, but not in terms of a dependency tree.

In reality there is no clear boundary, in particular between the institutional phrases and other collocations. Like many other traditional linguistic categories, cf. Manning (2003), this phenomenon seems to be more continuous than categorial.

For the purpose of this paper, however, it is not important at all. We simply try to find all instances of the expressions (subtrees) from a lexicon in a text, whatever form the expression may take in a sentence.

4 Data

In this work we use two datasets: Czech National Corpus (CNC), version SYN2006-PUB, and the

Prague Dependency Treebank (PDT), version 2.5. We run and compare results of our experiments on both manual annotation of PDT, and automatic analysis of both PDT and CNC (see Section 5.3). We also make use of SemLex, a lexicon of MWEs in the PDT featuring their dependency structures that is described in Section 4.3.

4.1 Corpora – Czech National Corpus and Prague Dependency Treebank

CNC is a large[3] corpus of Czech. Its released versions are automatically segmented and they contain automatic morphological tagging (Hajič, 2004).

PDT (Bejček et al., 2011) is a smaller news-domain corpus based on a subset of the news section of CNC. It contains approx. 0.8 million words that have three layers of annotation: morphological, analytical (surface syntax), and tectogrammatical (deep syntax).

Annotation of a sentence on the *morphological layer* consists of attaching morphological lemma and tag to the tokens. A sentence at the *analytical layer* is represented as a rooted ordered tree with labelled nodes. The dependency relation between two nodes is captured by an edge with a functional label. On the *tectogrammatical layer* only content words form nodes in a tree (t-nodes).[4] Auxiliary words are represented by various attributes of t-nodes, as they do not have their own lexical meaning, but rather modify the meaning of the content words. Each t-node has a t-lemma: an attribute whose value is the node's basic lexical form, and a dependency function that relates it to its parent. Figure 1 shows the relations between the neighbouring layers of PDT.

4.2 MWE in Prague Dependency Treebank 2.5

In the Functional Generative Description (Sgall et al., 1986, FGD)[5] the tectogrammatical layer is construed as a *layer of the linguistic meaning* of text. This meaning is composed by means of "deep" (tecto-grammatical) syntax from single-meaning-carrying units: monosemic lexemes.

[3]It contains 200 mil. words in SYN2000, 600 mil. in SYN2006-PUB; http://www.korpus.cz.

[4]with a few exceptions (personal pronouns or coord. heads)

[5]FGD is a framework for systematic description of a language, that the PDT project is based upon.

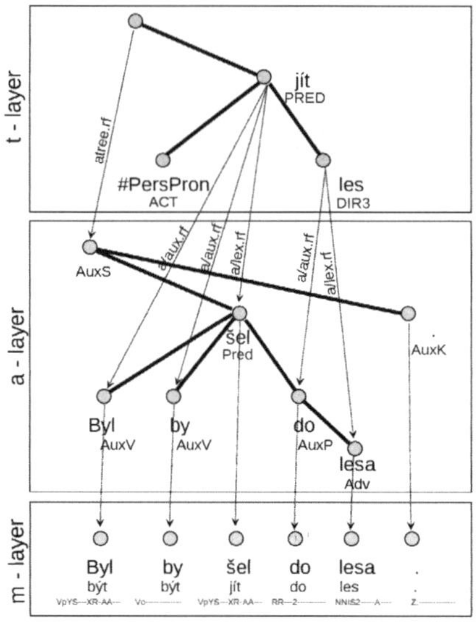

Figure 1: A visualisation of the annotation schema of PDT. Lit.: "[He] would have gone into forest."

In order to better facilitate this concept of t-layer, all multiword expressions in the release of PDT 2.5 (Bejček et al., 2011) have been annotated and they are by default displayed as single units, although their inner structure is still retained.

A lexicon of the MWEs has been compiled. A simple view of the result of this annotation is given in the Figure 2. A detailed description can be found in Bejček and Straňák (2010), and Straňák (2010). The MWEs in PDT 2.5 include both multiword lexemes (phrasemes, idioms) and named entities (NEs). In the present work we ignore the named entities, concentrating on the lexemes. Some NEs (names of persons, geographical entities) share characteristics of multiword lexemes, other NEs do not (addresses, bibliographic information).

We build on the PDT 2.5 data and MWE lexicon SemLex (Section 4.3) to evaluate the approach with various automatic methods for detection of MWEs.

4.3 Lexicon of MWEs – SemLex

SemLex is the lexicon of all the MWEs annotators identified during the preparation of PDT 2.5 t-layer. In the PDT 2.5 these instances of MWEs can then be displayed as single nodes and all the MWEs themselves are compiled in the SemLex lexicon. The lexicon itself is freely available. See `http://ufal.mff.cuni.cz/lexemann/mwe/`. Length (size)

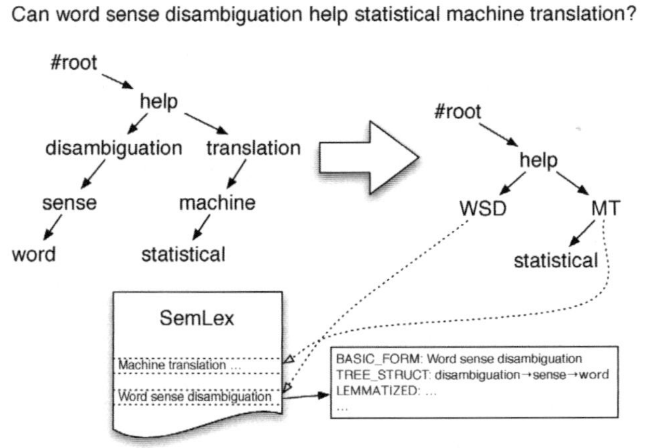

Figure 2: An illustration of changes in t-trees in PDT 2.5; every MWE forms a single node and has its lexicon entry

a) len	types	instances
2	7063	18914
3	1260	2449
4	305	448
5	100	141
6	42	42
7	16	15
8	4	5
9	4	3
11	1	0
12	2	2

b) len	types	instances
1[8]	148	534
2	7444	19490
3	843	1407
4	162	244
5	34	32
6	13	8
7	3	1
8	4	1
9	1	1
10	0	0

Table 1: Distribution of MWE length in terms of words (a) and t-nodes (b) in SemLex (types) and PDT (instances).

distribution of MWEs in PDT 2.5 is given in Table 1.

There are three attributes of SemLex entries crucial for our task:

BASIC_FORM – The basic form of a MWE. In many languages including Czech it often contains word forms in other than the basic form for the given word on its own. E.g. "vysoké učení" contains a neuter suffix of the adjective "vysoký" (high) because of the required agreement in gender with the noun, whereas the traditional lemma of adjectives in Czech is in the masculine form.

LEMMATIZED – "Lemmatised BASIC_FORM", i.e. take the basic form of an entry and substitute each form with its morphological lemma. This attribute is used for the identification of MWEs on the morphological layer. For more details see Section 5.

TREE_STRUCT (TS) – A simplified tectogrammatical dependency tree structure of an entry. Each node in this tree structure has only two attributes: its tectogrammatical lemma, and a reference to its effective parent.

4.4 Enhancing SemLex for the Experiments

SemLex contains all the information we use for the identification of MWEs on t-layer.[6] It also contains basic information we use for MWE identification on m-layer: the *basic form* and the *lemmatized form* of each entry. For the experiments with MWE identification on analytical (surface syntactic) layer we need to add some information about the surface syntactic structures of MWEs. Given the annotated occurrences of MWEs in the t-layer and links from t-layer to a-layer, the extraction is straightforward. Since one tectogrammatical TS can correspond to several analytical TSs that contain auxiliaries and use morphological lemmas, we add a list of a-layer TSs with their frequency in data to each SemLex entry (MWE). In reality the difference between t-layer and a-layer is unfortunately not as big as one could expect. Lemmas of t-nodes still often include even minute morphological variants, which goes against the vision of tectogrammatics, as described in Sgall et al. (1986).[7] Our methods would benefit from more unified t-lemmas, see also Section 6.2.

5 Methodology of Experiments

SemLex – with its almost 8,000 types of MWEs and their 22,000 instances identified in PDT – allows us to measure accuracy of MWE identification on various layers, since it is linked with the different layers of PDT 2.5. In this section, we present the method for identification of MWEs on t-layer in comparison with identification on a-layer and m-layer. The

[6]Automatic identification of MWES was, after all, one of the reasons for its construction.

[7]These variants are unified in FGD theory, but time consuming to annotate in practice. Therefore, this aspect was left out from the current version of PDT.

[8]Indeed, there are expressions that are multiword, but "single-node". E.g.: the preposition in *bez váhání* (without hesitation) does not have its own node on t-layer; the phrase *na správnou míru* (lit.: into correct scale) is already annotated as one phrasal node in PDT with the lemma "na_správnou_míru"; the verbal expression *umět si představit* (can imagine) has again only one node for reflexive verb "představit_si" plus an attribute for the ability (representing "umět" as explained in Section 4.1).

idea of using tectogrammatical TS for identification is that with a proper tectogrammatical layer (as it is proposed in FGD, i.e. with correct lemmatisation, added nodes in place of ellipses, etc.), this approach should have the highest Precision.

Our approach to identification of MWEs in this work is purely syntactic. We simply try to find MWEs from a lexicon in any form they may take (including partial ellipses in coordination, etc.). We do not try to exploit semantics, instead we want to put a solid baseline for future work which may do so, as mentioned in Section 2.

5.1 MWE Identification on t-layer

We assume that each occurrence of a given MWE has the same t-lemmas and the same t-layer structure anywhere in the text. During the manual construction of SemLex, these tectogrammatical *"tree structures"* (TSs) were extracted from PDT 2.5 and inserted into the lexicon. In general this approach works fine and for majority of MWEs only one TS was obtained. For the MWEs with more than one TS in data we used the most frequent one. These cases are due to some problems of t-layer, not deficiencies of the theoretical approach. See section 6.2 for the discussion of the problems.

These TSs are taken one by one and we try to find them in the tectogrammatical structures of the input sentences. Input files are processed in parallel. The criteria for matching are so far only t-lemmas and topology of the subtree.[9] Comparison of tree structures is done from the deepest node and we consider only perfect matches of structure and t-lemmata.

5.2 MWE Identification on a-layer and m-layer

We use identification of MWE occurrences on a-layer and m-layer mainly for comparison with our approach based on the t-layer.

We enhance SemLex with a-tree structures as explained in Section 4.4, and then **a-layer** is processed in the same manner as t-layer: analytical TS is taken from the SemLex and the algorithm tries to match it to all a-trees. Again, if more than one TS is offered in lexicon, only the most frequent one is used for searching.

MWE identification on the **m-layer** is based on matching lemmas (which is the only morphological information we use). The process is parametrised by a width of a window which restricts the maximum distance (in a sentence) of MWE components to span (irrespective of their order) measured in the surface word order. However, in the setting which does not miss any MWE in a sentence (100% Recall), this parameter is set to the whole sentence and the maximum distance is not restricted at all.

The algorithm processes each sentence at a time, and tries to find all lemmas the MWE consists of, running in a cycle over all MWEs in SemLex. This method naturally over-generates – it correctly finds all MWEs that have all their words present in the surface sentence with correct lemmatisation (high Recall), but it also marks words as parts of some MWE even if they appear at the opposite ends of the sentence by complete coincidence (false positives, low Precision).

In other experiments, the window width varies from two to ten and MWE is searched for within a limited context.

5.3 Automatic Analysis of Data Sets

The three MWE identification methods are applied on three corpora:

• **manually annotated PDT:** This is the same data, from which the lexicon was created. Results evaluated on the same data can be seen only as numbers representing the maximum that can be obtained.

• **automatically annotated PDT:** These are the same texts (PDT), but their analysis (morphological, analytical as well as tectogrammatical) started from scratch. Results can be still biased – first, there are no new lexemes that did not appear during annotation (that is as if we had a complete lexicon); second, it should be evaluated only on eval part of the data – see discussion in Section 6.1.

• **automatically annotated CNC:** Automatic analysis from scratch on different sentences. The

[9] It is not sufficient, though. Auxiliary words that are ignored on t-layer are occasionally necessary for distinguishing MWE from similar group of nodes. (E.g. *"v tomto směru"* (*"in this regard"*) is an MWE whereas *"o tomto směru"* (*"about this direction"*) is not.) There are also attributes in t-layer that are—although rarely—important for distinguishing the meaning. (E.g. words typeset in bold in *"Leonardo* ***dal*** *svým* ***gólem*** *signál."* (*"Leonardo signalled by his goal."*) compose exactly the same structure as in *"Leonardo* ***dal gól.***" (*"Leonardo scored a goal."*). I.e., the dependency relation is "*dal* governs *gól*" in both cases. The difference is in the dependency function of *gól*: it is either MEANS or DIRECT_OBJECT (CPHR).)

layer/span	PDT/man	PDT/auto	CNC/auto
tecto	61.99 / 95.95 / 75.32	63.40 / 86.32 / 73.11	44.44 / 58.00 / 50.33
analytical	66.11 / 88.67 / 75.75	66.09 / 81.96 / 73.18	45.22 / 60.00 / 51.58
morpho / 2	67.76 / 79.96 / 73.36	67.77 / 79.26 / 73.07	51.85 / 56.00 / 53.85
3	62.65 / 90.50 / 74.05	62.73 / 89.80 / 73.86	46.99 / 60.00 / 52.70
4	58.84 / 92.03 / 71.78	58.97 / 91.29 / 71.65	42.83 / 61.33 / 50.48
5	56.46 / 92.94 / 70.25	56.59 / 92.16 / 70.12	40.09 / 61.33 / 48.49
6	54.40 / 93.29 / 68.81	54.64 / 92.51 / 68.70	38.27 / 61.33 / 47.13
7	52.85 / 93.42 / 67.51	53.01 / 92.64 / 67.43	36.99 / 61.33 / 46.15
8	51.39 / 93.46 / 66.32	51.57 / 92.68 / 66.27	35.59 / 61.33 / 45.04
9	50.00 / 93.46 / 65.15	50.18 / 92.68 / 65.11	34.67 / 61.33 / 44.30
10	48.57 / 93.46 / 63.92	48.71 / 92.68 / 63.86	33.84 / 61.33 / 43.64
∞	35.12 / 93.51 / 51.06	35.16 / 92.72 / 50.99	22.70 / 62.00 / 33.24
	P / R / F	P / R / F	P / R / F

Table 2: Evaluation of all our experiments in terms of Precision (P), Recall (R) and F_1 score (F) in percent. Experiments on the m-layer are shown for different widths of window (see Section 5.2).

disadvantage here is the absence of gold data. Manual evaluation of results has to be accomplished.

For the automatic analysis we use the modular NLP workflow system Treex (Popel and Žabokrtský, 2010). Both datasets were analysed by the standard Treex scenario "Analysis of Czech" that includes the following major blocks:

1) standard rule-based Treex segmentation and tokenisation
2) morphology (Hajič, 2004) and Featurama tagger (Spousta, 2011) trained on the *train* part of the PDT
3) MST Parser with an improved set of features by Novák and Žabokrtský (2007)
4) and t-trees structure provided by standard rule-based Treex block.

6 Results

Effectiveness of our methods of identification of MWE occurrences is presented in Table 2. Numbers are given as percentages of Precision and Recall The first two columns show the results of the evaluation against gold data in PDT 2.5, the third column reflects the manual evaluation on 546 sentences. The results obtained for PDT (the first two columns) are also visualised in Figure 3.

The important issue to be decided when evaluating MWE identification is whether partial match between automatic identification and gold data MWE is to be counted. Because of cases containing ellipses (see Section 6.2), it can happen that longer MWE is used for annotation of its subset in text.[10] We do not want to penalise automatic identification (either performing this behaviour or confronted with it in the gold data), so we treated subset as a match.

Another decision is that although the MWEs cannot be nested in gold data, we accept it for automatic identification. Since one word can belong to several MWEs, the Recall rises, while Precision declines.[11]

6.1 Discussion of Results

The automatically parsed part of the CNC consists of 546 sentences. Thus the third column in Table 2 represents evaluation on a much smaller data set. During manual annotation of this data carried out by one annotator (different from those who annotated PDT data, but using the same methodology and a tool), 163 occurences of MWEs were found. Out

[10]Let us say, only elliptic term *Ministry of Industry* is seen in the data (instead of the full name *Ministry of Industry and Trade*) annotated by the full-term lexicon entry. Whenever *Ministry of Industry and Trade* is spotted in the test data, its first part is identified. Should that be qualified as a mistake when confronted with the gold annotation of the whole term? The assigned lexicon entry is the same – only the extent is different.

[11]For example, annotator had to choose only one MWE to annotate in *vládní návrh zákona o dani z příjmu* (lit.: government proposal of the Law on Income Tax), while it is allowed to automatically identify *vládní návrh zákona*, *zákon o dani* and *daň z příjmu* together with the whole phrase. Recall for this example is 1, whereas Precision is 0.25.

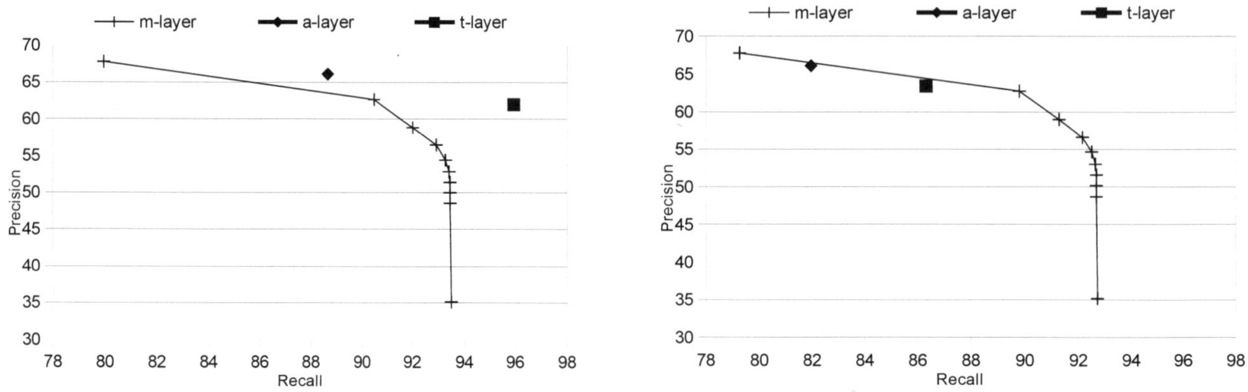

Figure 3: Precision–Recall scores of identification of MWE structures on manually/automatically annotated PDT.

of them, 46 MWEs were out-of-vocabulary expressions: they could not be found by automatic precedure using the original SemLex lexicon.

Note that results obtained using automatically parsed PDT are very close to those for manual data on all layers (see Table 2). The reasons need to be analysed in more detail. Our hypotheses are:

- M-layer identification reaches the same results on both data. It is caused by the fact that the accuracy of morphological tagging is comparable to manual morphological annotation: 95.68% (Spoustová, 2008).
- Both a- and t-parsers have problems mostly in complex constructions such as coordinations, that very rarely appear inside MWEs.

There are generally two issues that hurt our accuracy and that we want to improve to get better results. First, better data can help. Second, the method can always be improved. In our case, all data are annotated—we do nothing on plain text—and it can be expected that with a better parser, but also possibly a better manual annotation we can do better, too. The room for improvement is bigger as we go deeper into the syntax: data are not perfect on the a-layer (both automatically parsed and gold data) and on the significantly more complex t-layer it gets even worse. By contrast, the complexity of methods and therefore possible improvements go in the opposite direction. The complexity of tectogrammatic annotation results in a tree with rich, complex attributes of t-nodes, but simple topology and generalised lemmas. Since we only use tree topology and lemmas, the t-layer method can be really simple. It is slightly more complex on the a-layer (with auxiliary nodes, for example); and finally on the m-layer there is virtually unlimited space for experiments and a lot of literature on that problem. As we can see, these two issues (improving data and improving the method) complement each other with changing ratio on individual layers.

It is not quite clear from Table 2 that MWE identification should be done on the t-layer, because it is currently far from our ideal. It is also not clear that it should be done on the m-layer, because it seems that the syntax is necessary for this task.

6.2 Error Analysis and Possible Improvements

There are several reasons, why the t-layer results are not clearly better:

1. our representation of tree structures proved a bit too simple,
2. there are some deficiencies in the current t-layer parser, and
3. t-layer in PDT has some limitations relative to the ideal tectogrammatical layer.

Ad 1. We thought the current SemLex implementation of simple tree structures would be sufficient for our purpose, but it is clear now that it is *too simple* and results in ambiguities. At least auxiliary words and some further syntactico-semantic information (such as tectogrammatical functions) should be added to all nodes in these TSs.

Ad 2. Current tectogrammatical parser does not do several things we would like to use. E.g. it cannot properly generate t-nodes for elided parts of coordinated MWEs that we need in order to have the same TS of all MWE occurrences (see below).

Ad 3. The total of 771 out of 8,816 SemLex entries, i.e. 8.75%, have been used with more than one tectogrammatical tree structure in the PDT 2.5. That argues against our hypothesis (stated in Section 5.1) and cause false negatives in the output, since we currently search for only one TS. In this part we analyze two of the most important sources of these inconsistent t-trees and possible improvements:

• *Gender opposites, diminutives and lemma variations.* These are currently represented by variations of t-lemma. We believe that they should rather be represented by attributes of t-nodes that could be roughly equivalent to some of the lexical functions in the Meaning-text theory (see Mel'čuk (1996)). This should be tackled in some future version of PDT. Once resolved it would allow us to identify following (and many similar) cases automatically.

- *obchodní ředitel* vs. *obchodní ředitelka* (lit.: managing director-man vs. managing director-woman)
- *rodinný dům* vs. *rodinný domek* (lit.: family house vs. family little-house; but the diminutive *domek* does not indicate that the house is small)
- *občanský zákon* vs. *občanský zákoník* (lit.: citizen law vs. citizen law-codex, meaning the same thing in modern Czech)

These cases were annotated as instances of the same MWE, with a vision of future t-lemmas disregarding this variation. Until that happens, however, we cannot identify the MWEs with these variations automatically using the most frequent TS only.

• *Elided parts of MWEs in coordinations.* Although t-layer contains many newly established t-nodes in place of elided words, not all t-nodes needed for easy MWE annotation were there. This decision resulted in the situation, when some MWEs in coordinations cannot be correctly annotated, esp. in case of coordination of several multiword lexemes like *inženýrská, montážní a stavební společnost* (engineering, assembling and building company), there is only one t-node for *company*. Thus the MWE *inženýrská společnost / engineering company* is not in PDT 2.5 data and cannot be found by the t-layer identification method. It can, however, be found by the m-layer surface method, provided the window is large enough and MWEs can overlap.

7 Conclusions

Identification of occurrences of multiword expressions in text has not been extensively studied yet although it is very important for a lot of NLP applications. Our lexicon SemLex is a unique resource with almost 9 thousand MWEs, each of them with a tree-structure extracted from data. We use this resource to evaluate methods for automatic identification of MWE occurrences in text based on matching syntactic tree structures (tectogrammatical – deep-syntactic, and analytical – surface-syntactic trees) and sequences of lemmas in the surface sentence.

The theoretically ideal approach based on tectogrammatical layer turned out not to perform better, mainly due to the imperfectness of the t-layer implemented in PDT and also due to the low accuracy of automatic tectogrammatical parser. It still shows very high Recall, as expected – due to simple topology of the trees – however Precision is not ideal. Morphology-based MWE identification guarantees high Recall (especially when no limits are put on the MWE component distance) but Precision of this approach is rather low. On the other hand, if the maximum distance is set to 4–5 words we get a very interesting trade-off between Precision and Recall. Using analytical layer (and thus introducing surface syntax to the solution) might be a good approach for many applications, too. It provides high Precision as well as reasonable Recall.

Acknowledgements

This research was supported by the Czech Science Foundation (grant n. P103/12/G084 and P406/2010/0875). This work has been using language resources developed and/or stored and/or distributed by the LINDAT-Clarin project of the Ministry of Education of the Czech Republic (project LM2010013). We want to thank to our colleagues Michal Novák, Martin Popel and Ondřej Dušek for providing the automatic annotation of the PDT and CNC data.

References

Abhishek Arun and Frank Keller. 2005. Lexicalization in crosslinguistic probabilistic parsing: The case of French. In *Proceedings of the 43rd Annual Meeting of the Association for Computational Linguistics (ACL'05)*, pages 306–313, Ann Arbor, Michigan.

Laurie Bauer. 1983. *English Word-formation*. Cambridge Textbooks in Linguistics. Cambridge University Press.

Eduard Bejček and Pavel Straňák. 2010. Annotation of multiword expressions in the Prague dependency treebank. *Language Resources and Evaluation*, (44):7–21.

Eduard Bejček, Jarmila Panevová, Jan Popelka, Lenka Smejkalová, Pavel Straňák, Magda Ševčíková, Jan Štěpánek, Josef Toman, Zdeněk Žabokrtský, and Jan Hajič. 2011. Prague dependency treebank 2.5. `http://hdl.handle.net/11858/00-097C-0000-0006-DB11-8`. Data.

Marine Carpuat and Mona Diab. 2010. Task-based evaluation of multiword expressions: a pilot study in statistical machine translation. In *Human Language Technologies: The 2010 Annual Conference of the North American Chapter of the Association for Computational Linguistics*, HLT '10, pages 242–245, Stroudsburg, PA, USA.

Paul Cook, Afsaneh Fazly, and Suzanne Stevenson. 2007. Pulling their weight: exploiting syntactic forms for the automatic identification of idiomatic expressions in context. In *Proceedings of the Workshop on a Broader Perspective on Multiword Expressions*, MWE '07, pages 41–48.

Gülşen Eryiğit, Tugay İlbay, and Ozan Arkan Can. 2011. Multiword expressions in statistical dependency parsing. In *Proceedings of the Second Workshop on Statistical Parsing of Morphologically Rich Languages*, SPMRL '11, pages 45–55, Stroudsburg, PA, USA. Association for Computational Linguistics.

Richard Fothergill and Timothy Baldwin. 2011. Fleshing it out: A supervised approach to MWE-token and MWE-type classification. In *Proceedings of 5th International Joint Conference on Natural Language Processing*, pages 911–919, Chiang Mai, Thailand.

Spence Green, Marie-Catherine de Marneffe, and Christopher D. Manning. 2013. Parsing models for identifying multiword expressions. *Computational Linguistics*, 39(1):195–227.

Jan Hajič. 2004. *Disambiguation of Rich Inflection (Computational Morphology of Czech)*. Nakladatelství Karolinum.

Chikara Hashimoto and Daisuke Kawahara. 2008. Construction of an idiom corpus and its application to idiom identification based on WSD incorporating idiom-specific features. In *Proceedings of the Conference on Empirical Methods in Natural Language Processing*, EMNLP '08, pages 992–1001.

Deirdre Hogan, Conor Cafferkey, Aoife Cahill, and Josef van Genabith. 2007. Exploiting multi-word units in history-based probabilistic generation. In *EMNLP-CoNLL*, pages 267–276. ACL.

Graham Katz and Eugenie Giesbrecht. 2006. Automatic identification of non-compositional multi-word expressions using latent semantic analysis. In *Proceedings of the Workshop on Multiword Expressions: Identifying and Exploiting Underlying Properties*, MWE '06, pages 12–19.

Linlin Li and Caroline Sporleder. 2009. Classifier combination for contextual idiom detection without labelled data. In *Proceedings of the 2009 Conference on Empirical Methods in Natural Language Processing: Volume 1 - Volume 1*, EMNLP '09, pages 315–323.

Christopher D. Manning, 2003. *Probabilistic Linguistics*, chapter Probabilistic Syntax, pages 289–341. MIT Press, Cambridge, MA.

Igor Mel'čuk. 1996. Lexical functions: A tool for the description of lexical relations in a lexicon. In Leo Wanner, editor, *Lexical Functions in Lexicography and Natural Language Processing*, volume 31 of *Studies in Language Companion Series*, pages 37–102. John Benjamins.

Joachim Nivre and Jens Nilsson. 2004. Multiword units in syntactic parsing. In *Dias, G., Lopes, J. G. P. and Vintar, S. (eds.) MEMURA 2004 - Methodologies and Evaluation of Multiword Units in Real-World Applications, Workshop at LREC 2004*, pages 39–46, Lisbon, Portugal.

Václav Novák and Zdeněk Žabokrtský. 2007. Feature engineering in maximum spanning tree dependency parser. In Václav Matoušek and Pavel Mautner, editors, *Lecture Notes in Artificial Intelligence, Proceedings of the 10th International Conference on Text, Speech and Dialogue*, volume 4629 of *Lecture Notes in Computer Science*, pages 92–98, Berlin / Heidelberg. Springer.

Pavel Pecina. 2005. An extensive empirical study of collocation extraction methods. In *Proceedings of the ACL Student Research Workshop*, pages 13–18, Ann Arbor, Michigan.

Martin Popel and Zdeněk Žabokrtský. 2010. TectoMT: Modular NLP framework. In Hrafn Loftsson, Eirikur Rögnvaldsson, and Sigrun Helgadottir, editors, *Lecture Notes in Artificial Intelligence, Proceedings of the 7th International Conference on Advances in Natural Language Processing (IceTAL 2010)*, volume 6233 of *LNCS*, pages 293–304, Berlin / Heidelberg. Iceland Centre for Language Technology (ICLT), Springer.

Ivan A. Sag, Timothy Baldwin, Francis Bond, Ann Copestake, and Dan Flickinger. 2002. Multiword expressions: A pain in the neck for NLP. In *Computational Linguistics and Intelligent Text Processing: Third International Conference, CICLing*, volume 2276/2002 of *Lecture Notes in Computer Science*. Springer Berlin / Heidelberg.

Violeta Seretan. 2010. *Syntax-Based Collocation Extraction*, volume 44 of *Text, Speech and Language Technology*. Springer.

Petr Sgall, Eva Hajičová, and Jarmila Panevová. 1986. *The Meaning of the Sentence in Its Semantic and Pragmatic Aspects*. Academia/Reidel Publ. Comp., Praha/Dordrecht.

Miroslav Spousta. 2011. Featurama. `http://sourceforge.net/projects/featurama/`. Software.

Drahomíra "johanka" Spoustová. 2008. Combining statistical and rule-based approaches to morphological tagging of Czech texts. *The Prague Bulletin of Mathematical Linguistics*, 89:23–40.

Pavel Straňák. 2010. *Annotation of Multiword Expressions in The Prague Dependency Treebank*. Ph.D. thesis, Charles University in Prague.

Combining Different Features of Idiomaticity for the Automatic Classification of Noun+Verb Expressions in Basque

Antton Gurrutxaga
Elhuyar Foundation
Zelai Haudi 3, Osinalde industrialdea
Usurbil 20170. Basque Country
a.gurrutxaga@elhuyar.com

Iñaki Alegria
IXA group, Univ. of the Basque Country
Manuel Lardizabal 1
Donostia 20018. Basque Country
i.alegria@ehu.es

Abstract

We present an experimental study of how different features help measuring the idiomaticity of noun+verb (NV) expressions in Basque. After testing several techniques for quantifying the four basic properties of multiword expressions or MWEs (institutionalization, semantic non-compositionality, morphosyntactic fixedness and lexical fixedness), we test different combinations of them for classification into idioms and collocations, using Machine Learning (ML) and feature selection. The results show the major role of distributional similarity, which measures compositionality, in the extraction and classification of MWEs, especially, as expected, in the case of idioms. Even though cooccurrence and some aspects of morphosyntactic flexibility contribute to this task in a more limited measure, ML experiments make benefit of these sources of knowledge, allowing to improve the results obtained using exclusively distributional similarity features.

1 Introduction

Idiomaticity is considered the defining feature of the concept of multiword expressions (MWE). It is described as a non-discrete magnitude, whose "value" depends on a combination of features like institutionalization, non-compositionality and lexico-syntactic fixedness (Granger and Paquot, 2008).

Idiomaticity appears as a continuum rather than as a series of discrete values. Thus, the classification of MWEs into discrete categories is a difficult task. A very schematic classification that has achieved a fair degree of general acceptance among experts distinguishes two main types of MWEs at phrase-level: idioms and collocations.

This complexity of the concept of idiomaticity has posed a challenge to the development of methods addressing the measurement of the aforementioned four properties. Recent research has resulted in this issue nowadays being usually addressed through measuring the following phenomena: (i) cooccurrence, for institutionalization; (ii) distributional similarity, for non-compositionality; (iii) deviation from the behavior of free combinations, for morphosyntactic fixedness; and (iv) substitutability, for lexical fixedness. This is the broad context of our experimental work on the automatic classification of NV expressions in Basque.

2 Related Work

2.1 Statistical Idiosyncrasy or Institutionalization

Using the cooccurrence of the components of a combination as a heuristic of its institutionalization goes back to early research on this field (Church and Hanks, 1990), and is computed using association measures (AM), usually in combination with linguistic techniques, which allows the use of lemmatized and POS-tagged corpora, or the use of syntactic dependencies (Seretan, 2011). In recent years, the comparative analysis of AMs (Evert, 2005) and the combination of them (Lin et al., 2008; Pecina, 2010) have aroused considerable interest.

This approach has been recently explored in Basque (Gurrutxaga and Alegria, 2011).

2.2 Compositionality

The central concept in characterizing compositionality is the hypothesis of distributional similarity (DS) As proposed by Baldwin and Kim (2010), "the underlying hypothesis is that semantically idiomatic MWEs will occur in markedly different lexical contexts to their component words."

Berry-Rogghe (1974) proposed R-value to measure the compositionality of verb-particle constructions (VPCs), by dividing the overlap between the sets of collocates associated with the particle by the total number of collocates of the VPC. Wulff (2010) proposes two extensions to the R-value in her research on verb-preposition-noun constructions, combining and weighting in different ways individual R-values of each component.

The Vector Space Model (VSM) is applied, among others, by Fazly and Stevenson (2007), who use the cosine as a similarity measure. The shared task Distributional Semantics and Compositionality (DiSCo) at ACL-HLT 2011 shows a variety of techniques for this task, mainly association measures and VSM (Biemann and Giesbrecht, 2011). LSA (Latent Semantic Analysis) is used in several studies (Baldwin et al., 2003; Katz and Giesbrecht, 2006; Schone and Jurafsky, 2001).

Those approaches have been applied recently to Basque (Gurrutxaga and Alegria, 2012)

2.3 Morphosyntactic Flexibility (MSFlex)

Morphosyntactic fixedness is usually computed in terms of relative flexibility, as the statistical distance between the behavior of the combination and (i) the average behavior of the combinations with equal POS composition (Fazly and Stevenson, 2007; Wulff, 2010), or (ii) the average behavior of the combinations containing each one of the components of the combination (Bannard, 2007).

Fazly and Stevenson (2007) use Kullback-Leibler divergence (KL-div) to compute this distance. They analyze a set of patterns: determination (*a/the*), demonstratives, possessives, singular/plural and passive. They compute two additional measurements (dominant pattern and presence of absence of adjectival modifiers preceding the noun).

Wulff (2010) considers (i) tree-syntactic, (ii) lexico-syntactic and (iii) morphological flexibilities, and implements two metrics for these features: (i) an extension of Barkema proposal (NSSD, normalized sum of squared deviations), (ii) a special conception of "relative entropy" (H_{rel}).

Bannard (2007), using CPMI (conditional pointwise mutual information), analyses these variants: (i) variation, addition or dropping of a determiner; (ii) internal modification of the noun phrase; and (iii) verb passivation.

2.4 Lexical Flexibility (LFlex)

The usual procedure for measuring lexical flexibility is to compute the substitutability of each component of the combination using as substitutes its synonymous, quasi-synonyms, related words, etc.

The pioneering work in this field is Lin (1999), who uses a thesaurus automatically built from text. This resource is used in recent research (Fazly and Stevenson, 2007). They assume that the target pair is lexically fixed to the extent that its PMI deviates from the average PMI of its variants generated by lexical substitution. They compute flexibility using the z-score.

In Van de Cruys and Moirón (2007), a technique based on KL-div is used for Duch. They define R_{nv} as the ratio of noun preference for a particular verb (its KL-div), compared to the other nouns that are present in the cluster of substitutes. Similarly for R_{vn}. The substitute candidates are obtained from the corpus using standard distributional similarity techniques.

2.5 Other Methods

Fazly and Stevenson (2007) consider two other features: (i) the verb itself; and (ii) the semantic category of the noun according to WordNet.

2.6 Combined Systems

In order to combine several sources of knowledge, several studies have experimented with using Machine Learning methods (ML).

For Czech, Pecina (2010) combines only AMs using neural networks, logistic regression and SVM (Support Vector Machine). Lin et al. (2008) employ logistic linear regression model (LLRM) to combine scores of AMs.

Venkatapathy and Joshi (2005) propose a minimally supervised classification scheme that incorporates a variety of features to group verb-noun combinations. Their features drawn from AM and DS, but some of each type are tested and combined. They compute ranking correlation using SVM, achieving results of about 0.45.

Fazly and Stevenson (2007) use all the types of knowledge, and decision trees (C5.0) as a learning method, and achieve average results (F-score) near to 0.60 for 4 classes (literal, abstract, light verbs and idioms). The authors claim that the syntactic and combined fixedness measures substantially outperform measures of collocation extraction.

3 Experimental Setup

3.1 Corpus and Preprocessing

We use a journalistic corpus of 75 million words (MW) from two sources: (1) Issues published in 2001-2002 by the newspaper *Euskaldunon Egunkaria* (28 MW); and (2) Issues published in 2006-2010 by the newspaper *Berria* (47 MW).

The corpus is annotated with lemma, POS, fine grained POS (subPOS), case and number information using Eustagger developed by the IXA group of the University of the Basque Country. A precision of 95.42% is reported for POS + subPOS + case analysis (Oronoz et al., 2010).

3.2 Extraction of Bigram Candidates

The key data for defining a Basque NV bigram are lemma and case for the noun, and lemma for the verb. Case data is needed to differentiate, for example, *kontu hartu* ("to ask for an explanation") from *kontuan hartu* ("to take into account"), where *kontu* is a noun lemma in the inessive case.

In order to propose canonical forms, we need, for nouns, token, case and number annotations in bigram data. Those canonical forms can be formulated using number normalization, as described in Gurrutxaga and Alegria (2011). Bigrams belonging to the same key noun_lemma/noun_case+verb_lemma are normalized; a single bigram with the most frequent form is created, and the frequencies of bigrams and those of the noun unigrams summed.

We use the Ngram Statistics Package-NSP (Banerjee and Pedersen, 2010) to generate NV bigrams from a corpus generated from the output of Eustagger. Taking into account our previous results (Gurrutxaga and Alegria, 2011), we use a window span of ± 1 and a frequency threshold of $f > 30$. Before generation, some surface-grammar rules are applied to correct annotations that produce noise. For example, in most Basque AdjN combinations, the adjetive is a verb in a participe form (eg. *indar armatuak*, 'armed forces'). Similarly, those kind of participles can function as nouns (*gobernuaren aliatuak*, 'the allies of the government'). Not tagging those participles properly would introduce noise in the extraction of NV combinations.

3.3 Experiments Using Single Knowledge Sources

3.3.1 Cooccurrence

The cooccurrence data provided by NSP in the bigram extraction step is processed to calculate AMs. To accomplish this, we use Stefan Evert's UCS toolkit (Evert, 2005). The most common AMs are calculated: f, t-score, log-likelihood ratio, MI, MI^3, and chi-square (χ^2).

3.3.2 Distributional Similarity

The idea is to compare the contexts of each NV bigram with the contexts of its corresponding components, by means of different techniques. The more similar the contexts, the more compositional the combination.

Context Generation We extract the context words of each bigram from the sentences with contiguous cooccurrences of the components. The noun has to occur in the grammatical case in which it has been defined after bigram normalization.

The contexts of the corresponding noun and verb are extracted separately from sentences where they did not occur together. Only content-bearing lemmas are included in the contexts (nouns, verbs and adjectives).

Context Comparison We process the contexts in two different ways:

First, we construct a VSM model, representing the contexts as vectors. As similarity measures, we use Berry-Roghe's R-value (R_{BR}) and the two extensions to it proposed by Wulff (R_{W1} and R_{W2}), Jaccard index and cosine. For the cosine, different AMs have been tested for vector weights (f, t-score,

LLR and PMI). We experiment with different percentages of the vector and different numbers of collocates, using the aforementioned measures to rank the collocates. The 100 most frequent words in the corpus are stopped.

Second, we represent the same contexts as documents, and compare them by means of different indexes using the Lemur Toolkit (Allan et al., 2003). The contexts of the bigrams are used as queries against a document collection containing the context-documents of all the members of the bigrams. This can be implemented in different ways; the best results were obtained using the following:

- Lemur_1 (L1): As with vectors, the contexts of a bigram are included in a single query document, and the same is done for the contexts of its members
- Lemur_2 (L2): The context sentences of bigrams are treated as individual documents, but the contexts of each one of its members are represented in two separate documents

Due to processing reasons, the number of context sentences used in Lemur to generate documents is limited to 2,000 (randomly selected from the whole set of contexts).

We further tested LSA (using Infomap[1]), but the above methods yielded better results.

3.3.3 Morphosyntactic Flexibility

We focus on the variation of the N slot, distinguishing the main type of extensions and number inflections. Among left-extensions, we take into account relative clauses. In addition, we consider the order of components as a parameter. We present some examples of the free combination *liburua irakurri* ("to read a book")

- Determiner: *liburu bat irakurri dut* ("I have read one book"), *zenbat liburu irakurri dituzu?* ("how many books have you read?")
- Postnominal adjective: *liburu interesgarria irakurri nuen* ("I read an interesting book")
- Prenominal adjective: *italierazko liburua irakurri* ("to read a book in Italian")
- Relative clause: *irakurri dudan liburua* ("the book I have read"), *anaiak irakurritako liburu batzuk* ("some books read by my brother")
- Number inflection: *liburua/liburuak/ liburu/liburuok irakurri* ("to read a/some/∅/these book(s)")
- Order of components (NV / VN): *liburua irakurri dut* / *irakurri dut liburua* ("I have read a book")

We count the number of variations for each bigram, for all NV bigrams, and for each combination of the type bigram_component+POS of the other component (e.g, for *liburua irakurri*, the variations of all the combinations *liburua*+V and N+*irakurri*).

To calculate flexibility, we experiment with all the measures described in section 2.3: Fazly's KL-div, Wulff's NSSD and Hrel (relative entropy), and Bannard's CPMI.

3.3.4 Lexical Flexibility

In order to test the substitutability of the components of bigrams, we use two resources: (i) ELH: *Sinonimoen Kutxa*, a Basque dictionary of synonyms, published by the Elhuyar Foundation (for nouns and verbs, 40,146 word-synomyn pairs); (ii) WN: the Basque version of WordNet[2](68,217 word-synomyn pairs). First, we experimented with both resources on their own, but the results show that in many cases there either was no substitute candidate, or the corpus lacked combinations containing a substitute. In order to ensure a broader coverage, we combined both resources (ELHWN), and we expanded the set of substitutes including the siblings retrieved from Basque WordNet (ELHWNexpand).

To calculate flexibility, we experiment with the two measures described in section 2.4: z-score and KL-div based R.

3.4 Combining Knowledge Sources Using Machine Learning

We use some ML methods included in the *Weka* toolkit (Hall et al., 2009) in order to combine results obtained in experiments using single knowledge sources (described in section 3.3). The values

[1]http://infomap-nlp.sourceforge.net/

[2]http://ixa2.si.ehu.es/cgi-bin/mcr/public/wei.consult.perl

of the different measures obtained in those experiments were set as features.

We have selected five methods corresponding to different kind of techniques which have been used successfully in this field: Naive Bayes, C4.5 decision tree (j48), Random Forest, SVM (SMO algorithm) and Logistic Regression. Test were carried out using either all features, the features from each type of knowledge, and some subsets, obtained after manual and automatic selection. Following Fazly and Stevenson (2007), verbs are also included as features.

Since, as we will see in section 3.5, the amount of instances in the evaluation dataset is not very high (1,145), cross-validation is used in the experiments for model validation (5 folds). In the case of automatic attribute selection, we use *AttributeSelectedClassifier*, which encapsulates the attribute selection process with the classifier itself, so the attribute selection method and the classifier only see the data in the training set of each fold.

3.5 Evaluation

3.5.1 Reference Dataset and Human Judgments

As an evaluation reference, we use a subset of 1,200 combinations selected randomly from a extracted set of 4,334 bigrams, that is the result of merging the 2,000-best candidates of each AM ranking from the w = ± 1 and $f > 30$ extraction set.

The subset has been manually classified by three lexicographers into idioms, collocations and free combinations. Annotators were provided with an evaluation manual, containing the guidelines for classification and illustrative examples.

The agreement among evaluators was calculated using Fleiss' κ. We obtained a value of 0.58, which can be considered moderate, close to fair, agreement. Although this level of agreement is relatively low when compared to Krenn et al. (2004), it is comparable to the one reported by Pecina (2010), who attributed his "relatively low" value to the fact that "the notion of collocation is very subjective, domain-specific, and also somewhat vague." Street et al. (2010) obtain quite low inter-annotator agreement for annotation of idioms in the ANC (American National Corpus). Hence, we consider that the level of agreement we have achieved is acceptable.

For the final classification of the evaluation set, cases where agreement was two or higher were automatically adopted, and the remaining cases were classified after discussion. We removed 55 combinations that did not belong to the NV category, or that were part of larger MWEs. The final set included 1,145 items, out of which 80 were idioms 268 collocations, and 797 free combinations.

3.5.2 Procedure

In order to compare the results of the individual techniques, we based our evaluation on the rankings provided by each measure. If we were to have an ideal measure, the set of bigram categories ('id', 'col' and 'free') would be an ordered set, with 'id' values on top of the ranking, 'col' in the middle, and 'free' at the bottom. Thus, the idea is to compute the distance between a rank derived from the ideally ordered set, which contains a high number of ties, and the rank yielded by each measure. To this end, we use Kendall's τ_B as a rank-correlation measure. Statistical significance of the Kendall's τ_B correlation coefficient is tested with the Z-test. The realistic topline, yielded by a measure that ranks candidates ideally, but without ties, would be 0.68.

In addition, average precision values (AP) were calculated for each ranking.

In the case of association measures, similarity measures applied to VSM, and measures of flexibility, the bigrams were ranked by means of the values of the corresponding measure. In the case of experiments with Lemur, the information used to rank the bigrams consisted of the positions of the documents corresponding to each member of the bigram in the document list retrieved ('rank' in Table 1). For the experiments in which the context sentences have been distributed in different documents, average positions were calculated and weighted, in relation to the amount of documents for each bigram analysis ('rank_weight'). The total number of documents in the list (or 'hits') is weighted in the same manner ('hit_rel').

When using ML techniques, several measures provided by Weka were analyzed: percentage of Correctly Classified Instances (CCI), F-measures for each class (id, col, free), Weighted Average F-measure and Average F-measure.

	measure	τ_B	AP_MWE	AP_id	AP_col
	random rank	(-0.02542)	0.30879	0.0787	0.23358
AM	f	0.18853	0.43573	0.07391	0.37851
	t-score	0.19673	0.45461	0.08442	0.38312
	log-likelihood	0.15604	0.42666	0.10019	0.33480
	PMI	(-0.12090)	0.25732	0.08648	0.18234
	chi-squared	(-0.03699)	0.30227	0.11853	0.20645
DS	R_{BR}_NV (MI_-50%)	0.27034	0.47343	0.21738	0.30519
	R_{W1}(2000_MI_f3_50%)	0.26206	0.47152	0.19664	0.30967
	L1_Indri_rankNV	0.31438	0.53536	0.22785	0.35299
	L1_KL_rankNV	0.29559	0.51694	0.23558	0.33607
	L2_Indri_hit_rel_NV	**0.32156**	**0.56612**	0.29416	0.35389
	L2_KL_hit_rel_NV	0.30848	0.55146	**0.31977**	0.33241
	L2_Indri_rankN_weight	0.21387	0.45567	0.26148	0.28025
	L2_Indri_rankV_weight	0.31398	0.55208	0.12837	**0.43143**
MSFlex	H_{rel}_Det	0.07295	0.38995	0.12749	0.27704
	H_{rel}_PostAdj	(-0.05617)	0.31673	0.04401	0.29597
	H_{rel}_PreAdj	0.11459	0.38561	0.09897	0.29223
	H_{rel}_Rel	0.09115	0.40502	0.12913	0.29012
	H_{rel}_Num	0.11861	0.43381	0.13387	0.31318
	H_{rel}_ord	(0.02319)	0.31661	0.08124	0.24052
	CPMI (components)	0.05785	0.41917	0.12630	0.30831
LFlex	R_{nv}_ELHWN	(0.08998)	0.36717	0.07521	0.29896
	R_{vn}_ELHWN	(0.03306)	0.31752	0.08689	0.24369
	z-score_V_ELHWNexpand	0.10079	0.35687	0.12232	0.25019
	z-score_N_ELHWNexpand	0.08412	0.35534	0.07245	0.29005

Table 1: Kendall's τ_B rank-correlations relative to an ideal idiomaticity ranking, obtained by different idiomaticity measures. Non-significant values of τ_B in parentheses ($p > 0.05$). Average precisions for MWEs in general, and specific values for idioms and collocations.

4 Experimental Results

4.1 Single Knowledge Experiments

The results for Kendall's τ_B and AP for MWEs and separate AP values for idioms and collocations are summarized in Table 1 (only the experiments with the most noteworthy results are included).

The best results are obtained in the Lemur experiments, most notably in the Lemur_2 type, using either Indri or KL-div indexes. In the MWE rankings, measures of the R-value type only slightly outperform AMs.

In the case of idioms, DS measures obtain significantly better ranks than the other measures. Idioms being the least compositional expressions, his result is expected, and supports the hypothesis that semantic compositionality can better be characterized using measures of DS than using AMs.

Regarding collocations, no such claim can be made, as the AP values for t-score and f outperform DS values, with a remarkable exception: the best AP is obtained by an Indri index that compares the semantic similarity between the verb in combination with the noun and the verb in contexts without the noun (L2_Indri_rankV_weight), accordingly with the claim that the semantics of the verb contribute to the semicompositionality of collocations. By contrast, the corresponding measure for the noun (L2_Indri_rankN_weight) works quite a bit better with idioms than the previous verb measure.

Figure 1 shows the precision curves for the extraction of MWEs by the best measure of each component of idiomaticity.

In Figure 2 and 3, we present separately the preci-

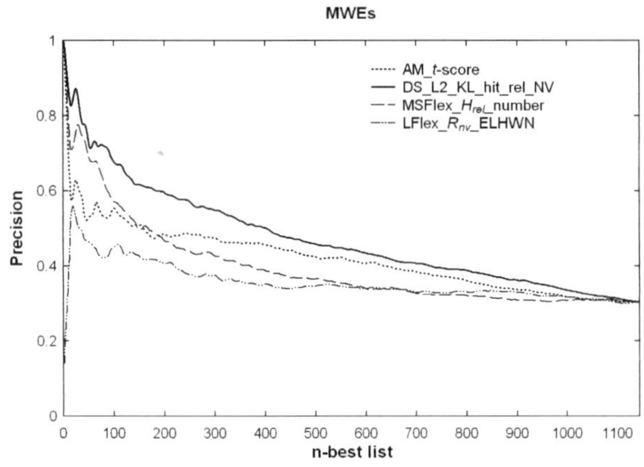

Figure 1: Precision results for the compositionality rankings of MWEs.

sion curves for idioms and collocations. We plot the measures with the best precision values.

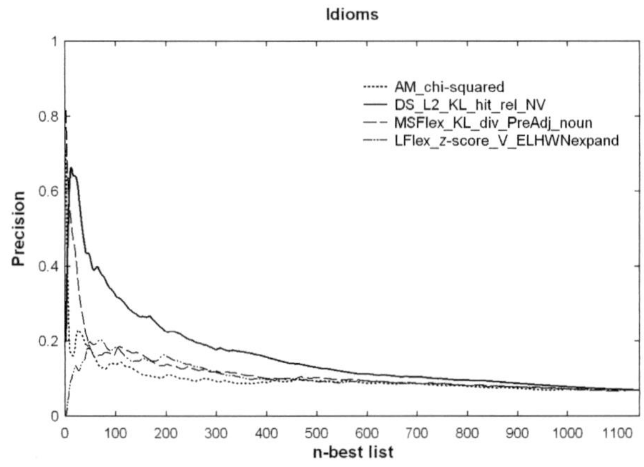

Figure 2: Precision results for the compositionality rankings of idioms.

Regarding the precision for collocations in Figure 3, the differences are not obviously significant. Even though the DS measure has the better performance, precision values for the t-score are not too much lower, and the t-score has a similar performance at the beginning of the ranking ($n < 150$).

4.2 Machine Learning Experiments

We report only the results of the three methods with the best overall performance: Logistic Regression (LR), SMO and RandomForest (RF).

In Table 2, we present the results obtained with datasets containing only DS attributes (the source of knowledge with the best results in single experiments); datasets containing all features corresponding to the four properties of idiomaticity; and datasets obtained adding the verb of the bigram as a string-type attribute.

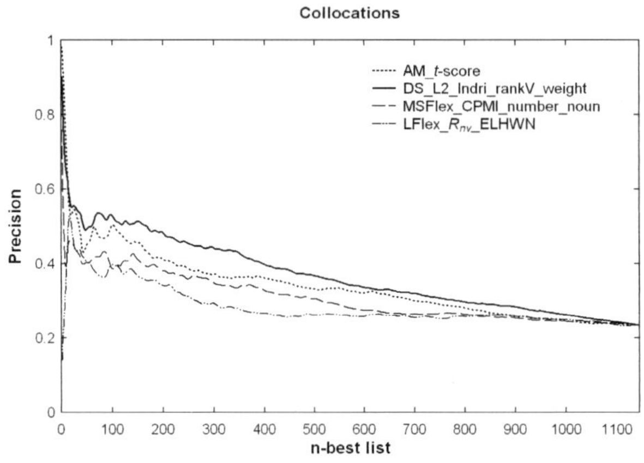

Figure 3: Precision results for the compositionality rankings of collocations.

As the figures show, it is difficult to improve the results obtained using only DS. The results of SMO are better when the features of the four components of idiomaticity are used, and even better when the verb is added, especially for idioms. The verb causes the performance of RF be slightly worse; in the case of LR, it generates considerable noise.

It can be observed that the figures for LR are more unstable. Using SMO and RF, convergence does not depend on how many noisy variables are present (Biau, 2012). Thus, feature selection could improve the results when LR is used.

In a complementary experiment, we observed the impact of removing the attributes of each source of knowledge (without including verbs). The most evident result was that the exclusion of LFlex features contributes the most to improving F. This was an expected effect, considering the poor results for LFlex measures described in section 4.1. More interesting is the fact that removing MSFlex features had a higher negative impact on F than not taking AMs as features.

Table 3 shows the results for two datasets generated through two manual selection of attributes: (1) manual_1: the 20 attributes with best AP average results; and (2) manual_2: a manual selection of the attributes from each knowledge source with the best AP_MWE, best AP_id and best AP_col. The third

Features	Method	CCI	F_id	F_col	F_free	F_W.Av.	F_Av.
DS	LR	72.489	0.261	0.453	0.838	0.707	0.517
	SMO	74.061	0.130	0.387	0.824	0.575	0.447
	RF	71.441	0.295	0.440	0.821	0.695	0.519
all idiom. properties	LR	71.703	0.339	0.514	0.821	0.716	0.558
	SMO	**76.507**	0.367	0.505	**0.857**	0.740	0.576
	RF	74.498	0.323	0.486	0.844	0.724	0.551
all + verb	LR	60.000	0.240	0.449	0.726	0.627	0.472
	SMO	75.808	**0.400**	**0.540**	0.848	**0.744**	**0.596**
	RF	74.061	0.243	0.459	0.846	0.713	0.516

Table 2: Results of Machine Learning experiments combining knowledge sources in three ways: (i) DS: distributional similarity features; (ii) knowledge related to the four components of idiomaticity (AM+DS+MSFlex+LFlex); (iii) previous features+verb components of bigrams.

section presents the results obtained with *AttributeSelectedClassifier* using *CfsSubsetEval* (CS) as evaluator[3] and *BestFirst* (BS) as search method. Looking at the results of the selection process in each fold, we saw that the attributes selected in more than 2 folds are 36: 1 AM, 20 from DS, 7 from MSFlex, 1 from LFlex and 7 verbs.

Features	Method	F_W.Av.	F_Av.
manual_1	LR	0.709	0.525
	SMO	0.585	0.304
	RF	0.680	0.485
manual_2	LR	0.696	0.518
	SMO	0.581	0.286
	RF	0.688	0.519
CS-BF	LR	**0.727**	**0.559**
	SMO	0.693	0.485
	RF	0.704	0.531

Table 3: F Weighted average and F average results for experiments using: (1) the 20 attributes with best AP average results; (2) a manual selection of the 3 best attributes from each knowledge source; and (3) *AttributeSelectedClassifier* with automatic attribute selection using *CfsSubsetEval* as evaluator and *BestFirst* as search method

The results show that, for each method, automatic selection outperforms the two manual selections. Most of the attributes automatically selected are DS measures, but it is interesting to observe that MSFlex and the verb slot contribute to improving the results. Using automatic attribute selection and LR, the results are close to the best figure of F_W.Av. using SMO and all the features (0.727 vs 0.744).

[3]http://wiki.pentaho.com/display/DATAMINING/CfsSubsetEval

5 Discussion

The most important conclusions from our experiments are the following:

- In the task of ranking the candidates, the best results are obtained using DS measures, and, in particular, Indri and KL-div in L2 experiments. This is true for both type of MWEs, and is ratified in ML experiments when automatic attribute filtering is carried out. It is, however, particularly notable with regard to idioms; in the case of collocations, the difference between the performance of DS and that of and MS and AM were not that significant.

- MSFlex contributes to the classification task when used in combination with DS, but get poor results by themselves. The most relevant parameter MSFlex is number inflection.

- SMO is the most precise method when a high amount of features is used. It gets the best overall F-score. The other methods need feature selection to obtain similar results.

- Automatic attribute selection using CS-BF filter yields better results than manual selections. The method that takes the most advantage is LR, whose scores are little bit worse than those of SMO using the whole set of attributes.

Some of these conclusions differ from those reached by earlier works. In particular, the claims in Fazly and Stevenson (2007) and Van de Cruys and Moirón (2007) that syntactic as well as lexical flexibility outperform other techniques of MWE characterization are not confirmed in this work for Basque. Some hypothesis could be formulated to explain those differences: (1) Basque idioms could be syntactically more flexible, whereas some free combinations could present a non-negligible level of fixedness; (2) Basque, especially in the journalistic register, could be sociolinguistically less fixed than, say, English or Spanish; thus, the lexical choice of the collocate could be not so clearly established; (3) the Basque lexical resources to test substitutability could have insufficient coverage; and (4) Fazly and Stevenson (2007) use the cosine for DS, a measure which in our experiments is clearly below other measures. Those hypotheses require experimental testing and deeper linguistic analysis.

6 Conclusions and Future Work

We have presented an in-depth analysis of the performance of different features of idiomaticity in the characterization of NV expressions, and the results obtained combining them using ML methods. The results confirm the major role of DS, especially, as expected, in the case of idioms. It is remarkable that the best results have been obtained using Lemur, an IR tool. ML experiments show that other features contribute to improve the results, especially some aspects of MSFlex, the verb of the bigram and, to a more limited extent, AMs. The performance of DS being the best one for idioms confirm previous research on other languages, but MSFlex and LFlex behave below the expected. The explanations proposed for this issue require further verification.

We are planning experiments using these techniques for discriminating between literal and idiomatic occurrences of MWEs in context. Work on parallel corpora is planned for the future.

Acknowledgments

This research was supported in part by the Spanish Ministry of Education and Science (TACARDI-TIN2012-38523-C02-011) and by the Basque Government (Berbatek project, Etortek-IE09-262; KONBITZ project, Saiotek 2012). Ainara Estarrona and Larraitz Uria (IXA group) and Ainara Ondarra and Nerea Areta (Elhuyar) are acknowledged for their work as linguists in the manual evaluation. Maddalen Lopez de la Calle and Iñaki San Vicente (Elhuyar) and Oier Lopez de la Calle (IXA group) have contributed with their expertise to the design of the experiments with Lemur and Infomap. Finally, special thanks goes to Olatz Arregi (IXA group) for having guided us in the experiments with Weka, and to Yosu Yurramendi from the University of the Basque Country, for his advice on the statistics in the evaluation step.

References

Allan, J., J. Callan, K. Collins-Thompson, B. Croft, F. Feng, D. Fisher, J. Lafferty, L. Larkey, T. Truong, P. Ogilvie, et al. (2003). The Lemur Toolkit for language modeling and information retrieval.

Baldwin, T., C. Bannard, T. Tanaka, and D. Widdows (2003). An empirical model of multiword expression decomposability. In *Proceedings of the ACL 2003 workshop on Multiword expressions: analysis, acquisition and treatment-Volume 18*, pp. 96.

Baldwin, T. and S. Kim (2010). Multiword expressions. *Handbook of Natural Language Processing, second edition. Morgan and Claypool.*

Banerjee, S. and T. Pedersen (2010). The design, implementation, and use of the Ngram Statistics Package. *Computational Linguistics and Intelligent Text Processing*, 370–381.

Bannard, C. (2007). A measure of syntactic flexibility for automatically identifying multiword expressions in corpora. In *Proceedings of the Workshop on a Broader Perspective on Multiword Expressions*, pp. 1–8.

Berry-Rogghe, G. (1974). Automatic identification of phrasal verbs. *Computers in the Humanities*, 16–26.

Biau, G. (2012). Analysis of a random forests model. *The Journal of Machine Learning Research 98888*, 1063–1095.

Biemann, C. and E. Giesbrecht (2011). Distributional semantics and compositionality 2011:

Shared task description and results. *Workshop on Distributional semantics and compositionality 2011. ACL HLT 2011*, 21.

Church, K. and P. Hanks (1990). Word association norms, mutual information, and lexicography. *Computational linguistics 16*(1), 22–29.

Evert, S. (2005). *The statistics of word cooccurrences: Word pairs and collocations*. Ph. D. thesis, University of Stuttgart.

Fazly, A. and S. Stevenson (2007). Distinguishing subtypes of multiword expressions using linguistically-motivated statistical measures. In *Proceedings of the Workshop on A Broader Perspective on Multiword Expressions*, pp. 9–16. Association for Computational Linguistics.

Granger, S. and M. Paquot (2008). Disentangling the phraseological web. *Phraseology. An interdisciplinary perspective*, 27–50.

Gurrutxaga, A. and I. Alegria (2011). Automatic extraction of NV expressions in Basque: basic issues on cooccurrence techniques. *Proc. of the Workshop on Multiword Expressions. ACL HLT 2011*, 2–7.

Gurrutxaga, A. and I. Alegria (2012). Measuring the compositionality of nv expressions in basque by means of distributional similarity techniques. *LREC2012*.

Hall, M., E. Frank, G. Holmes, B. Pfahringer, P. Reutemann, and I. H. Witten (2009). The weka data mining software: an update. Volume 11, pp. 10–18. ACM.

Katz, G. and E. Giesbrecht (2006). Automatic identification of non-compositional multi-word expressions using latent semantic analysis. In *Proceedings of the Workshop on Multiword Expressions: Identifying and Exploiting Underlying Properties*, pp. 12–19. Association for Computational Linguistics.

Krenn, B., S. Evert, and H. Zinsmeister (2004). Determining intercoder agreement for a collocation identification task. In *Proceedings of KONVENS*, pp. 89–96.

Lin, D. (1999). Automatic identification of non-compositional phrases. In *Proceedings of the 37th annual meeting of the ACL*, pp. 317–324. Association for Computational Linguistics.

Lin, J., S. Li, and Y. Cai (2008). A new collocation extraction method combining multiple association measures. In *Machine Learning and Cybernetics, 2008 International Conference on*, Volume 1, pp. 12–17. IEEE.

Oronoz, M., A. D. de Ilarraza, and K. Gojenola (2010). Design and evaluation of an agreement error detection system: testing the effect of ambiguity, parser and corpus type. In *Advances in Natural Language Processing*, pp. 281–292. Springer.

Pecina, P. (2010). Lexical association measures and collocation extraction. *Language resources and evaluation 44*(1), 137–158.

Schone, P. and D. Jurafsky (2001). Is knowledge-free induction of multiword unit dictionary headwords a solved problem. In *Proc. of the 6th EMNLP*, pp. 100–108. Citeseer.

Seretan, V. (2011). *Syntax-Based Collocation Extraction*. Text, Speech and Language Technology. Dordrecht: Springer.

Street, L., N. Michalov, R. Silverstein, M. Reynolds, L. Ruela, F. Flowers, A. Talucci, P. Pereira, G. Morgon, S. Siegel, et al. (2010). Like finding a needle in a haystack: Annotating the american national corpus for idiomatic expressions. In *Proc. of LREC'2010*.

Van de Cruys, T. and B. Moirón (2007). Semantics-based multiword expression extraction. In *Proceedings of the Workshop on A Broader Perspective on Multiword Expressions*, pp. 25–32. Association for Computational Linguistics.

Venkatapathy, S. and A. Joshi (2005). Measuring the relative compositionality of verb-noun (vn) collocations by integrating features. In *Proceedings of HLT/EMNLP*, pp. 899–906. Association for Computational Linguistics.

Wulff, S. (2010). *Rethinking Idiomaticity*. Corpus and Discourse. New York: Continuum International Publishing Group Ltd.

Semantic Roles for Nominal Predicates: Building a Lexical Resource

Ashwini Vaidya and **Martha Palmer** and **Bhuvana Narasimhan**
Dept of Linguistics
Institute of Cognitive Science
University of Colorado, Boulder
Boulder, CO 80309
{vaidyaa, mpalmer, narasimb}@colorado.edu

Abstract

The linguistic annotation of noun-verb complex predicates (also termed as light verb constructions) is challenging as these predicates are highly productive in Hindi. For semantic role labelling, each argument of the noun-verb complex predicate must be given a role label. For complex predicates, frame files need to be created specifying the role labels for each noun-verb complex predicate. The creation of frame files is usually done manually, but we propose an automatic method to expedite this process. We use two resources for this method: Hindi PropBank frame files for simple verbs and the annotated Hindi Treebank. Our method perfectly predicts 65% of the roles in 3015 unique noun-verb combinations, with an additional 22% partial predictions, giving us 87% useful predictions to build our annotation resource.

1 Introduction

Ahmed et al. (2012) describe several types of complex predicates that are found in Hindi e.g. morphological causatives, verb-verb complex predicates and noun-verb complex predicates. Of the three types, we will focus on the noun-verb complex predicates in this paper. Typically, a noun-verb complex predicate *chorii* 'theft' *karnaa* 'to do' has two components: a noun *chorii* and a light verb *karnaa* giving us the meaning 'steal'. Complex predicates [1] may be found in English e.g. *take a walk* and many other languages such as Japanese, Persian, Arabic and Chinese (Butt, 1993; Fazly and Stevenson, 2007).

The verbal component in noun-verb complex predicates (NVC) has reduced predicating power (although it is inflected for person, number, and gender agreement as well as tense-aspect and mood) and its nominal complement is considered the true predicate, hence the term 'light verb'. The creation of a lexical resource for the set of true predicates that occur in an NVC is important from the point of view of linguistic annotation. For semantic role labelling in particular, similar lexical resources have been created for complex predicates in English, Arabic and Chinese (Hwang et al., 2010).

1.1 Background

The goal of this paper is to produce a lexical resource for Hindi NVCs. This resource is in the form of 'frame files', which are directly utilized for PropBank annotation. PropBank is an annotated corpus of semantic roles that has been developed for English, Arabic and Chinese (Palmer et al., 2005; Palmer et al., 2008; Xue and Palmer, 2003). In Hindi, the task of PropBank annotation is part of a larger effort to create a multi-layered treebank for Hindi as well as Urdu (Palmer et al., 2009).

PropBank annotation assumes that syntactic parses are already available for a given corpus. Therefore, Hindi PropBanking is carried out on top of the syntactically annotated Hindi Dependency Treebank. As the name suggests, the syntactic representation is dependency based, which has several advantages for the PropBank annotation process (see Section 3).

The PropBank annotation process for Hindi follows the same two-step process used for other PropBanks. First, the semantic roles that will occur with each predicate are defined by a human expert. Then,

[1] They are also otherwise known as light verb, support verb or conjunct verb constructions.

these definitions or 'frame files' are used to guide the annotation of predicate-argument structure in a given corpus.

Semantic roles are annotated in the form of *numbered arguments*. In Table 1 PropBank-style semantic roles are listed for the simple verb *de*;'to give':

de.01	'to give'
Arg0	the giver
Arg1	thing given
Arg2	recipient

Table 1: A frame file

The labels ARG0, ARG1 and ARG2 are always defined on a verb-by-verb basis. The description at the verb-specific level gives details about each numbered argument. In the example above, the numbered arguments correspond to the giver, thing given and recipient. In the Hindi treebank, which consists of 400,000 words, there are nearly 37,576 predicates, of which 37% have been identified as complex predicates at the dependency level. This implies that a sizeable portion of the predicates are NVCs, which makes the task of manual frame file creation time consuming.

In order to reduce the effort required for manual creation of NVC frame files, we propose a novel automatic method for generating PropBank semantic roles. The automatically generated semantic roles will be used to create frame files for each complex predicate in the corpus. Our method accurately predicts semantic roles for almost two thirds of the unique nominal-verb combinations, with around 20% partial predictions, giving us a total of 87% useful predictions.

For our implementation, we use linguistic resources in the form of syntactic dependency labels from the treebank. In addition we also have manually created, gold standard frame files for Hindi **simple** verbs[2]. In the following sections we provide linguistic background, followed by a detailed description of our method. We conclude with an error analysis and evaluation section.

[2]http://verbs.colorado.edu/propbank/framesets-hindi/

2 The Nominal and the Light Verb

Semantic roles for the arguments of the light verb are determined jointly by the noun as well as the light verb. Megerdoomian (2001) showed that the light verb places some restrictions on the semantic role of its subject in Persian. A similar phenomenon may be observed for Hindi. Compare example 1 with example 2 below:

(1) *Raam-ne cycle-kii chorii kii*
Ram-erg cycle-gen theft do.prf
'Ram stole a bicycle'

(2) *aaj cycle-kii chorii huii*
Today cycle-gen theft be.pres
'Today a bicycle was stolen'

PropBank annotation assumes that sentences in the corpus have already been parsed. The annotation task involves identification of arguments for a given NVC and the labelling of these arguments with semantic roles. In example 1 we get an agentive subject with the light verb *kar* 'do'. However, when it is replaced by the unaccusative *ho* 'become' in Example 2, then the resulting clause has a theme argument as its subject. Note that the nominal *chorii* in both examples remains the same. From the point of view of PropBank annotation, the NVC *chorii kii* will have both ARG0 and ARG1, but *chorii huii* will only have ARG1 for its single argument *cycle*. Hence, the frame file for a given nominal must make reference to the type of light verb that occurs with it.

The nominal as the true predicate also contributes its own arguments. In example 3, which shows a full (non-light) use of the verb *de* 'give', there are three arguments: giver(agent), thing given(theme) and recipient. In contrast the light verb usage *zor de* 'emphasis give; emphasize', seen in example 4, has a locative marked argument *baat par* 'matter on' contributed by the nominal *zor* 'emphasis'.

(3) *Raam-ne Mohan ko kitaab dii*
Ram-erg Mohan-dat book give.prf
'Ram gave Mohan a book'

(4) *Ram ne is baat par zor diyaa*
Ram-erg this matter loc emphasis give.prf
'Ram emphasized this matter'

As both noun and light verb contribute to the semantic roles of their arguments, we require linguistic knowledge about both parts of the NVC. The semantic roles for the nominal need to specify the co-occurring light verb and the nominal's argument roles must also be captured. Table 2 describes the desired representation for a nominal frame file.

Frame file for *chorii*-n(oun)	
chorii.01: theft-n	light verb: *kar*'do; to steal'
Arg0 Arg1	person who steals thing stolen
chorii.02 : theft-n	light verb: *ho* 'be/become; to get stolen'
Arg1	thing stolen

Table 2: Frame file for predicate noun chorii 'theft' with two frequently occurring light verbs *ho* and *kar*. If other light verbs are found to occur, they are added as additional rolesets as chorii.03, chorii.04 and so on.

This frame file shows the representation of a nominal *chorii* 'theft' that can occur in combination with a light verb *kar* 'do' or *ho* 'happen'. For each combination, we derive a different set of PropBank roles: agent and patient for chorii.01 and theme for chorii.02. Note that the nominal's frame actually contains the roles for the combination of nominal and light verb, and not the nominal alone.

Nominal frame files such as these have already been defined for English PropBank.[3] However, for English, many nominals in NVCs are in fact nominalizations of full verbs, which makes it far easier to derive their frame files (e.g. *walk* in *take a walk* is a full verb). For Hindi, this is not the case, and a different strategy needs to be employed to derive these frames automatically.

3 Generating Semantic Roles

The Hindi Treebank has already identified NVC cases by using a special label pof or 'part-of'. The Treebank annotators apply this label on the basis of native speaker intuition. We use the label given by the Treebank as a means to extract the NVC cases (the issues related to complex predicate identification are beyond the scope of this paper). Once this extraction step is complete, we have a set of nominals and a corresponding list of light verbs that occur with them.

[3]http://verbs.colorado.edu/propbank/framesets-noun/

In Section 2, we showed that the noun as well as the light verb in a sentence influence the type of semantic roles that will occur. Our method builds on this idea and uses two resources in order to derive linguistic knowledge about the NVC: PropBank frame files for simple verbs in Hindi and the Hindi Treebank, annotated with dependency labels. The next two sections describe the use of these resources in some detail.

3.1 *Karaka* to PropBank Mapping

The annotated Hindi Treebank is based on a dependency framework (Begum et al., 2008) and has a very rich set of dependency labels. These labels (also known as *karaka* labels) represent the relations between a head (e.g. a verb) and its dependents (e.g. arguments). Using the Treebank we extract all the dependency *karaka* label combinations that occur with a unique instance of an NVC. We filter them to include argument labels and discard those labels that are usually used for adjuncts. We then calculate the most frequently occurring combination of labels that will occur with that NVC. Finally, we get a tuple consisting of an NVC, a set of *karaka* argument labels that occur with it and a count of the number of times that NVC has occurred in the corpus. The *karaka* labels are then mapped onto PropBank labels. We reproduce in Table 3 the numbered arguments to *karaka* label mapping found in Vaidya et al., (2011).

PropBank label	**Treebank label**
Arg0 (agent)	k1 (karta); k4a (experiencer)
Arg1 (theme, patient)	k2 (karma)
Arg2 (beneficiary)	k4 (beneficiary)
Arg2-ATR(attribute)	k1s (attribute)
Arg2-SOU(source)	k5 (source)
Arg2-GOL(goal)	k2p (goal)
Arg3 (instrument)	k3 (instrument)

Table 3: Mapping from *Karaka* labels to PropBank

3.2 Verb Frames

Our second resource consists of PropBank frames for full Hindi verbs. Every light verb that occurs in

Hindi is also used as a full verb, e.g. *de* 'give' in Table 1 may be used both as a 'full' verb as well as a 'light' verb. As a full verb, it has a frame file in Hindi PropBank. The set of roles in the full verb frame is used to generate a "canonical" verb frame for each light verb. The argument structure of the light verb will change when combined with a nominal, which contributes its own arguments. However, as a default, the canonical argument structure list captures the fact that most *kar* 'do' light verbs are likely to occur with the roles `ARG0` and `ARG1` respectively or that *ho* 'become', an unaccusative verb, occurs with only `ARG1`.

3.3 Procedure

Our procedure integrates the two resources described above. First, the tuple consisting of *karaka* labels for a particular NVC is mapped to PropBank labels. But many NVC cases occur just once in the corpus and the *karaka* label tuple may not be very reliable. Hence, the likelihood that the mapped tuple accurately depicts the correct semantic frame is not very high. Secondly, Hindi can drop mandatory subjects or objects in a sentence e.g., *(vo) kitaab paRegaa*; '(He) will read the book'. These are not inserted by the dependency annotation (Bhatia et al., 2010) and are not easy to discover automatically (Vaidya et al., 2012). We cannot afford to ignore any of the low frequency cases as each NVC in the corpus must be annotated with semantic roles. In order to get reasonable predictions for each NVC, we use a simple rule. We carry out a mapping from karaka to PropBank labels only if the NVC occurs at least 30 times in the corpus. If the NVC occurs fewer than 30 times, then we use the "canonical" verb list.

4 Evaluation

The automatic method described in the previous section generated 1942 nominal frame files. In order to evaluate the frame files, we opted for manual checking of the automatically generated frames. The frame files were checked by three linguists and the checking focused on the validity of the semantic roles. The linguists also indicated whether annotation errors or duplicates were present. There was some risk that the automatically derived frames could bias the linguists' choice of roles as it is quicker to accept a given suggestion than propose an entirely new set of roles for the NVC. As we had a very large number of automatically generated frames, all of which would need to be checked manually anyway, practical concerns determined the choice of this evaluation.

After this process of checking, the total number of frame files stood at 1884. These frame files consisted of 3015 rolesets i.e. individual combinations of a nominal with a light verb (see Table 2). The original automatically generated rolesets were compared with their hand corrected counterparts (i.e. manually checked 'gold' rolesets) and evaluated for accuracy. We used three parameters to compare the gold rolesets with the automatically generated ones: a full match, partial match and no match. Table 4 shows the results derived from each resource (Section 3) and the total accuracy.

Type of Match	Full	Partial	None	Errors
Karaka Mapping	25	31	4	0
Verbal Frames	1929	642	249	143
Totals	1954	673	245	143
% Overall	65	22	8	5

Table 4: Automatic mapping results, total frames=3015

The results show that almost two thirds of the semantic roles are guessed correctly by the automatic method, with an additional 22% partial predictions, giving us a total of 87% useful predictions. Only 8% show no match at all between the automatically generated labels and the gold labels.

When we compare the contribution of the karaka labels with the verb frames, we find that the verb frames contribute to the majority of the full matches. The karaka mapping contributes relatively less as only 62 NVC types occur more than 30 times in the corpus. If we reduce our frequency requirement from of 30 to 5, the accuracy drops by 5%. The bulk of the cases are thus derived from the simple verb frames. We think that the detailed information in the verb frames, such as unaccusativity contributes towards generating the correct frame files.

It is interesting to observe that nearly 65% accuracy can be achieved from the verbal information alone. The treebank has two light verbs that occur with high frequency i.e. *kar* 'do' and *ho* 'become'. These combine with a variety of nominals but per-

Light verb	Full (%)	None (%)	Total Uses*
kar'do'	**64**	8	1038
ho 'be/become'	**81**	3	549
de 'give'	55	**34**	157
A 'come'	31	**42**	36

Table 5: Light verbs 'do' and 'be/become' vs. 'give' and 'come'. *The unique total light verb usages in the corpus

form more consistently than light verbs such as *de* 'give' or *A* 'come'. The light verb *kar* adds intentionality to the NVC, but appears less often with a set of semantic roles that are quite different from its original 'full' verb usage. In comparison, the light verbs such as *de* 'give' show far more variation, and as seen from Table 4, will match with automatically derived frames to a lesser extent. The set of nominals that occur in combination with *kar*, usually seem to require only a doer and a thing done. Borrowed English verbs such *dijain*'design' or *Pona*'phone' will appear preferentially with *kar* in the corpus and as they are foreign words they do not add arguments of their own.

One of the advantages of creating this lexical resource is the availability of gold standard frame files for around 3000 NVCs in Hindi. As a next step, it would be useful to use these frames to make some higher level generalizations about these NVCs. For example, much work has already been done on automatic verb classification for simple predicates e.g. (Merlo and Stevenson, 2001; Schulte im Walde, 2006), and perhaps such classes can be derived for NVCs. Also, the frame files do not currently address the problem of polysemous NVCs which could appear with a different set of semantic roles, which will be addressed in future work.

Acknowledgments

I am grateful to Archna Bhatia and Richa Srishti for their help with evaluating the accuracy of the nominal frames. This work is supported by NSF grants CNS-0751089, CNS-0751171, CNS-0751202, and CNS-0751213.

References

Tafseer Ahmed, Miriam Butt, Annette Hautli, and Sebastian Sulger. 2012. A reference dependency bank for analyzing complex predicates. In *Proceedings of the Eight International Conference on Language Resources and Evaluation (LREC'12*.

Rafiya Begum, Samar Husain, Arun Dhwaj, Dipti Misra Sharma, Lakshmi Bai, and Rajeev Sangal. 2008. Dependency Annotation Scheme for Indian Languages. In *Proceedings of The Third International Joint Conference on Natural Language Processing (IJCNLP). Hyderabad, India*.

Archna Bhatia, Rajesh Bhatt, Bhuvana Narasimhan, Martha Palmer, Owen Rambow, Dipti Misra Sharma, Michael Tepper, Ashwini Vaidya, and Fei Xia. 2010. Empty Categories in a Hindi Treebank. In *Proceedings of the 7th International Conference on Language Resources and Evaluation (LREC'10)*, pages 1863–1870.

Miriam Butt. 1993. The Light Verb Jungle. In G. Aygen, C. Bowers, and C. Quinn, editors, *Harvard Working Papers in Linguistics: Papers from the GSAS/Dudley House workshop on light verbs*, volume 9.

Afsaneh Fazly and Suzanne Stevenson. 2007. Automatic Acquisition of Knowledge about Multiword Predicates. In *Proceedings of PACLIC 19, the 19th Asia-Pacific Conference on Language, Information and Computation*.

Jena D. Hwang, Archna Bhatia, Claire Bonial, Aous Mansouri, Ashwini Vaidya, Nianwen Xue, and Martha Palmer. 2010. PropBank Annotation of Multilingual Light Verb Constructions. In *Proceedings of the Linguistic Annotation Workshop held in conjunction with ACL-2010*.

Karine Megerdoomian. 2001. Event Structure and Complex Predicates in Persian. *Canadian Journal of Linguistics*, 46:97–125.

Paola Merlo and Suzanne Stevenson. 2001. Automatic Verb Classification Based on Statistical Distributions of Argument Structure. *Computational Linguistics*, 27(3):373–408.

Martha Palmer, Daniel Gildea, and Paul Kingsbury. 2005. The Proposition Bank: An annotated corpus of semantic roles. *Computational Linguistics*, 31(1):71–106.

Martha Palmer, Olga Babko-Malaya, Ann Bies, Mona Diab, Mohammed Maamouri, Aous Mansouri, and Wajdi Zaghouani. 2008. A pilot Arabic PropBank. In *Proceedings of the 6th International Language Resources and Evaluation*.

Martha Palmer, Rajesh Bhatt, Bhuvana Narasimhan, Owen Rambow, Dipti Misra Sharma, and Fei Xia. 2009. Hindi Syntax: Annotating Dependency, Lexical

Predicate-Argument Structure, and Phrase Structure. In *Proceedings of ICON-2009: 7th International Conference on Natural Language Processing*, Hyderabad.

Sabine Schulte im Walde. 2006. Experiments on the Automatic Induction of German Semantic Verb Classes. *Computational Linguistics*, 32(2):159–194.

Ashwini Vaidya, Jinho D. Choi, Martha Palmer, and Bhuvana Narasimhan. 2011. Analysis of the Hindi proposition bank using dependency structure. In *Proceedings of the 5th Linguistic Annotation Workshop - LAW V '11*.

Ashwini Vaidya, Jinho D. Choi, Martha Palmer, and Bhuvana Narasimhan. 2012. Empty Argument Insertion in the Hindi PropBank. In *Proceedings of the Eighth International Conference on Language Resources and Evaluation - LREC-12, Istanbul.*

Nianwen Xue and Martha Palmer. 2003. Annotating the Propositions in the Penn Chinese Treebank. In *Proceedings of the 2nd SIGHAN workshop on Chinese language processing*, SIGHAN'03, pages 47–54.

Constructional Intensifying Adjectives in Italian

Sara Berlanda
Università Roma Tre
Via Ostiense, 234
Rome, Italy
sara.berlanda@gmail.com

Abstract

Grading is a primary cognitive operation that has an important expressive function. Information on degree is grammatically relevant and constitutes what Lazard (2006) calls a *primary domain of grammaticalization*: According to typological studies (Cuzzolin & Lehmann, 2004), many languages of the world have in fact at their disposal multiple grammatical devices to express gradation. In Italian, the class of superlativizing structures alternative to the morphological superlative is very rich and consists, among others, of adverbs of degree, focalizing adverbs and prototypical comparisons. This contribution deals with a particular analytic structure of superlative in Italian that is still neglected in the literature. This is what we will call Constructional Intensifying Adjectives (CIAs), adjectives which modify the intensity of other adjectives on the basis of regular semantic patterns, thus giving rise to multiword superlative constructions of the type: ADJ_X+ADJ_{INTENS}. A comparative quantitative corpus analysis demonstrates that this strategy, though paradigmatically limited, is nonetheless widely exploited: From a distributional point of view, some of these CIAs only combine with one or a few adjectives and form MWEs that appear to be completely lexicalized, while some others modify wider classes of adjectives thus displaying a certain degree of productivity.

1 Introduction

The functional category of degree formally expresses the intensity with which a property or, to a lesser extent, a state of affairs, applies to an entity.

Adjectives are gradable words *par excellence* and, indeed, all adjectival inflections in languages – except those expressing agreement with the head – have to do with grading (Croft, 1991: 134-135). Even when gradation is not realized through morphology, languages show numerous alternative analytical forms for expressing the extent to which the quality expressed by the adjective applies to an entity.

In this paper we will focus on a particular strategy of *absolute superlative* in Italian: The absolute superlative indicates that the quality expressed by the predicate is present at the highest degree, without making any comparison with other entities (1a), or at least to a very high degree on the scale of the corresponding values (Sapir, 1944), (1b):

1) a. *Questo libro è* ***bellissimo***.
'this book is very beautiful'
b. *Il tuo bambino è* ***molto vivace***.
'your child is very lively'

Due to the "human fondness of exaggeration" (Bolinger, 1972), the array of processes employed to realize the superlative degree is very wide, both cross- and intralinguistically. As for morphological strategies, the highest grade is generally formed by means of reduplication or affixation; however, the most common process to form the superlative among the world's languages is the use of an unbound lexeme. Indeed, "almost every language has a word meaning roughly *very* which, preposed or postposed, combines with the adjective" (Cuzzolin & Lehmann, 2004: 1215).

Section 2 briefly describes the most exploited analytical and synthetic superlative forms in Italian, which will be part of the quantitative comparison carried out in our research, and then focuses on CIAs, a multiword strategy still largely unexplored

1	**Affixes**	superlative suffixation	Adj + -issimo (or irregular superlative suffixes) *bellissimo* 'very beautiful', *acerrimo* 'very bitter'
2		superlative prefixation	stra-/ultra-/arci-/super-/… + Adj *straricco* 'very rich', *arcinoto* 'very famous'
3	**Intensifiers**	adverbs of quantity	*molto buono* 'very good', *troppo stupido* 'very stupid'
4		adverbs of degree	*terribilmente solo* 'terribly lonely'
5a		resultative adverbs	*particolarmente comodo* 'particularly comfortable'
5b		adverbs of completeness	*interamente solo* 'completely lonely'
6		indexical expressions	*così brusco* 'very abrupt'
7		multiword adverbs	*del tutto nuovo* 'totally new'
8		prototypical comparisons	NX+Adj+come+NProtoype *NX pieno come un uovo* 'full as an egg'

'Tab.1 Absolute superlative forms in Italian'

in the literature. In Section 3 the tools and the methodology used for data extraction and analysis will be introduced; the results will be presented and discussed in Section 4. The conclusion (Section 5) offers an overview of possible future developments of the present research.

2 The Absolute Superlative in Italian

2.1 Adverbial Devices

Italian, like other Romance languages, forms the absolute superlative with the Latin-derived suffix *-issimo* (Tab.1 #1) or with some intensifying prefixes derived from Greek or Latin, limited to colloquial varieties (Tab.1 #2).

Adjectives can also be graded by means of lexical elements ('degree words' (Bolinger, 1972), 'degree modifiers' (Kennedy & Nally, 2005) or 'adverbs of degree') which intensify them by scaling upwards the property they express. As Klein (1998: 26-27) suggests, the class of intensifiers comprises elements that, from a crosslinguistic perspective, always seem to derive from the same sources. Consequently, in Italian as in many other languages, the prototypical intensifiers are represented by the closed class of adverbs of quantity (Tab.1 #3). Then we find derived adverbs of degree in *–mente* (Tab.1 #4), "implicitly grading" (Bosque, 1999) since they contain the feature of 'maximum' in their semantics. Similarly, resultative adverbs, which include the subset of those denoting completeness, assume a grading function after a "semantic bleaching" (Lorenz, 2002) of the original lexical motivation that their morphology would suggest (Tab.1 #5a,b).

Adverbs derived from indexical and comparative expressions are other common devices capable of attributing the highest degree (Bolinger, 1972) (Tab.1 #6), as well as the large class of multiword adverbs (Tab.1 #7), and the so-called prototypical comparisons (Guil, 2006) – formally similative constructions relating two entities, one of which is prototypical with respect to a particular property, and in which the comparison with a prototype triggers a hyperbolizing, and thus superlativizing, interpretation (Tab.1 #8).

2.2 Constructional Intensifying Adjectives

Intensifiers forming the absolute superlative in Italian (cf. list in Tab.1) are generally adverbial and preferably occur in pre-adjectival position.

CIAs, on the other hand, are adjectives that intensify their adjectival head by placing themselves in the typical position of prepositional complements, as in (2):

2) $[ADJ_X + ADJ_{INTENS}]_{MW\text{-}AbsSup}$

There are about a dozen constructional adjectives that are employed to attribute the value of maximum degree to the adjective they combine with, leading to superlative MWEs:

3) *Bagnato* ***fradicio***, 'soaking wet'; *sudato* ***fradicio*** 'very sweaty'; *ubriaco* ***fradicio***, 'dead-drunk'; *buio* ***fitto***, 'very dark'; *buio* ***pesto***, 'very dark'; *morto* ***stecchito***, 'stone dead'; *nuovo* ***fiammante***, 'brand new'; *incazzato* ***nero***, 'very pissed off'; *innamorato* ***pazzo***, *innamorato* ***cotto***, *innamorato* ***perso***, 'crazy in love'; *pieno* ***zeppo***, 'crammed full'; *ricco* ***sfondato***, 'very wealthy'; *sporco* ***lurido***, 'very dirty'; *stanco* ***morto***, 'dead tired'; *stufo* ***marcio***, 'sick and tired'.[1]

While some of these CIAs can hardly be used to intensify adjectives other than the ones that normally select them lexically, there are others which show a certain degree of productivity. So CIAs can either be used to form a single, fixed MWE or to modify wider classes, as shown in (4):

4) a. X $_{ADJ}$ + *perso* > *innamorato perso* 'crazy in love', *sbronzo perso* 'dead-drunk', ...
b. X $_{ADJ}$ + *marcio* > *ubriaco marcio* 'dead-drunk', *spocchioso marcio* 'very arrogant', ...
c. X $_{ADJ}$ + *fradicio* > *geloso fradicio* 'very gealous', *innamorato fradicio* 'crazy in love', ...[2]

The phenomenon of grading an adjective by using another adjective is also known to other languages – also limited to few adjectives. Evidence of similar constructions can be found in Spanish (5a), English (5b), German (5c), Afrikaans (5d) and Dutch (5e):

5) a. Sp. *histerica perdida*, 'extremely hysterical'; *quieto parado* 'extremely quiet' (Guil, 2006);
b. Eng. *dead-tired* (Bolinger, 1972); *bored stiff* (Cacchiani, 2010);
c. Ger. *schwerreich*, 'very rich'; *gesteckt voll*, 'crammed full';
d. Afr. *dolgelukkig*, 'very happy'; *malverlief*, 'madly in love';
e. Dut. *doodmoeg*, 'very tired' (Klein, 1998).

But while in Italian and Spanish the components of these MWEs tend to keep part of their morphosyntactic and phonological autonomy (i.e. agreement and accent), in the other languages they rather give rise to compound words.

3 Data Extraction

3.1 Corpora and Tools

The data used in our analysis were extracted from two of the main corpora of written Italian, namely CORIS-CODIS (120 million tokens) and *LaRepubblica* (380 million tokens), both lemmatized and morphosyntactically annotated. Starting from these resources, a list of superlatives formed with CIAs was built and intensifiers able to modify more than one base adjective were isolated. The automatic identification was facilitated by the strong syntactic cohesion of the investigated structures: CIAs occur always in post-adjectival position and the resulting superlative MWEs never admit any insertion between the two composing elements.

We then cross-checked the data in GRADIT (*GRAnde Dizionario ITaliano dell'uso*), used as a gold standard to verify the results and the lexicographical status of every combination.

The objects of the present research mostly belong to colloquial Italian and, in general, to a non-standard variety. In order to verify their effective vitality in the Italian lexicon, we considered it worthwhile to exploit the web as a corpus in the case of intensifiers that were scarcely represented in the corpora.

Sketch Engine (Kilgarriff et al., 2004) was also used as a basis for our comparative analysis: 'Word sketch' tables were in fact employed to verify the most frequent superlativizing strategies for each ADJ_X.

3.2 Methodology

Firstly, occurrences of each MW superlative in (3) were compared to the occurrences of the general intensifying strategies (cf. Table 1) applicable to the same adjective.

When useful and possible, such comparison was differentiated depending on ADJ_X and further extended to each one's most typical intensification device – according to the data suggested by Sketch Engine tables – and to the superlative obtained by combining ADJ_X with the adverbial intensifier cor-

[1] We provide below the translation of the CAIs only: ***Cotto***, 'cooked', (*fig.*) 'very much in love'; ***fiammante***, 'flaming', (*fig.*) 'new'; ***fitto***, 'thick', 'dense'; ***fradicio***, 'soaked', 'rotten'; ***lurido***, 'filthy'; ***marcio***, 'rotten'; ***morto***, 'dead'; ***nero***, 'black', (*fig.*) 'very angry'; ***pazzo***, 'crazy'; ***perso***, 'lost'; ***pesto***, (*fig.*) 'dense'; ***sfondato***, 'bottomless', (*fig.*) 'limitless'; ***stecchito***, 'skinny', (*fig.*) 'dead'; ***zeppo***, 'packed'.

[2] Even if these CIAs happen to modify similar classes of adjectives, there seem to be differences in their semantics, having *marcio* and *fradicio* a more negative connotation than *perso*.

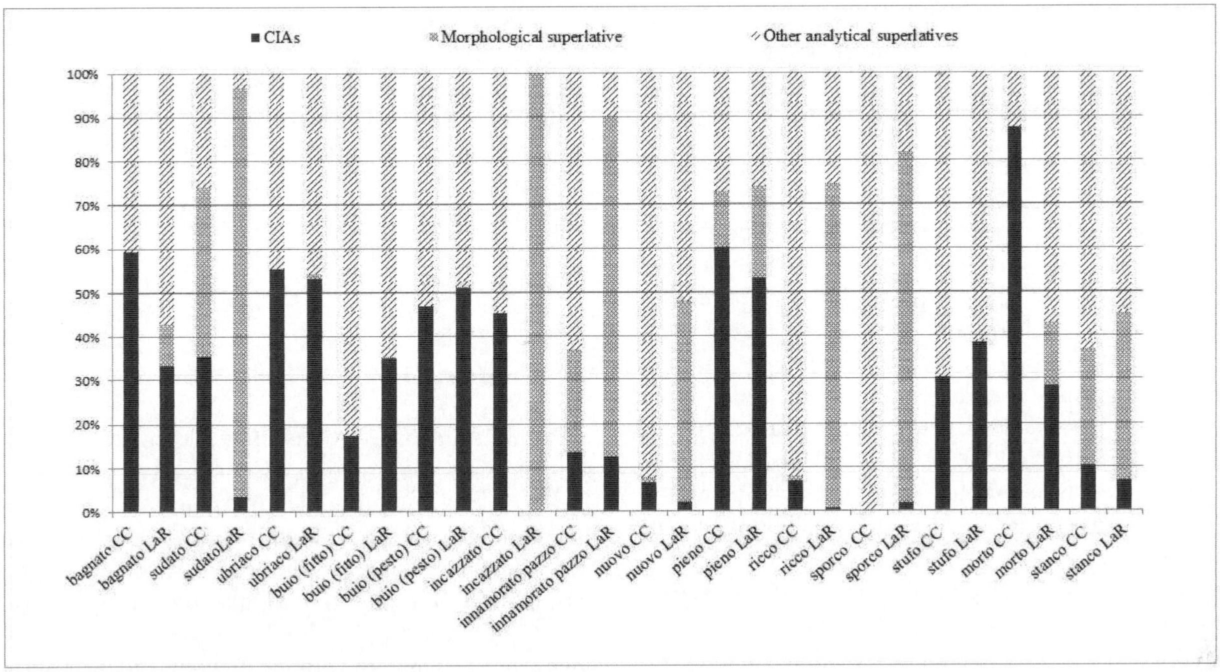

'Tab.2 Data from CORIS-CODIS (here CC) and LaRepubblica (here LaR) standardized to 100%'

responding to the ADJ_{INTENS}. To give an example, occurrences of *pieno zeppo* were compared to those of *pienissimo, molto pieno, tanto pieno, ...* (cf. Tab.1) but also to those of *completamente pieno* and *pieno fino all'orlo*, which Sketch Engine indicates as the most typical modifications of this adjective; since an adverb derived from *zeppo* does not exist (>**zeppamente*), this last comparison was not possible in this specific case (cf. however *innamorato* ***pazzo*** *~ innamorato* ***pazzamente***).

4 Comparative Quantitative Analysis

4.1 Distribution

The comparative quantitative analysis showed that CIAs are generally much exploited as compared to their rival strategies, even though we mainly considered a written variety of Italian. As we can notice from Tab.2, MWEs as *buio pesto, pieno zeppo, stufo marcio, morto stecchito, bagnato fradicio, ubriaco fradicio* seem to be the most used strategies compared to other superlative devices for the same ADJ_X taken individually.

In other cases, (*buio fitto, incazzato nero, sudato fradicio*), this MW strategy seems to compete against the "canonical" means of intensification, i.e. morphological superlative and degree adverbs, or appears just slightly less frequently than those (*stanco morto*). Cases where the CIAs are scarcely represented seem to depend on the fact that they belong to some particularly marked expression (as for the MWE *sporco lurido*, 'very filthy', which is diatopically marked). A comparison with web data suggests that they have however a pretty high number of occurrences in proportion to the other strategies.

These results appear of even greater interest if one considers that the analyzed corpora were written. Furthermore, while the occurrences we counted for the patterns in (3) reflect pretty accurately the effective number of uses (since they are fixed and easily identifiable), the margin of error for the alternative strategies is higher, since they have often been computed together with occurrences belonging to similar but not equal syntactic structures[3].

It is also worth noting that in cases like *nuovo fiammante* or *ricco sfondato*, where the modified adjective is highly polysemic, the great differences with the alternative superlatives taken into account is mainly due to the fact that the intensifier here acts on the grade of ADJ_X only in one of its possible senses, while the traditional strategies appear

[3] This is particularly true for the web data, where the search tools do not allow to automatically exclude some interfering constructions, such as the verbal MWE *essersi innamorato pazzo*, 'to fall crazy in love'.

more "neutral" in this sense and tend to modify the ADJ_X's degree in all or most of its senses.

4.2 Productivity

At a second stage, we tested whether CIAs in (3) could extend their grading function to other adjectives. As a result, the intensifiers in (4) were isolated. In cases like *nero* and *fradicio*, the intensifier combines with the synonyms of the main bases (for example, *arrabbiato* and *incavolato,* both synonyms of *incazzato*, can occur with *nero*). Furthermore, regarding *fradicio*, its use can not only be extended metaphorically and metonymically to the whole semantic field of *bagnato* (cf. its bases in 3) but it can also be employed with adjectives denoting emotions or behaviours (maybe for one of its senses' synonymy with *marcio*, which already modifies the same category): *Geloso/emozionato/... fradicio.*

4.3 CIAs as Constructions: Semantic Models

CIAs are primitive or participial modifiers denoting a quality which triggers the intensity of the modified adjective's quality according to two main abstract semantic schemes:

a) *Semantic feature copying* (Lorenz, 2002). The two adjectives of the construction share the same property and are thus associated to the same grading scale; but ADJ_{INTENS} is on a higher position, since it represents the implicit superlative of ADJ_X. See *bagnato fradicio*, *innamorato cotto*, *pieno zeppo* among others. This highly iconic pattern gives rise to completely specified constructions which often appear as already registered in the lexicon.

b) *Metonymic/metaphoric scale association.* The extreme degree of intensity is here expressed by the contiguity between two scales that are normally associated to different semantic fields. Thanks to a semantic shift, the property of one scale is perceived as designating the maximum grade of a property which actually identifies a different scale of values. A typical example is the metaphorical process "NEGATIVE FEELING - DARK COLOUR", according to which *nero* represents the highest expression of being *incazzato*. Other examples are *buio pesto*, *buio fitto*, *stufo marcio*. A subclass of this group is formed by couples of adjectives which display a metonymical "CAUSE – EFFECT" relation. If we talk about an *innamorato pazzo*, we intend somebody who is so much in love to become/look like crazy.

The origin of these modifiers, which especially in this latter case seem to be very productive, is clearly propositional (Bosque, 1999): Their status of intensifiers is fulfilled by means of a formerly "consecutive" interpretation (*stanco morto*, 'dead tired' indicate somebody who is so tired that she is/looks as if she was dead).

5 Conclusions

We focused on CIAs as lexical elements which contribute to the creation of superlative constructions. As revealed by the distributional analysis, this strategy, though paradigmatically limited, is nevertheless extremely interesting given its large exploitation if compared to its competing strategies. As for the productivity, semantic regularities where noticed in the relation between the components of each MWE, and the schemas which underlie the most productive patterns were identified.

As this kind of word formation seems to function through analogy or semantic contiguity (Siller-Runggaldier, 2006), it is legitimate to think that it appears firstly in the *discourse* space and then into the *system* (in Coseriu's sense; cf. Coseriu, 1962). That's why a direct follow up of this research could be that of extending the analysis to other corpora representative of those language varieties which are more sensitive to experimentation.[4]

Moreover, the computational comparison between competitive superlative constructions could be deepened in order to understand which kind of syntactic or pragmatic constraints influence the use of different strategies: In this perspective a collostructional analysis (Stefanowitsch and Gries, 2003) ought to be more informative of the data extracted so far. Such a method could also profitably be extended to the analysis of analogous intensification strategies applied to different parts of speech. Indeed, many nouns show intensification patterns comparable to the one presented here (*freddo polare*, *idiota completo*) and also some verbs exists which are often intensified by means of oblique uses of some particular adjectives (*studiare duro*, *lavorare sodo*).

[4] First experiments with the web-derived corpus Paisà (250 million tokens) showed however that this corpus is considerably closer to written than to spoken language.

References

Paul K. Andersen. 1992. Gradation. In William Bright (Ed.), *International Encyclopedia of Linguistics* , Vol. 2:79. Oxford University Press, New York, Oxford.

Dwight Bolinger. 1972. *Degree Words*. Mouton, Den Haag.

Ignacio Bosque. 1999. El sintagma adjetival. Modificadores y complementos del adjetivo. Adjetivo y participio. In Ignacio Bosque and Violeta Demonte (Eds.), *Gramática descriptiva de la Lengua Española*, Vol. I: 217-230. Espasa Calpe, Madrid.

Karl Bühler. 1983[1934]. *Teoria del linguaggio*. Armando, Roma.

Silvia Cacchiani. 2009. Lexico-functional categories and complex collocations. The case of intensifiers. In Ute Römer and Rainer Schulze (Eds.), *Exploring the Lexis-Grammar Interface*: 229-246. John Benjamins, Amsterdam.

Silvia Cacchiani. 2010. A CL perspective on complex intensifying adjectives. In *TEXTUS 2010/3*:601-618.

Eugenio Coseriu. 1962. *Teoría del lenguaje y lingüística general*. Gredos, Madrid.

William Croft. 1991. *Syntactic Categories and Grammatical Relations: The Cognitive Organization of Information*. The University of Chicago Press, Chicago.

Pierluigi Cuzzolin and Christian Lehmann. 2004. Comparison and gradation. In Gerd Booij et al. (Eds.), *Morphologie. Ein internationales Handbuch zur Flexion und Wortbiltung*, 2:1212-1220. Mouton de Gruyter, Berlin.

Charles J. Fillmore, Paul Kay and Catherine O'Connor 1988, Regularity and idiomaticity in grammatical constructions: The case of *let alone*. In *Language*, 64:501-538.

Adele Goldberg. 2006. *Constructions at work*. Oxford University Press, Oxford.

José Manuel González Calvo. 1984. Sobre la expresión de lo *superlativo en español*. In *Anuario de Estudios Filológicos*. Cáceres, VII:173-205. Universidad de Extremadura.

Pura Guil. 2006. Modificatori dell'aggettivo. In Emanuela Cresti (Ed.), *Prospettive nello studio del lessico italiano*, Atti SILFI 2006, Vol. 2:491-496. FUP, Firenze.

Christopher Kennedy and Louise McNally. 2005. Scale Structure, Degree Modification, and the Semantics of Gradable Predicates. In *Language*, 81:345-381.

Adam Kilgarriff, Pavel Rychly et al. The Sketch Engine. In *Proc EURALEX 2004*:105-116. Lorient, France.

Henny Klein. 1998. *Adverbs of Degree in Dutch and Related Language*. John Benjamins, Amsterdam.

Gilbert Lazard. 2006. *La quête des invariantes interlangues. La linguistique est-elle une science*? Honoré Champion, Paris.

Alessandro Lenci, Nicoletta Montemagni and Vito Pirrelli. 2005. *Testo e computer. Elementi di linguistica computazionale*. Roma, Carocci.

Gunter Lorenz. 2002. A corpus-based approach to the delexicalization and grammaticalization of intensifiers in Modern English. In Ilse Wischer and Gabriele Diewald (Eds.), *New Reflections on Grammaticalization*. John Benjamins, Amsterdam.

Edward Sapir. 1944. Grading: A Study in Semantics. In *Philosophy of Science*, 11:93-116.

Heidi Siller-Runggaldier. 2006. Le collocazioni lessicali: strutture sintagmatiche idiosincratiche? In Emanuela Cresti (Ed.), *Prospettive nello studio del lessico italiano*, Atti SILFI 2006, Vol. 2:591-598. FUP, Firenze.

Raffaele Simone. 2010. Verbi sintagmatici come categoria e costruzione. In Monica Cini (Ed.), *Verbi sintagmatici*: 13-30. Peter Lang, Berlin.

Anatol Stefanowitsch and Stefan. Th. Gries. 2003. Collostructions: Investigating the interaction of words and constructions. In *International Journal of Corpus Linguistics*, 8.2: 209-43.

Tullio De Mauro (Ed.). 1999. *GRADIT = Grande dizionario italiano dell'uso*. UTET, Torino.

Corpora and Tools

CORIS-CODIS – CORpus di Riferimento di Italiano Scritto. http://corpora.dslo.unibo.it/TCORIS.

LaRepubblica Corpus. http://sslmit.unibo.it/repubblica.

Paisà. Corpus. http://www.corpusitaliano.it.

Sketch Engine. http://www.sketchengine.co.uk.

The Far Reach of Multiword Expressions in Educational Technology

Jill Burstein
Educational Testing Service
660 Rosedale Road
Princeton, NJ 08541 USA
JBurstein@ets.org

Abstract

Multiword expressions as they appear as nominal compounds, collocational forms, and idioms are now leveraged in educational technology in assessment and instruction contexts. The talk will focus on how multiword expression identification is used in different kinds of educational applications, including automated essay evaluation, and teacher professional development in curriculum development for English language learners. Recent approaches developed to resolve polarity for noun-noun compounds in a sentiment system being designed to handle evaluation of argumentation (sentiment) in test-taker writing (Beigman-Klebanov, Burstein, and Madnani, to appear) will also be described.

About the Speaker

Jill Burstein is a managing principal research scientist in the Research & Development division at Educational Testing Service in Princeton, New Jersey. Her background and expertise is in computational linguistics with a focus on educational applications for writing, reading, and teacher professional development. She holds 13 patents for educational technology inventions. Jills inventions include e-rater, an automated essay scoring and evaluation system. And, in more recent work, she has leveraged natural language processing to develop Language MuseSM, a teacher professional development application that supports teachers in the development of language-based instruction that aids English learner content understanding and language skills development. She received her B.A. in Linguistics and Spanish from New York University, and her M.A. and Ph.D. in Linguistics from the Graduate Center, City University of New York.

References

Beigman Klebanov, B., Burstein, J., and Madnani, N. (to appear) *Sentiment Profiles of Multi-Word Expressions in Test-Taker Essays: The Case of Noun-Noun Compounds.* In V. Kardoni, C. Ramisch, and A. Villavicencio (eds.) ACM Transactions for Speech and Language Processing, Special Issue on Multiword Expressions: From Theory to Practice.

Construction of English MWE Dictionary and its Application to POS Tagging

Yutaro Shigeto, Ai Azuma, Sorami Hisamoto, Shuhei Kondo, Tomoya Kose, Keisuke Sakaguchi, Akifumi Yoshimoto, Frances Yung, Yuji Matsumoto
Nara Institute Science of Technology (NAIST)
Ikoma, Nara 630-0192 Japan
yutaro-s@is.naist.jp

Abstract

This paper reports our ongoing project for constructing an English multiword expression (MWE) dictionary and NLP tools based on the developed dictionary. We extracted functional MWEs from the English part of Wiktionary, annotated the Penn Treebank (PTB) with MWE information, and conducted POS tagging experiments. We report how the MWE annotation is done on PTB and the results of POS and MWE tagging experiments.

1 Introduction

While there have been a great progress in POS tagging and parsing of natural language sentences thanks to the advancement of statistical and corpus-based methods, there still remains difficulty in sentence processing stemming from syntactic discrepancies. One of such discrepancies is caused by multiword expressions (MWEs), which are known and defined as expressions having "idiosyncratic interpretations that cross word boundaries (or spaces)" (Sag et al., 2002).

Sag et al. (2002) classifies MWEs largely into the following categories:

- Lexicalized phrases
  - fixed expressions: Those having fixed word order and form (e.g. *by and large*).
  - semi-fixed expressions: Those having fixed word order with lexical variation such as inflection, determiner selection, etc. (e.g. *come up with*).
  - syntactically flexible expressions: Those having a wide range of syntactic variability (e.g. phrasal verbs that take an NP argument between or following the verb and the particle).
- Institutionalized phrases
  - Phrases that are semantically and syntactically compositional, such as collocations (e.g. *traffic light*).

This paper reports our ongoing project for developing an English MWE dictionary of a broad coverage and MWE-aware natural language processing tools. The main contributions of this paper are as follows:

1. Construction of an English MWE dictionary (mainly consisting of functional expressions) through extraction from Wiktionary[1].
2. Annotation of MWEs in the Penn Treebank (PTB).
3. Implementation of an MWE-aware POS tagger and evaluation of its performance.

2 Related work

While there is a variety of MWE researches only a few of them focus on MWE lexicon construction. Though some examples, such as French adverb dictionaries (Laporte and Voyatzi, 2008; Laporte et al., 2008), a Dutch MWE dictionary (Grégoire, 2007) and a Japanese MWE dictionary (Shudo et al., 2011) have been constructed, there is no freely available English MWE dictionary with a broad coverage.

Moreover, MWE-annotated corpora are only available for a few languages, including French and

[1] https://en.wiktionary.org

Swedish. While the British National Corpus is annotated with MWEs, its coverage is far from complete. Considering this situation, we started construction of an English MWE dictionary (with functional expressions first) and classified their occurrences in PTB into MWE or literal usage, obtaining MWE-annotated version of PTB.

The effect of MWE dictionaries have been reported for various NLP tasks. Nivre and Nilsson (2004) investigated the effect of recognizing MWEs in syntactic dependency parsing of Swedish. Korkontzelos and Manandhar (2010) showed performance improvement of base phrase chunking by annotating compound and proper nouns. Finlayson and Kulkarni (2011) reported the effect of recognizing MWEs on word sense disambiguation.

Most of the previous approaches to MWE recognition are based on frequency or collocation measures of words in large scale corpora. On the other hand, some previous approaches tried to recognize new MWEs using an MWE lexicon and MWE-annotated corpora. Constant and Sigogne (2011) presented MWE recognition using a Conditional Random Fields (CRFs)-based tagger with the BIO schema. Green et al. (2011) proposed an MWE recognition method using Tree Substitution Grammars. Constant et al. (2012) compared two phrase structure analysis methods, one that uses MWE recognition as preprocessing and the other that uses a reranking method.

Although MWEs show a variety of flexibilities in their appearance, most of the linguistic analyses consider the fixed type of MWEs. For example, the experiments by Nivre and Nilsson (2004) focus on fixed expressions that fall into the following categories:

1. Multiword names
2. Numerical expressions
3. Compound function words
    (a) Adverbs
    (b) Prepositions
    (c) Subordinating conjunctions
    (d) Determiners
    (e) Pronouns

Multiword names and numerical expressions behave as noun phrases and have limited syntactic functionalities. On the other hand, compound function words have a variety of functionalities that may affect language analyses such as POS tagging and parsing. In this work, we extract compound functional expressions from the English part of Wiktionary, and classify their occurrences in PTB into either literal or MWE usages. We then build a POS tagger that takes MWEs into account. In implementing this, we use CRFs that can handle a sequence of tokens as a single item (Kudo et al., 2004). We evaluate the performance of the tagger and compare it with the method that uses the BIO schema for identifying MWE usages (Constant and Sigogne, 2011).

3 MWEs Extraction from Wiktionary

To construct an English MWE dictionary, we extract entries from the English part of Wiktionary (as of July 14, 2012) that include white spaces. We extract only fixed expressions that are categorized either as adverbs, conjunctions, determiners, prepositions, prepositional phrases or pronouns. We exclude compound nouns and phrasal verbs since the former are easily recognized by an existing method such as chunking and the latter need more sophisticated analyzing methods because of their syntactic flexibility. We also exclude multiword adjectives since many of them are semi-fixed and behave differently from lexical adjective, having predicative usage only. Table 1 summarizes the numbers of MWE entries in Wiktionary and the numbers of them that appear at least once in PTB.

4 Annotation of MWEs in PTB

While it is usually not easy to identify the usage of an MWE as either an MWE or a literal usage, we initially thought that the phrase structure tree annotations in PTB would have enough information to identify their usages. This assumption is correct in many cases (Figures 1(a) and 1(b)). The MWE usage of "*a bit*" in Figure 1(a) is analyzed as "`NP-ADV`", suggesting it is used as an adverb, and the literal usage of "*a bit*" in Figure 1(b) is labeled as "`NP`", suggesting it is used literally. However, there are a number of examples that are annotated differently while their usages are the same. For example, Figures 1(c), 1(d) and 1(e) all show RB us-

Table 1: Number of MWE types in Wiktionary and Penn Treebank

	Adverb	Conjunction	Determiner	Preposition	Prepositional Phrase	Pronoun
Wiktionary	1501	49	15	110	165	83
PTB	468	35	9	77	66	18
Examples	*after all*	*as wll as*	*a number of*	*according to*	*against the law*	*no one*

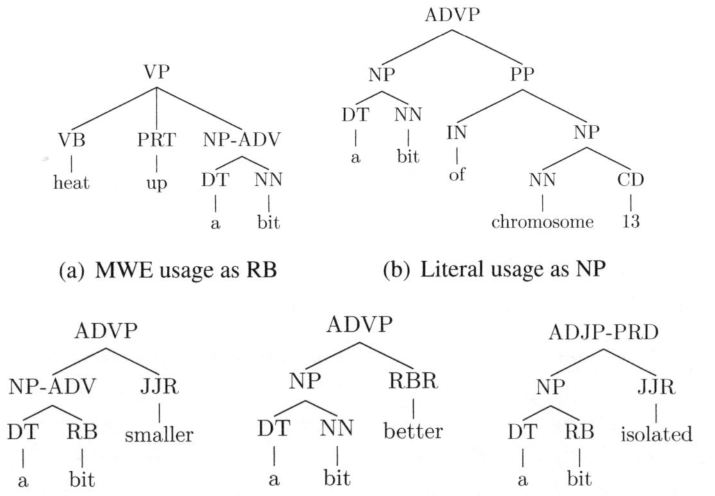

(a) MWE usage as RB (b) Literal usage as NP

(c) MWE usage as RB (d) MWE usage as RB (e) MWE usage as RB

Figure 1: Examples of phrase structures annotated to "*a bit*"

age of "*a bit*" while they are annotated differently [2]. Sometimes, the same structure tree is annotated to instances of different usages (Figures 1(b) and 1(d)).

Therefore, for each MWE candidate, we first cluster its occurrences in PTB according to their phrase tree structures. Some of the clusters clearly indicate MWE usages (such as "NP-ADV" trees in Figures 1(a) and 1(c)). In such cases, we regarded all instances as MWE usages and annotated them as such. For inconsistent or ambiguous cases (such as "NP" trees in Figures 1(b), 1(d) and 1(e)), we manually classify each of them into either MWE or literal usage (some MWEs have multiple MWE usages). We find a number of inconsistent POS annotations on some internal words of MWEs (e.g. "*bit*" in Figures 1(c) and 1(e) are annotated as RB while they should be NN). We correct such inconsistent cases (correction is only done on internal words of MWEs, selecting the majority POS tags as correct). The total number of POS tag corrections made on PTB (chapter 00-24) was 1084.

[2]The POS tags in the trees are: RB(adverb), IN(preposition), DT(determiner), NN(common noun) ...

5 Experiments of POS tagging and MWE recognition

5.1 Experiment Setting

We conduct POS tagging experiments on the MWE-annotated PTB, using sections 0-18 for training and sections 22-24 for test as usual.

For the experiments, we use four versions of PTB with the following POS annotations.

(a) Original: PTB with the original POS annotation
(b) Revised: PTB with correction of inconsistent POS tags
(c) BIO MWE: MWEs are annotated with the BIO schema
(d) MWE: MWEs are annotated as single words

Concerning the MWE annotation in (c) and (d), the total number of MWE tokens in PTB is 12131 (9417 in the training chapters, 1396 in the test chapters, and 1319 for the remaining (development) chapters).

Each word is annotated with the following in-

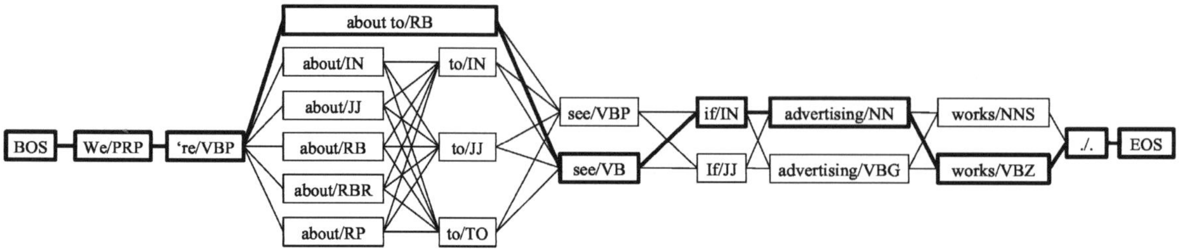

Figure 2: Example of lattice containing MWE ("*about to*/RB") (correct path is marked with bold boxes.)

Table 2: Examples of MWE annotations in four versions

Version	Word/POS
(a) Original	*about*/RB *to*/TO
(b) Revised	*about*/IN *to*/TO
(c) BIO MWE	*about*/RB-B *to*/RB-I
(d) MWE	*about to*/RB

formation: coarse-grained POS tag (CPOS), fine-grained POS tag (FPOS) and surface form. Each MWE is further annotated with its POS tag, surface form, its internal words with their POS tags.

Table 2 shows sample annotations of MWE "*about to*" in each of the four versions of PTB. In (a), "*about*/RB" is annotated incorrectly, which is corrected in (b). In (c), "-B" indicates the beginning token of an MWE and "-I" indicates an inside position of an MWE. In (d), "*about to*" is annotated as an RB (we omit the POS tags for its internal words, which are IN and TO).

We use a CRF-based tagger for training and test on all the four PTB versions. Our CRF can handle "words with spaces" (e.g. "*about to*" as a single token as well as separated tokens) as shown in Figure 2. This extension is only relevant to the case of the (d) MWE version.

Table 3 summarizes the set of feature templates used in the experiments. In Table 3, "Head POS" means the POS tag of the beginning token of an MWE. In the same way, "Tail POS" means the POS tag of the last token of an MWE. For example, for "*a lot of* /DT", its Head POS is DT and its Tail POS is IN.

We evaluate POS tagging accuracy and MWE recognition accuracy. In POS evaluation, each token receives a tag in the cases of (a), (b) and (c), so the tagging accuracy is straightforwardly calculated.

Table 3: Feature templates used in CRF training

Unigram features
Surface form
FPOS, Surface form
CPOS, Surface form
Bigram features (left context / right context)
Surface form / FPOS, Surface form
FPOS, Surface form / Surface form
Tail POS, Surface form / Head POS, Surface form
Surface form / Head POS
Tail POS / Head POS
Tail POS / Surface form

In the case of (d), since MWEs are analyzed as single words, they are expanded into the internal words with their POS tags and the evaluated on the token basis.

MWE recognition accuracy is evaluated for the cases of (c) and (d). For the purpose of comparison, we employ a simple baseline as well. This baseline assigns each occurrence of an MWE its most frequent usage in the training part of PTB. Evaluation of MWE recognition accuracy is shown in precision, recall and F-measure.

We use the standard set of features based on unigram/bi-gram of words/POS. For our MWE version, we add the word forms and POS tags of the first and the last internal words of MWEs as shown in Table 3.

5.2 Experimental Results

Table 4 shows the results of POS tagging. A slight improvement is observed in (b) compared with (a) because some of inconsistent tags are corrected. Further improvement is achieved in (d). The experiment on (c) does not show improvement even over correct: · · · · who/WP <u>after all/RB</u> is/VBZ really/RB <u>a/DT</u> <u>bit/JJ</u> player/NN on/IN the/DT stage/NN · · · ·

system: · · · · who/WP <u>*after/IN</u> <u>*all/DT</u> is/VBZ really/RB <u>*a bit/RB</u> player/NN on/IN the/DT stage/NN · · · ·

Figure 3: Example of errors: "*after all* /RB" and "*a* /DT *bit* /JJ."

Table 4: Per token accuracy (precision)

Version	Accuracy
(a) Original	97.54
(b) Revised	97.56
(c) BIO MWE	97.32
(d) split MWE	97.62

Table 5: Recognition performance of MWEs

	Precision	Recall	F-measure
Baseline	78.79	80.26	79.51
(c) BIO	92.81	90.90	90.18
(d) MWE	95.75	97.16	96.45

(a). The reason may attribute to the data sparseness caused by the increased size of POS tags.

Table 5 shows the results of MWE recognition. Our MWE-aware CRF model (d) shows the best results. While the BIO model (c) significantly outperforms the baseline, it gives significantly lower results than our model.

We investigated errors in (d) and categorized them into three types.

- False Positive: System finds an MWE, while it is actually literal.
- False Negative: System misses to identify an MWE.
- Misrecognition: System finds an MWE wrongly (correct answer is another MWE).

Table 6 shows number of recognition errors of MWEs.

An example of the False Positive is "*a bit* /RB" in Figure 3, which actually is a literal usage and should be tagged as "*a* /DT, *bit* /NN".

An example of the False Negative is "*in black and white* /RB", which is not recognized as an MWE. One reason of this type of errors is low or zero frequency of such MWEs in training data. "*after all* /RB" (in Figure 3) is another False Negative example.

Table 6: Recognition error of MWEs

Error types	# of errors
False Positives	33
False Negatives	19
Misrecognition	17

One example of Misrecognition errors stems from ambiguous MWEs. For example, while "*how much*" only has MWE usages as RB, there are two RB usages of "*how much*" that have different POS tag sequences for the internal words. Other examples of Misrecognition are due to zero or low frequency MWEs, whose substrings also matches shorter MWEs: "*quite*/RB, *a few*/PRP" while correct analysis is "*quite a few*/RB", and "*the hell* /RB, *out of* /IN" while the correct analysis is "*the hell out of* /RB".

6 Conclusion and Future work

This paper presented our ongoing project for construction of an English MWE dictionary, and its application to MWE-aware POS tagging. The experimental results show that the MWE-aware tagger achieved better performance on POS tagging and MWE recognition. Although our current MWE dictionary only covers fixed types of functional MWEs, this dictionary and MWE annotation information on PTB will be made publicly available.

We plan to handle a wider range of MWEs such as phrasal verbs and other semi-fixed and syntactically flexible MWEs, and to develop a POS tagger and a syntactic parser on top of them.

References

Matthieu Constant and Anthony Sigogne. 2011. MWU-Aware Part-of-Speech Tagging with a CRF Model and Lexical Resources. In *Proceedings of the Workshop on Multiword Expressions: from Parsing and Generation to the Real World*, MWE '11, pages 49–56.

Matthieu Constant, Anthony Sigogne, and Patrick Watrin. 2012. Discriminative Strategies to Integrate Multiword Expression Recognition and Parsing. In *Proceedings of the 50th Annual Meeting of the Association for Computational Linguistics*, ACL '12, pages 204–212.

Mark Alan Finlayson and Nidhi Kulkarni. 2011. Detecting Multi-Word Expressions improves Word Sense Disambiguation. In *Proceedings of the Workshop on Multiword Expressions: from Parsing and Generation to the Real World*, MWE '11, pages 20–24.

Spence Green, Marie-Catherine de Marneffe, John Bauer, and Christopher D Manning. 2011. Multiword Expression Identification with Tree Substitution Grammars: A Parsing *tour de force* with French. In *Proceedings of the Conference on Empirical Methods in Natural Language Processing*, EMNLP '11, pages 725–735.

Nicole Grégoire. 2007. Design and Implementation of a Lexicon of Dutch Multiword Expressions. In *Proceedings of the Workshop on a Broader Perspective on Multiword Expressions*, MWE '07, pages 17–24.

Ioannis Korkontzelos and Suresh Manandhar. 2010. Can Recognising Multiword Expressions Improve Shallow Parsing? In *Human Language Technologies: The 2010 Annual Conference of the North American Chapter of the Association for Computational Linguistics*, HLT '10, pages 636–644.

Taku Kudo, Kaoru Yamamoto, and Yuji Matsumoto. 2004. Applying conditional random fields to japanese morphological analysis. In *Proceedings of the Conference on Empirical Methods in Natural Language Processing*, EMNLP '04, pages 230–237.

Eric Laporte and Stavroula Voyatzi. 2008. An Electronic Dictionary of French Multiword Adverbs. In *Language Resources and Evaluation Conference. Workshop Towards a Shared Task for Multiword Expressions*, MWE '08, pages 31–34.

Eric Laporte, Takuya Nakamura, and Stavroula Voyatzi. 2008. A French Corpus Annotated for Multiword Nouns. In *Proceedings of the Language Resources and Evaluation Conference. Workshop Towards a Shared Task on Multiword Expressions*, MWE '08, pages 27–30.

Joakim Nivre and Jens Nilsson. 2004. Multiword Units in Syntactic Parsing. In *Workshop on Methodologies and Evaluation of Multiword Units in Real-World Applications*, MEMURA '04, pages 39–46.

Ivan A Sag, Timothy Baldwin, Francis Bond, Ann A Copestake, and Dan Flickinger. 2002. Multiword Expressions: A Pain in the Neck for NLP. In *Proceedings of the Third International Conference on Computational Linguistics and Intelligent Text Processing*, CICLing '02, pages 1–15.

Kosho Shudo, Akira Kurahone, and Toshifumi Tanabe. 2011. A Comprehensive Dictionary of Multiword Expressions. In *Proceedings of the 49th Annual Meeting of the Association for Computational Linguistics: Human Language Technologies*, HLT '11, pages 161–170.

Author Index